GROW MORE WITH LESS
VINCENT A. SIMEONE

FIRST PUBLISHED IN 2013 BY COOL SPRINGS PRESS, A MEMBER OF QUAYSIDE PUBLISHING GROUP INC.,
400 FIRST AVENUE NORTH, SUITE 400, MINNEAPOLIS, MN 55401

COOL SPRINGS PRESS TITLES ARE ALSO AVAILABLE AT DISCOUNTS IN BULK QUANTITY FOR INDUSTRIAL OR SALES-
PROMOTIONAL USE. FOR DETAILS WRITE TO SPECIAL SALES MANAGER AT COOL SPRINGS PRESS, 400 FIRST AVENUE NORTH,
SUITE 400, MINNEAPOLIS, MN 55401 USA. TO FIND OUT MORE ABOUT OUR BOOKS, VISIT US ONLINE AT
WWW.COOLSPRINGSPRESS.COM.

LIBRARY OF CONGRESS CATALOGING-IN-PUBLICATION DATA

SIMEONE, VINCENT A.
  GROW MORE WITH LESS : SUSTAINABLE GARDEN METHODS FOR GREAT LANDSCAPES WITH LESS WATER, LESS WORK, LESS
MONEY / VINCENT A. SIMEONE.
    P. CM.
  INCLUDES INDEX.
  ISBN 978-1-59186-551-3 (SC)
  1. SUSTAINABLE HORTICULTURE. 2. ORGANIC GARDENING. 3. LANDSCAPE GARDENING. 4. GARDENING--ENVIRONMENTAL
ASPECTS. I. TITLE.

  SB319.95.S56 2013
  635'.048--DC23

                    2013028507

ACQUISITIONS EDITOR: BILLIE BROWNELL
DESIGN MANAGER: CINDY SAMARGIA LAUN
DESIGN AND LAYOUT: PAULINE MOLINARI
COVER DESIGN: KARL LAUN

PRINTED IN CHINA
10 9 8 7 6 5 4 3 2

DISCLAIMER
THE OPINIONS AND STATEMENTS CONTAINED IN THIS BOOK ARE THE AUTHOR'S AND DO NOT REPRESENT THE OPINIONS OR
INTERESTS OF THE NEW YORK STATE OFFICE OF PARKS, RECREATION AND HISTORIC PRESERVATION.

GROW MORE WITH LESS

VINCENT A. SIMEONE

Cool
Springs
Press

Home and Garden Experts™

MINNEAPOLIS, MINNESOTA

Dedication & Acknowledgments

This book is dedicated to my parents, Vincent and Rosemary Simeone, who instilled in me the value of hard work, loyalty, and respect. They are in my thoughts and memories every day. They both made great sacrifices in life to ensure our family was always whole. I also dedicate this book to the craft of horticulture, for which I am honored to have made my career.

From the time when I was a little boy, the wonders of nature always fascinated me. It is not at all surprising to me that forty-plus years later, I am still engaged and amazed at all of the gifts that our natural world has to offer. My appreciation for trees and my love for horticulture are partly fueled by the endless possibilities that this outdoor classroom reveals each day. My passion is equally ignited by the infinite supply of talented professionals who make me a better horticulturist each time I interact with them. The more gardens I visit and the more gardeners I meet, the more I realize how fortunate I am to be in this rewarding field. The gardening community on Long Island, New York, and all over the United States, for that matter, is indeed rich and continuously prospering. I have traveled all over the world to visit gardens and their dedicated gardeners and, without question, plants are the common denominator that pulls us together as a gardening community.

How do I even begin to thank all of the family, friends, and colleagues who have touched my life so deeply and profoundly? The list could go on forever, and I'm sure I will inadvertently miss someone, so forgive my abridged version.

For the past twenty-one years I have had the pleasure of working at Planting Fields Arboretum in Oyster Bay, New York, one of many magnificent state historic parks in New York State. This horticultural jewel inspires me to teach, lecture, write, and pursue the next great garden plant to enhance our landscapes.

To so many mentors and positive influences in my life: Allan and Susan Armitage, Dave and Eileen Barnett, Michael Coe, Michael and Bonnie Dirr, Steve and Linda Finley, Gordon and Thelma Jones, and John and Connie Norbeck, just to name a few. These incredible people continue to keep me on the straight and narrow and make me a better person.

To the colleagues and family members who contributed in many ways such as motivating, editing, typing, proofreading, and sometimes suffering through endless phone calls, e-mails, and conversations about plants: Alexis Alvey, Allan Armitage, Mia Broder, Linda Copeland, Margery Daughtery, Dan Gilrein, Joanne Macrelli, Sal Pezzino, John Simeone, Ken Spencer, Michael Veracka, and Richard Weir III.

Last, but definitely not least, to my entire family who always have my back. Also, to my wife Gloria and to Chuckles and Sophie, the crazy Smooth Fox Terriers who keep me moving, and to Chauncey the cat. My animals are my salvation.

This book proved challenging and inspiring all at the same time. As I get older, I realize more and more that humans are only a part of a greater whole and that the natural world around us is a gift that we must protect and nurture. Too often we view natural resources as an entitlement that is to be used as we see fit. But it is time to realize that we are only a piece of a bigger puzzle, and we are not guaranteed the virtues of tomorrow. Sustainability is an evolving phenomenon that gives us the opportunity to ensure a better way of life for future generations. It is a responsible way of life that should be embraced as a necessary part of our culture.

TABLE OF CONTENTS

Introduction

Sustainable Gardening: Grow More with Less

The term *sustainability* is a catchy phrase that has garnered a lot of attention the past few years. But unlike many catch phrases, sustainability has substance, credibility, and the potential to change life as we know it. For those who accept sustainability as a way of life, it will undoubtedly pay long-term dividends. Sustainability is a complex issue that affects every facet of our lives. But sustainability requires an investment of time and resources that will yield positive results over years to come. This commitment of time, hard work, and patience is a worthwhile effort that reduces the impact that we as human beings have on our environment. Like many worthwhile endeavors, sustainability offers us a chance to lead a responsible, healthy life and provide an example for others to learn from.

Environmental destruction is one of several reasons why sustainability has become such an important issue for so many. Human nature is to advance both intellectually and physically and that means more building, more consumption, and more resources needed. This progress comes with a price, though, usually at the cost of the environment. In the past while we built roadway systems, housing developments, shopping malls, and resorts, the long-term impact to the environment was often not considered or anticipated. But that is slowly changing and everything from large developments to residential homes has the ability to become more sustainable.

For the home gardener, the sustainability movement has taken giant steps forward over the past decade. The concept of becoming more environmentally sensitive to the natural world around us has gained momentum to the point where it now seems to be an unavoidable, irresistible force. It's no revelation that many of us have been unknowingly practicing sustainable living for many years without even realizing it. The difference is that today, sustainability isn't just an option anymore; it truly is a necessary way of life. The days of casually practicing sustainable living when it is convenient are in the past. The time has come to embrace sustainability as an everyday part of life.

But sustainability is a relative and subjective term that can mean different things to different people. Sustainability will be influenced by many factors including economics, size and complexity of your property, climate, and available resources. It is difficult to put a specific definition on the term with the idea that it will apply to all, or even most, situations that we encounter daily. Because we live in such a dynamic, changing environment with an incredibly diverse population, sustainability will need to change and adapt along with us as a society. In order to successfully create a more sustainable environment, we must understand what it takes to create a lifestyle that supports this way of living. There is no question that there are general beliefs and practices about sustainability that are most accepted in our society.

DEFINING SUSTAINABILITY

By definition sustainability is the capacity to endure. It is the belief that living systems can persevere and adapt no matter what the circumstances. For humans, sustainability is the long-term maintenance of the world around us, which has environmental, economic, and social implications, and encompasses the concept of stewardship and the responsible management of natural resources. Most important, the sustainability movement must include the idea that what we do today should not negatively affect future generations. In the context of nature, sustainability relates to how biological systems remain diverse and productive over time, a necessary element for the long-term well being of humans and other organisms.

With threatened ecosystems, limited natural resources, and a changing environment, developing more sustainable ways to manage and survive has become a necessity that cannot be ignored. For example, ecotourism has become very popular and economically viable for many communities around the world. But the human interaction and impact in these environmentally sensitive areas requires careful oversight. If an old growth forest or a diverse barrier reef is being negatively impacted by human activity, there are sustainable ways to manage these issues. These management techniques include limited or seasonal use or alternate use that reduces impact. In the case of hunting and fishing, the legal limits put on the numbers of fish or deer that can be harvested during a given season is an excellent example of sustainable practices. Without these guidelines, animal populations would be greatly reduced or become extinct. In the grand scheme of things, sustainability evokes the reality that humans are a smaller part of a bigger picture and we must do our part to ensure the viability of future generations. There has long been a debate about where we as humans fit along the hierarchy of the environmental system. The reality today is that what we do ultimately affects the world around us and we must do our part to protect the symbiotic relations we have with the earth.

"Sustainability is the ability for diverse populations to survive over a long period of time and which allows us to satisfy the demands of today without sacrificing the needs of future generations."

As consumers and users of the land, humans have both positive and negative impacts to the environment. There is some debate on whether recent climate change has been caused by human activity, but there is little debate that it is occurring. Many experts feel that global climate change is causing severe weather patterns, droughts and floods, and variations in temperature patterns and is impacting where plants grow. Whether this is a short-term or long-term trend remains to be seen. Obviously, our hope is that the weather patterns return to "normal" and that what we are currently experiencing is just a minor speed bump in terms of long-range weather trends.

One common way of measuring the effect that humans have on their environment is known as a carbon footprint. A carbon footprint offers us the opportunity to quantify the impact that we have with the resources that we use everyday. A carbon footprint is measured as the greenhouse gas emissions (GHG) as a result of an organization, activity, product, or people. Greenhouse gases can be emitted through transportation, clearing of land, and the production and consumption of food, fuels, manufactured goods, materials, roads, buildings, and so forth. These activities cause the emission of harmful amounts of carbon dioxide or other GHGs. The negative effects of these damaging gases can even be generated from household power equipment such as lawn mowers, leaf blowers, weed trimmers, or any equipment that uses fossil fuels. Of course, cars, the burning of heating oil, and factories that create harmful pollutants to manufacture products can all have huge impacts to the environment. As we know from

Cultivated landscapes can be layered with different levels of vegetation, just like the forest.

popular terms such as global warming or the "greenhouse effect," these emissions can cause climate change.

There has long been a debate on the extent and direct causes of global warming but few doubt that it is occurring. This impact that is directly caused by human consumption and activity affects our entire ecosystem. This realization has most certainly accelerated the need to look for ways to be more responsible.

SUSTAINABILITY FOR THE HOME GARDENER

On a smaller and more comprehensible scale, the sustainability movement can *definitely* be applied to your home landscape. On a more manageable level, sustainability influences what and how we grow plants and how we manage our gardens. For far too long sustainability considerations have not been incorporated into the planning and development of both residential and commercial landscapes. *You*, as the designer of a new or completely renovated landscape, have the opportunity to start fresh and incorporate the innovations that sustainable techniques have to offer. Even if some landscapes only receive a partial makeover, sustainable practices can be incorporated to make them better. In many cases, gardeners are attempting to enhance the existing conditions of a well-established landscape. If this is the case for you, trying to improve or change years of accumulated or inherited mishaps and poor gardening practices can be a challenging and often frustrating task. Don't give up. The key is to make these improvements part of an overall, strategic plan that is manageable and prioritized. Superior and innovative design techniques work hand in hand with proper sustainability initiatives. A landscape with flowing lines and well-used space provides a great foundation on which to build. In addition to the design of the landscape, sustainability is an integral part of many other aspects of gardening including Integrated Pest Management, plant healthcare, recycling, composting, organic gardening, energy efficiency, alternative fuels, fuel-efficient equipment, and water conservation.

An example of a well-designed landscape with multiple seasons of interest includes Ogon spirea (back left), variegated redtwig dogwood (back right), blue star amsonia, (middle), iris (front left), daylily (front right), and dwarf blue spruce (front center).

Gardening is extremely popular among a large portion of the worldwide population on both professional and hobbyist levels. While gardening originated in Europe and Asia centuries ago, it continues to evolve along with new technologies and research. Probably the single most attractive feature of gardening that makes it so popular is the ever-changing and exciting challenge that it presents on a daily, monthly, seasonal, and annual basis. Gardening has important social and economic impacts to our society affecting millions of people and generating billions of dollars each year. Popular opinion is that gardening is one of the most admired hobbies in America today. Gardeners will tell you first-hand that it is certainly the most rewarding. However, gardening has far exceeded the confines of a hobby and has transformed itself into one of the most meaningful professions on the planet. The main reason for this is that gardening is accessible and appealing to a broad audience. Gardening affects people in a wide variety of ethnic, social, and economic backgrounds and transcends each of them.

But with an ever-changing climate that often includes extreme and unpredictable weather conditions, finite and often strained resources,

and increased pressures such as new pest problems, gardening has become increasingly challenging. These challenges affect casual hobbyist gardeners as well as professionals. So it's no surprise that sustainable gardening has emerged as an innovative, efficient, and responsible way to grow plants and manage landscapes. Until recently, the concept of living a more sustainable lifestyle in the garden had mostly been an afterthought in American households. But that is rapidly changing first in the professional horticultural and landscape design industry and now in home gardening.

Within a garden setting, sustainability directly relates to proper management of soil, composting to enhance soil properties, responsible water usage, sound maintenance practices for plants, managing invasive species, and most important, proper plant selection. Putting the right plant in the right place is not only important, it is essential to garden success. Sound landscape design to support a lower maintenance, healthy, and functional landscape is equally important. One of the most important components of sustainability is the development and selection of plants that require less care and resources. These are plants selected for their genetic superiority such as superior ornamental qualities, pest resistance, drought tolerance, cold tolerance, and so forth. New varieties of landscape plants and agricultural crops are regularly being developed to accommodate the needs of a growing and more demanding population of gardeners. Many universities have plant evaluation and breeding programs to introduce these superior plants into the landscape. The results from these programs are filtered down to farmers, nurserymen, gardeners, retailers, and eventually homeowners. Today all types of plants are being developed for the garden from new species and varieties of trees, shrubs, annuals, perennials, and even agricultural crops that can also be used as ornamentals in the garden. Plant selection and diversity are two of the most important components in an effective sustainability program to keep landscapes healthy and thriving.

These and other sound gardening techniques are vital to the long-term success of our landscapes. Sustainable gardening reaches far beyond traditional horticultural practices of gardening for aesthetics. In fact it is more about the function of landscape plants these days than just how pretty the plants are. While having a colorful and aesthetically pleasing garden is still a priority,

reducing the resources needed to maintain that beauty is achievable. If sound, responsible, and well-planned gardening techniques are employed utilizing sustainability practices, the dedicated gardeners can have their cake and eat it too.

> "By managing the garden in a more sustainable manner, we can protect the environment and simultaneously save time and money."

THE KEY TO SUSTAINABLE GARDENING

Sustainable gardening is influenced by many factors including size of the garden, budget, climate, soil conditions, and local regulatory restrictions. A large private estate or public municipality will have more resources available than a small home garden. But the key to successful sustainable gardening isn't dictated only by economics. You can accomplish your desired goals by following consistent, sound gardening principles that apply to large, commercial sites as well as smaller, residential ones. Essentially, a good, well-thought-out

This well-balanced landscape is designed in layers to offer a succession of bloom as well as a multi-tiered arrangement with larger plants in the back and smaller plants in the front.

plan is the blueprint to success regardless of the size or scope of a project.

During the late part of the nineteenth century and the early part of the twentieth centuries, large, grand private estates designed by famous landscape architects of the era such as Thomas Church, Miriam Cruger Coffin, Beatrix Ferrand, Fredrick Law Olmsted, and Flecter Steele all had one common theme. These landscapes had undeniable character, ingenuity, and an identity that is still alive and well today. But these landscapes were also built with the idea that they would serve future generations and leave long-lasting impressions on our society. Although it is true that many of these projects had vast amounts of resources, they also had a long-term vision and strategic plan to last the test of time.

THE END OF DISPOSABLE LANDSCAPES

Today home gardens tend to have a much shorter lifespan. Homeowners seem content to get 5, 10, or 15 years out of a newly designed landscape before it is renovated or replaced. These "disposable" landscapes are often poorly designed and managed with little or no planning or thought to function, soil health, proper siting of plant material, or important infrastructure such as irrigation or hardscape elements. While I am not suggesting that expansive, commercial landscapes with large amounts of resources from 100 years ago can be compared to small, postage-stamp-sized residential landscapes on a fixed budget of today, it does highlight the need for good planning and consistency. The same gardening principles and long-term planning that went into developing these great, sustainable landscapes can be applied to smaller home gardens. There is no doubt that good planning and design are the common thread that ties these two very different types of landscapes together. I have visited many gardens throughout the world and some of the most impressive ones have been residential landscapes with a clear focus and goal. By creating a solid, functional design and good foundation, any landscape is bound to succeed.

Less Is More: The Importance of the Sustainability Movement

So why is sustainable gardening so important? It's important for the same reason living a more responsible, sustainable lifestyle is. Less is more and gardeners have to find creative ways to do more with less. Today natural resources are more limited than ever and the competing demand for them is at an all-time high. With rising costs for fossil fuel, food, other forms of energy, and other products, efficiency is essential. The impact humans have made on the environment over the last century proves that conservation, preservation, reducing water, and using fewer resources is essential to our future. With a growing population and increased demands on our environment, more attention needs to be paid to protecting water supplies, reducing chemical use and pollution, managing invasive species, and nurturing animal and plant life.

The notion that home gardeners can go to a local retail store and purchase chemical fertilizers, pesticides, and other products and apply them at will is old-fashioned. Traditional practices such as these just aren't feasible anymore. *Now* is the time to act responsibly and resist the urge to maintain the garden in a conventional way. *Now* is the time to pay more attention to the health and longevity of the garden by supporting healthy soil biology, responsible use of water, and the introduction of new and improved plant species and varieties into the landscape.

"On a smaller scale, home gardeners can implement the same philosophies that created great American landscapes by using sound garden design principles and maintenance practices."

USDA Plant Hardiness Zone Map

USDA Plant Hardiness Zone Map, 2012. Agricultural Research Service, U.S. Department of Agriculture. Accessed from http://planthardiness.ars.usda.gov.

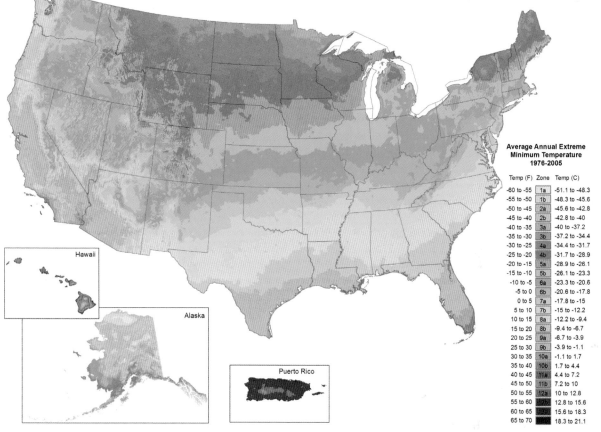

Average Annual Extreme Minimum Temperature 1976-2005

Temp (F)	Zone	Temp (C)
-60 to -55	1a	-51.1 to -48.3
-55 to -50	1b	-48.3 to -45.6
-50 to -45	2a	-45.6 to -42.8
-45 to -40	2b	-42.8 to -40
-40 to -35	3a	-40 to -37.2
-35 to -30	3b	-37.2 to -34.4
-30 to -25	4a	-34.4 to -31.7
-25 to -20	4b	-31.7 to -28.9
-20 to -15	5a	-28.9 to -26.1
-15 to -10	5b	-26.1 to -23.3
-10 to -5	6a	-23.3 to -20.6
-5 to 0	6b	-20.6 to -17.8
0 to 5	7a	-17.8 to -15
5 to 10	7b	-15 to -12.2
10 to 15	8a	-12.2 to -9.4
15 to 20	8b	-9.4 to -6.7
20 to 25	9a	-6.7 to -3.9
25 to 30	9b	-3.9 to -1.1
30 to 35	10a	-1.1 to 1.7
35 to 40	10b	1.7 to 4.4
40 to 45	11a	4.4 to 7.2
45 to 50	11b	7.2 to 10
50 to 55	12a	10 to 12.8
55 to 60	12b	12.8 to 15.6
60 to 65	13a	15.6 to 18.3
65 to 70	13b	18.3 to 21.1

But besides the obvious benefits I've listed, practicing sustainable gardening ensures the long-term viability of the landscape and over time creates a low-maintenance environment. This low-maintenance environment will ultimately support beneficial insects, birds, and other important wildlife, and also reduce the impact of invasive plants and the reliance on chemicals. It will also encourage the use of organic measures to maintain a well-balanced landscape. Again, while the short-term benefits of chemicals and traditional gardening practices are tempting to use, sustainability offers greater options and alternatives. Sustainability is without a doubt a "marathon" that requires endurance and patience over the shorter term "sprint" or quick fix that has been the main theme within the home garden.

CLIMATE CHANGE

One of the most important issues influencing sustainability today is climate change. Many experts feel there is consistent evidence to suggest that the earth is getting warmer and climate change is a reality we must face now. But more than just a warming trend, there is a bigger picture in terms of what climate change means to us. Climate change is thought to affect overall weather patterns causing extreme weather conditions, variations in temperature, both hot and cold, drought, excessive rain, and flooding. In the gardening world climate change is believed to be affecting plant growth and blooming times (with some plants migrating from their traditional hardiness zones). These shifting weather patterns are directly responsible for longer growing seasons. This is why there have been recent changes to the USDA hardiness zone map, in most cases showing a warming trend in the United States.

While it is impossible to predict what the future holds, groups like the National Oceanic and Atmospheric Administration (NOAA) are closely monitoring this issue and the future impact it will have on our environment. This is why the sustainability movement is so important right now. Many scientists feel that by reducing the human impact to the environment, it will decrease these effects, or at the very least not make them any worse in the future. Climate change adds a sense of urgency to becoming more sustainable, especially from a landscape perspective. Practicing smart horticulture and sound landscape design practices can play major roles in improving the community we live in. Protecting our natural resources, wildlife habitats, and plant life one garden at a time will undoubtedly help the cause. It's especially important since large corporations, farmers, golf course managers, nurseries, and just about everyone around us have already started some sort of sustainability program. If large, commercial land managers can become sustainable, then so can you.

WHAT'S OLD IS NEW AGAIN: THE HISTORY OF THE SUSTAINABILITY MOVEMENT

The history of sustainability is a complex and fascinating story. The word "sustain," from the Latin *sustinere* (*sus* from below and *tenere* to hold) means to keep in existence or maintain; it implies long-term support or permanence. Sustainable practices can be traced back 8,000 to 10,000 years. Agrarian communities depended largely on their environment and the creation of a "structure of permanence." Societies outgrowing their local food supply or depleting critical resources either moved or faced collapse. Archeological evidence suggests that the early civilizations arose in Sumer, now Iraq and Egypt, dating back to 3000 B.C. The example of Sumer illustrates issues vital to sustainability and human survival. Sumerian cities practiced year-round agriculture. The surplus of storable food created by this civilization allowed its population to settle in one place instead of migrating in search of food. The inhabitants learned to use agricultural techniques to their benefit rather than depleting the land.

The Industrial Revolution of the eighteenth to nineteenth centuries maximized the growth potential of the energy created by fossil fuels. Over time these innovations took their toll on the environment. In the mid-twentieth century, a global environmental movement highlighted that there were environmental costs associated with the many benefits that human innovations had provided. In the late twentieth century, these environmental issues became most evident with the energy crisis of 1973 and 1979, which brought to the forefront our dependence on non-renewable energy resources.

In the twenty-first century, there is much more awareness and sensitivity to the pitfalls and past environmental impacts created by humans. During the modern era, sustainability as it relates to agriculture began in the early 1980s. In this context, sustainable agriculture was developed to create farming systems that were capable of maintaining their productivity and usefulness to society over a long period of time. Like all sustainable systems, farming had to become more efficient and resource conserving, socially supportive, commercially competitive, and environmentally sound. Sustainable agriculture was addressed by Congress in the 1990 Farm Bill. Under that law, the term "sustainable agriculture" means an integrated system of plant and animal production practices having a site-specific application that over time will satisfy human food needs, enhance environmental quality and the natural resources, create more efficient use of nonrenewable resources and on-farm resources and integrate, where appropriate, natural biological cycles and controls and sustain economic viability and quality of life as a whole.

Using the Same Practices

Many of the eco-friendly principles and ideas that are used in sustainable gardening today embody the same practices and beliefs established during the sustainable agricultural movement years ago. These practices were established as initiatives for resource saving, self-sufficiency, and small-scale farming based on eco-friendly principles including biodynamic agriculture, no till farming, forest gardening, and of course, organic gardening. On a larger scale there is the more recent "whole farm planning," which is a holistic approach to farm management used to identify and prioritize environmental issues on a farm without compromising the farm business. There is also eco-agriculture, first recognized in 2001, which was developed to enhance rural livelihoods by conserving and enhancing biodiversity and ecosystems and developing more sustainable and productive agricultural systems.

One of the most influential of these sustainable approaches is permaculture, which relates to ecological design and engineering and develops sustainable human settlements and self-maintained agricultural systems influenced by natural ecosystems.

It was some time later that sustainable horticulture (gardening) became recognized as an important part of human culture. Sustainable horticulture was first addressed on a global scale at the International Society of Horticultural Science's First International Symposium on Sustainability in Horticulture held at the International Horticultural Congress in Toronto in 2002. This symposium produced tangible conclusions on sustainability in horticulture for the twenty-first century. The principles and objectives outlined at this conference were discussed in more practical terms at the following conference at Seoul, South Korea, in 2006.

> "Sustainability was born from the efforts of the agricultural industry and is now a household word on a global scale."

While sustainable agricultural programs influenced the development of what we now know as sustainable horticulture, there is one significant difference, which is that agriculture primarily relates to developing food while horticulture specifically relates to enhancing the aesthetics and functionality of the landscape. But the principles are indeed the same and the main goal tied to both disciplines is saving resources and creating a low-maintenance environment.

LOW MAINTENCE IS A GOAL

Low-maintenance gardening is one of the main benefits of developing a sustainable landscape and vise versa. The two are integrated, but this takes an investment of time and patience, at least initially. While many gardeners enjoy working in their gardens, reducing maintenance is worthwhile for several reasons. First, by reducing the overall maintenance of the garden, gardeners can focus their time and efforts on future planning, enhancement, and expansion of the garden, as well as the acquisition of new plants and garden features. Second, a low-maintenance garden requires fewer resources and will ultimately cost less to care for. If these landscapes are maintained using a more natural, organic approach in a holistic, comprehensive manner, the long-term benefits include saving resources, reducing health risks, and ultimately reducing intense maintenance and day-to-day care. How much time is needed to accomplish this really depends on the type, size, and complexity of the garden and the environmental conditions in it. But in general, even within a few years great strides can be made to reduce garden maintenance if sustainable practices are implemented. Some examples of using sustainable practices to reduce maintenance are proper mulching and composting to enhance soil biology, creating habitat for beneficial insects, and proper siting and selection of superior plant species. A few good examples of low-maintenance practices that will lead to a more sustainable landscape include raising mowing heights of turf, using a mulching mower, and designing the garden with smooth curving lines that are easy to mow along. These maintenance practices are a few of many ways that dedicated gardeners can create a more sustainable garden.

Soil is the Foundation

One very important example described is soil biology and health of the soil, which plays a huge part in supporting a sustainable garden. Soil is the foundation that sustains life in the garden. If it is lacking or compromised, sustainable gardening is unrealistic and hard to achieve. Everything starts in the soil and it is important to investigate your soil conditions first before investing any time in enhancing your garden. While it is true that certain plants will thrive in poor, depleted soils, by making efforts to improve soil drainage and friability (ability to be "crumbled"), pH, organic matter content, and the microorganisms that live in soil, your garden success is much greater. The best way to learn more about the condition and type of soil you have in the garden is to take a soil sample to your local agricultural Extension agency and have it tested for pH, nutrients, and organic content. While improving soil health takes time, the benefits will have long-lasting rewards. It is similar to a building contractor who creates a strong foundation on a house, uses quality building materials, and does fine quality craftsmanship—you have a better home. The hard work and investment of time and money in your landscape will pay off in the future.

THE BENEFITS OF GOING GREEN

So, what are the advantages of "going green" and what does that mean? Probably the most logical explanation for the term is to live more responsibly with the goal to reduce consumption and negative impact on the environment. Using renewable energy and recycling or reusing recycled products can accomplish this goal. The term "going green" sounds like a responsible thing to do to protect our environment. But to truly embrace the green movement, one must be committed and motivated to follow this greener path. This decision will have many benefits that will save money and time. There are many reasons and tangible benefits to going green in your home and garden. These benefits can include increasing energy efficiency and cost savings, increasing property value, and reducing health risks. In business, green products also help foster healthy competition, which helps our economy. In a garden setting, going green can translate into the reduction of exposure to harmful chemicals and materials and an overall healthier, thriving garden.

So what specific things can you do as a homeowner to practice more sustainable living? There are many ways even outside the realm of gardening. For example, besides recycling cans and paper, using double-sided copies can save a significant amount of copy paper. Of course, as computer technology has increased over the past two decades, electronic means of communication have greatly reduced the need for paper. Collecting batteries and taking them to a local retail outlet or recycling center will reduce the chance of them ending up in a landfill. Time and money can also be saved by using rechargeable batteries. Using alternative fuel vehicles that run on renewable energy is quickly becoming a popular trend that is an efficient, reliable, and eco-friendly way of traveling. New vehicles can be powered by electricity and recharged, or powered by natural gas. New hybrid vehicles have become quite popular that run on a combination of gasoline and electricity and gas mileage is exceptionally good. New technology has resulted in electric- or battery- operated power tools and gardening tools that reduce pollution and are easier to use for home gardeners. All of these new innovations support the idea that sustainable living is much more within our grasp now than it was twenty years ago. New technology continues to be the driving force that guides us to a greener future.

DEVELOPING A PLAN

Within the framework of the landscape, whether natural or cultivated, there are several examples of where responsible, objective thinking can be an important asset when developing a sustainability plan. These two examples highlight the notion of thinking outside the box on a more global scale rather than just our own backyard.

Poison Ivy Isn't Always a Weed

The first example involves a gardener's constant battle with poison ivy (*Toxicodendron radicans*), a member of the sumac family often

Poison ivy fruit is high in protein and is a valuable source of food for a wide variety of birds.

associated with causing rashes or blistering of the skin. Within a cultivated garden we spend an enormous amount of time eradicating this garden pest and maligning its very existence, but poison ivy is actually a very important native plant.

Poison ivy is dioecious, meaning it has male and female flowers on separate plants, like hollies. The female plants produce silvery gray fruit, which are a highly valuable food source for birds such as cardinals, robins, chickadees, bluebirds, and other native birds. The fruit is high in lipids and is an ideal food source for birds migrating for the winter. In addition, white tailed deer, rabbits, and raccoons will feed on the new foliage and fruit of poison ivy. Poison ivy also provides shelter for small mammals such as rabbits, squirrels, chipmunks, and birds.

> "Going green involves a strong commitment and the ability to accept change in everyday life."

Another role that poison ivy plays in our natural environment is that it is essential to the stabilization of barrier beaches as it holds down sand dunes that would otherwise be swept away by wind and damaging storms. This is true from the maritime providences of Canada all the way to Florida, and beyond. In fact, poison ivy is native in all states east of the Rocky Mountains.

So within a garden setting poison ivy is an unwanted guest but within the natural world that surrounds our garden, it plays a vital role and therefore has its place without us even realizing it.

Another example of a so-called "weed" plant that plays an important role in our environment is black cherry (*Prunus serotina*). It is native from eastern Canada south to Florida and Texas. This fast-growing, somewhat invasive tree has spiky white flowers in spring, smooth green leaves, and dark brown to gray, rough bark. While it's not considered an ornamental worthy of inclusion in a garden, black cherry is a very important food source for a wide variety of insects and birds. For example, Dr. Douglas Tallamy from the University of Delaware compiled important research data about species of plants that most support butterfly and moth species. The table below shows black cherry with the second highest number (456) of insect species supported behind oaks. These insects are central in the pollination of plants and in turn also support a wide variety of bird species as well.

Butterfly/Moth Species Supported

TREE	LATIN NAME	
Oak	*Quercus*	534
Black cherry	*Prunus*	456
Willow	*Salix*	455
Birch	*Betula*	413
Poplar	*Populus*	368
Crabapple	*Malus*	311
Blueberry	*Vaccinium*	288
Maple	*Acer*	285
Elm	*Ulmus*	213
Pine	*Pinus*	203
Hickory	*Carya*	200
Hawthorn	*Crataegus*	159
Spruce	*Picea*	156
Alder	*Alnus*	156
Basswood	*Tilia*	150
Ash	*Fraxinus*	150
Rose	*Rosa*	139
Filbert	*Corylus*	131
Walnut	*Juglans*	130
Beech	*Fagus*	126
Chestnut	*Castanea*	125

This is an example of a well-planned, sustainable garden at Farmingdale State College in New York, which encompasses wildlife friendly plants, a rain garden, edible plants and native plants including meadow grasses.

In both of these scenarios, it is easy to see how plants that we often take for granted serve a vital role to the world around us. In areas where we can, such as woodlands, seashores, and native borders, maybe we should give these types of plants a second thought. It's not only about how plants serve us but how they serve the environment as a whole.

Here are two examples that the sustainability movement is alive and well. Professor Michael Veracka, a landscape gardener and chairman of the ornamental horticulture program at Farmingdale State College in Farmingdale, New York, has created a sustainability garden for the purpose of teaching students enrolled in the program as well as homeowners the virtues of sustainable living. Students have access to many innovative and educational components of the garden, which is still evolving. Each spring the staff hosts a sustainability conference for the community featuring knowledgeable speakers, vendors, and demonstrations about sustainability. It is a great example of how college universities can incorporate a sustainability program into their horticulture, landscape architecture, environmental science, and ecology programs nationwide. Today many universities are doing just that, not only developing management programs for campuses to practice sustainability, but by also incorporating course work on sustainability into their curriculums.

is an excellent way for golf courses to provide an educational and environmentally sound management plan while still providing quality golf to their patrons. The goal of this program is to protect our environment and preserve the natural tradition of golf. Today many golf courses around the country participate in this program. If a golf course can become more sustainable, so can a home gardener. In fact, golf courses, parks, public gardens, nature preserves, and other public facilities play a vital role in environmental education and the advancement of the sustainability movement.

> "Sustainability affects properties, private and public, large and small with the same relatively positive results."

EMBRACING SUSTAINABILITY

To make sustainability work for you, you must embrace the notion that human beings have a great effect on their environment and accept the fact that you are a part of a much larger equation. The idea that humans are at the top of the food chain and should be allowed to consume what we need without taking responsibility is irresponsible and short sighted. It is important to understand that we need to respect and share our natural world and its resources with a vision towards protecting future generations. It is equally important to understand that we need animals, plants, clean air and water, a reliable food source, and healthy soil to survive. The environment is not ours to use and sometimes misuse as we see fit. The more products and materials that can be reused rather than wasted, the cleaner our environment will be. Sustainability gives us the opportunity to protect our natural resources while creating a healthier, more productive life for everyone. If there was ever a mantra that typifies what sustainability is all about it is this:

Rethink, Reuse, and Reduce

Equally impressive is Beth Page State Park Golf Course, located close by the Farmingdale campus on Long Island. It is one of the most famous public golf courses in the United States. The legendary black course played host to the 2002 and 2009 U.S. Open, an honor that is at the pinnacle of the golf world. But while Bethpage had been managed as a traditional golf course with intensely manicured greens, they have also made a great effort to make the course more sustainable. Working with Audubon International, an organization that helps golf courses and other facilities manage natural areas, they have planted native species and encouraged wildlife habitats while minimizing potentially harmful impacts of the golf course operations. It

CHAPTER 1

Eco-Friendly Strategic Planning for Your Garden

Setting Up a Blueprint for the Future

The term *eco-friendly* is used quite often, but do you truly know the meaning and intent of the term? Many people don't. *Eco-friendly* is an abbreviated version of *ecologically friendly* or *environmentally friendly* and basically means the activities, products, practices, and policies that do the least amount of harm to the environment. Companies and organizations have used this term regularly as a marketing tool to make their products more attractive to consumers. In the garden realm, *eco-friendly* can have very specific and direct significance. For example, compost and processed organic products are marketed as eco-friendly products because they are derived from plant and animal matter. It seems only natural that this recycling process of returning to the earth what came from it is the right thing to do. Eco-friendly products can be a wide range of recyclables, such as fertilizer, paper, and cardboard; recycled plastic and rubber products; recycled wood products; and more. Eco-friendly activities can range from using grey water (recycling wastewater as a source of nonpotable water to wash clothes or water the lawn) to riding a bike to school or the mall rather than using a car. Using energy conservation initiatives and equipment that reduces harmful emissions is not only eco-friendly but is economical as well.

Eco-friendly strategic planning takes the term *eco-friendly* to a whole new level and validates why sustainability is so meaningful. There is no question that in order to be successful at creating a sustainable garden, you have to do a little research, be prepared, and have a plan in place before starting. A gardener without a plan is destined to waste time and money trying to piece together various sustainability practices with no clear sense of direction. Planning gives you the opportunity to map out a schedule, prioritize, and list the goals that will undoubtedly make your life easier in the long run. That's what this chapter is about—helping you plan.

LONG-TERM PLANNING AND SUSTAINABILITY

Long-term planning is a key element in developing a sustainable garden. Proper planning and design will enable your home landscape to survive the stress of an ever-changing, challenging world that includes extreme environmental conditions, increased pressure from pests, and other environmental challenges. If we have learned anything from the history of the American landscape, it is that the landscape is a dynamic entity. The late part of the nineteenth century until the middle part of the twentieth century brought ingenuity and the great American ideals that open space and the interaction between the landscape and humans are critical. Back then, landscapes were built with long-term goals and great aspirations of making a difference. But slowly our public and private landscapes have become shorter-term propositions with little regard for long-term viability. The ideals and life lessons that worked in our favorite community gardens can be applied to our own residential landscapes. As home gardeners, we love the open space of our own backyards and that connection with nature. This open space does not have to be a large, expansive lawn but can be something more long-term, such as a diverse landscape planting that you can enjoy growing old with. It is time to start reinventing our gardens and infusing in them the same passion and long-term planning that previous generations felt so committed to.

This commitment to the future starts with planting the garden for the long-term and not worrying about now. Today, in the context of new plantings, many home gardeners focus on how their landscape looks *right now*. It's all about "how do I screen the neighbor's fence?" or "how fast will my perennial garden grow so I can have instant color in the garden?" But that is not how sustainability in the garden works. We should not be focused on the short-term benefits of the garden as much as what it will offer and look like years down the road. So when you're designing your garden—and *before* you add plants—you've got to do some research to fully understand how the plants you are considering grow and what their ultimate size will be. Many times I have seen

gardeners just plant whatever they want wherever they want, with the idea that if the plant gets too big or becomes a problem, it can just be pruned or transplanted sometime in the future. This is the complete opposite of sustainable gardening. A better approach would be to provide your plants with the space and growing environment that will maximize plant growth and function in the landscape. Plants that have been put in the right situation have a much better chance of thriving in that situation and requiring little care while providing big dividends.

Believe me, as the director of Planting Fields Arboretum, I know firsthand that plants aren't as easy to control as we would like to think! The notion of pruning a shrub that has been misplaced in the garden because we don't want it to outgrow its bounds is shortsighted. Frankly, misplaced plants will either become misshapen or eventually outgrow the rate you prune them; they become eyesores or burdens on the landscape. Misplacement or poor planning can cause plants to perform so poorly that we lose sight of what the original purpose was. Sustainability gives us an opportunity to realize that we are not in control of our environment and we need to work with nature rather than against it. It is a hard lesson to learn, and many gardeners have had to experience this firsthand in order to truly understand it.

The long-term planning of the landscape is especially important in planting trees, shrubs, and evergreens. These plants typically live for a long time compared to other plants, such as herbaceous and tropical plants. More often than not, these woody plants are not given adequate room to grow, outgrowing their allocated space way before they reach maturity. I have witnessed many an evergreen grouping shoehorned into an area too small to accommodate it with spacing of only a few feet between plants. In five years' time, these plants are competing with one another and shading one another instead of complementing one another in the garden.

THE ONE-HALF RULE

One basic rule that I recommend you should follow, whether you're planting a shrub, shade tree, or evergreen, is the One-Half Rule. Whatever

Properly spacing your shrubs so they have adequate room to grow is important.

plant you select for your yard, find out how large it will ultimately grow. Then assume it will grow *at least* half that size in your lifetime. This will help you determine how far the plant should be planted from the house, fence, garage, or other plants. For example, if you choose to plant a row of American arborvitaes (*Thuja occidentalis*), and the plant tags state they will grow 30 feet tall and 15 feet wide at maturity, then at the very least, you should assume that each arborvitae would grow 15 feet tall and 7.5 feet wide in your lifetime. That means that you should plant these arborvitaes farther apart than just a few feet—in this case, more than 5 feet apart. Yes, it will take longer for your plants to touch or fill in, but ample space will allow them to reach their ultimate size unobstructed by an overcrowded garden. Obviously the One-Half Rule depends on the specific growth of your plants, your climate, your soil, and many other factors, but you get the idea. This rule may seem a bit extreme, but many modern landscapes become overgrown with poorly shaped plants because we want an instant landscape. This rule supports the idea of a more open, airy landscape with plenty of air circulation and light, which will create better growing conditions. The goal here is to spend time planning your garden design and to implement sound gardening practices. It depends on what you are trying to accomplish. For example, I might space my arborvitae a bit closer if I am creating a screen or hedge versus if I want a grouping to soften the foundation of the house.

Proper spacing, siting, plant selection, and understanding of the specific growing conditions for the plants in your yard are all important factors that must be considered when planning the garden. Plants that are given the proper growing environment and spacing will be healthier, will require less maintenance, and will offer the most function and ornamental qualities possible. The more tinkering you do to control the natural environment that plants live in, the more you create an artificial, unsuitable environment for your favorite garden plants. Planting for the long term ensures that the landscape will be able to survive, even through adverse conditions, for a long time.

Besides proper gardening practices, choosing long-lived, adaptable plants—such as long-lived hardwood trees like oaks—is an important part of any long-range landscape plan. The garden culture today seeks plants that grow and establish quickly. We want things now and don't want to wait years for something to look good. But with the exception of perennials, annuals, and tropical plants, many fast-growing plants such as willow, Leyland cypress, maple, and poplar are considered short-lived compared to native hardwoods and long-lived plants such as oak, cherry, elm, and dogwood. This is why it is so important to select a diverse collection of plants for your garden. With the right mixture of slow-growing, long-lived plants and shorter-term species, the garden will be balanced and productive.

> "It is important that you provide your trees and shrubs with adequate space, light, and air circulation, which will help them reach their full potential. Know how big your plant will get at maturity and assume it will get at least half that size and space during your lifetime."

SITE ANALYSIS

The concept of site analysis is derived from a series of steps in urban planning. It involves research, analysis, and synthesizing findings to develop a plan. This formal and often complex process is used widely in architecture, landscape architecture, and engineering. But within the context of garden sustainability, this can be a much simpler process. (The principles are still the same.)

The goal of a site analysis is to evaluate your garden and record your observations. This is critical before designing the garden and implementing that design. Whether you are planting or altering part or all of the landscape, a site analysis gives you the opportunity to fix past failures or issues. Without a site analysis, gardeners will likely repeat the same mistakes over and over because they've given too little time to the planning process. A sound, well-thought-out, organized strategic plan will lay the foundation upon which your sustainable garden will be built, making the most of your efforts. How many times have we purchased plants, pottery, garden ornaments, furniture, and so forth at a local store and just placed them where we had room? A thorough site analysis will help you determine where things should go in the garden—sort of like arranging a room in your house. Many gardeners think of their landscape as an extension of their living space, which it is.

In addition, a site analysis gives you an opportunity to evaluate existing conditions in your garden. This is when you should be evaluating soil type and drainage capacity, light conditions, exposure and wind issues, erosion problems, and so forth. Site analysis will also enable you to reconfigure your garden if something is not working well for you. Perhaps your patio is in the wrong location, or you would prefer to have more shade on the western part of the house in the afternoon and need an evergreen screen.

When performing your site analysis, rarely are you dealing with a blank page that can be easily manipulated. More often you will be evaluating a site within an established landscape. If you move into a newly built home and you have a fairly blank slate with a lawn and a few new trees, it does make things a bit simpler. But if you own or inherit a mature landscape, you will have to decide how to work around existing features such as large trees, shrub borders, walkways, patios, and so on. This is all the more reason why a site analysis is so important in the process of creating a sustainable landscape. It gives you the option to erase past blunders and enhance the functionality, aesthetic qualities, and long-term sustainability of your garden.

Drawing a Simple Site Analysis

Before you begin your site analysis, you will need a few materials to complete the survey of your property.

- Clipboard and notepad to document your findings
- Deed map (This can be obtained at your local county clerk's office. It is a simple map that will show property lines, outline of the house, and other important information.)
- Measuring tape and helper to measure bed dimensions, widths of walkways, placement of trees, and other important information
- Digital camera to take "before" pictures, which will help you determine what you like and dislike about your garden

If a deed map of your property is not available, simply get some drawing paper and sketch out the basic areas of your property: house, driveway, walkways, any other significant landscape features, and so forth. If you are reconfiguring the garden, you would only want to draw in any existing features that will remain and then draw in any new features—plantings and such that you want to obtain. For example, if, while doing your site analysis, you notice a small depression in the garden where water collects after a rainstorm, you should note that. Perhaps the best plan of action for that area would be to create a rain garden.

Plant Inventory

Other important information that you should be recording is a plant inventory. This is especially true if you plan to move or redesign a particular area of the garden. This inventory should include plants you want to salvage as well as ones you want to remove. All of this information should be noted on your sketch. A simple chart can be created to easily organize and record inventory of your garden.

By recording this valuable information, you will learn a lot about the plants that are growing in your garden. For example, if your hydrangeas are performing poorly in the area where you have them currently, it may be wise to look closer at the conditions they are growing in and move them to a more suitable area of the garden. Or if the Japanese maple is getting too close to the house and is in poor condition anyway, maybe it is time to replace it with something more suitable.

Once you have documented existing conditions of the site, you can determine where specific plants will grow best, where the lawn should go, where the compost bins would work best, and so on. Obviously you would want to site the vegetable garden or the lawn in a sunny location with good drainage and place shade-loving perennials and shrubs along the perimeter of the garden in more protected areas. Since sustainability is doing (and growing) more with less, maximizing the space that you have and finding the right place for plants, hardscape features, recreational areas, and even just an area to sit and enjoy your handiwork is important. Putting everything in its proper place will give the garden organization and proper perspective.

Sample Plant Inventory Chart

Plant Name	Type	Quantity	Size	Location	Condition
JAPANESE MAPLE	TREE	1	20 FT. TALL BY 12 FT. WIDE	NORTHEAST CORNER OF THE HOUSE	POOR
KURUME AZALEA	EVERGREEN SHRUB	5	24x24 IN.	NORTHWEST SIDE OF GARAGE	FAIR
VARIEGATED HOSTA	PERENNIAL	12	12x15 IN.	UNDER MAPLE TREE ON NORTHEAST SIDE OF PROPERTY	GOOD
AMERICAN ARBORVITAE	EVERGREEN SCREEN	7	4 FT. TALL	SOUTH SIDE OF THE PROPERTY ALONG THE FENCE LINE	GOOD
HYDRANGEA	FLOWERING SHRUB	3	4x5 FT.	FRONT YARD NEAR BAY WINDOW	FAIR

Other information to consider when doing a site analysis:

- Pay close attention to where underground utilities such as water, electric, telephone, and natural gas are. Call 811 to have a markout done by a trained professional before doing any digging.
- Over several days, weeks, or months, observe how sunlight hits the garden and what areas are in shade, partial shade, or sun most of the day. Taking a photograph in the exact same spot each time you do your observation will give you an excellent perspective on how sunlight illuminates your garden over a period of time.
- Check for overhead wires, tree branches, fences, and other obstacles that may interfere with the canopies of new trees or shrubs.
- Take soil samples from various parts of the garden to determine soil types, fertility, and drainage. This will help you determine which plants—flowers, shrubs, trees, vegetable, or lawn—are best suited for a specific location.

A proper site analysis is the first step in creating a garden that will work best for you. Without one, you are walking around blindfolded and not seeing your garden for what it really is. Knowing what you have, what you need, and how to obtain it should be priority number one. You will not be able to truly maximize the potential of the garden without this critical first step.

> "The first step in developing a sustainable garden is to put together a site plan by evaluating your soil, light, and wind conditions and then selecting plants that are adapted to grow in those conditions."

SIZE REALLY DOESN'T MATTER

As you have already learned, sustainability has no real boundaries and can be applied to the smallest postage stamp–sized garden as well as the large, expansive landscape. The size of your garden really is irrelevant in terms of whether sustainable practices are appropriate for your particular site. Sustainability can be valuable no matter what size, shape, or type of garden you prefer. What is more important than size is the know-how to make the most of the resources you have available to you in your specific situation. Not all gardens are created equal, nor should they be. The attraction we all have to gardening is partly because of the fact that gardens are ever-changing features that never cease to amaze us and always entice us to want more.

What is also important is not only how your garden is arranged but also how you maintain it. Overusing chemicals, misusing water, neglecting soil health, and planting and pruning improperly can all contribute to a poorly performing garden. So once you have set up your garden the way you like, and once it is designed with sustainability in mind, it is time to implement those ideals that make sustainability so effective. Keep working at improving your garden and do not complicate what should be a rather simple and sensible approach to garden maintenance. I am a strong believer that simple is better and that gardeners should not overthink things.

THE DOS AND DON'TS OF PESTICIDES

Although the issue of pesticides is discussed in more detail under "Integrated Pest Management" (Chapter 4), it is important to discuss pesticides as they relate to the strategic plan for your garden. Pesticides have been vilified over the past four or five decades because of their overuse and sometimes misuse. There is no question that the heavy debate over this issue has changed the way garden maintenance and pest management are approached forever. The gardening community and the environment are better for it, because we are using chemicals less but more responsibly, and new products are much safer than old ones. By no means am I suggesting that all pesticides should be banned for garden use.

When used judiciously and responsibly, pesticides can be effective at protecting valuable plant crops. On the other hand, if integrated pest management (IPM) and sustainability have taught us anything, it is that finding less toxic alternatives to pesticides is in everyone's best interest. Pesticides should be used only when necessary, and quite frankly, I think in most cases, leaving pesticide applications up to a landscape professional who is trained to do so is the best-case scenario.

The fact of the matter is that no matter how safe pesticides are, they are still products that are designed to kill or suppress pests. Even something as safe as horticultural oil or soap should be used with the utmost care. The best advice I can give to you, the home gardener, is don't always run to the cabinet to get a pesticide to deal with a pest issue. Sometimes it is better to handle this issue another way. A more responsible approach would be to take a pest problem or question to your local agricultural Extension office for further analysis. It may be able to recommend a nonchemical solution to your problem. This approach is more eco-friendly and supports the principles of IPM and sustainability.

It is true that pest management technology has advanced substantially over the years, now including more biological controls, biopesticides, and even strategies such as use of insect sex pheromones for mating disruption. Many of the more toxic or problematic products are being phased out or have been cancelled altogether by the Environmental Protection Agency (EPA). Examples of these include dicofol (a once-popular miticide also known as Kelthane), endosulfan (an insecticide also known as Thiodan), and chlordane (used on home lawns for soil insects and around homes as a termiticide). One of the most dramatic and interesting stories to make headlines early in the pesticide debate surrounded the federal ban on use of DDT in 1973; it (and a metabolite, DDE) leaves persistent residues that accumulate, leading to significant health effects on some wildlife, including the American bald eagle.

Pesticides—which include even seemingly benign insecticidal soap, horticultural oil, insect repellents, and minimum-risk products containing plant essential oils—can be helpful in the home garden but should be used judiciously and only as a last resort after other strategies (pest and disease

resistance, hand removal, sanitation, screening or mechanical control, trapping, biological control, and so forth) have been employed or considered. There is scientific evidence showing some of these products may harm or even kill helpful organisms that are not the intended target, such as beneficial insects and mites. These products can even hurt animals and fish and other aquatic life when they are used improperly. My best advice to any gardener experiencing difficult pest, disease, or weed problems in home gardens and landscapes is to discuss concerns with knowledgeable individuals such as local agricultural Extension specialists, experienced gardeners, and other horticultural professionals. In some cases these problems may not be threatening to plant health and are only of a short-term cosmetic nature. In some cases pesticide applications may be prescribed, but if you feel unsure or uncomfortable applying pesticides yourself, you can hire a licensed pesticide applicator to handle the trickier situations.

Some particularly difficult situations where pesticides are typically used:

- Targeted systemic treatments to rescue valuable specimen trees threatened by invasive pests, such as hemlock woolly adelgid or emerald ash borer
- Selective herbicides for invasive or troublesome weeds not easily managed by mechanical means, such as giant hogweed and poison ivy
- Repellents for ticks, mosquitoes, or other pests that may carry disease-causing organisms
- Structural treatments to prevent destruction by wood-infesting insects, such as termites and carpenter ants

The keys to proper pesticide use are to read the label, use as directed, and use only when necessary. If your roses have blackspot, either live with the fact that they will defoliate every few weeks, use organic pest control or cultural measures, or replace the roses with disease-resistant ones. If your hemlocks have succumbed to woolly adelgid, instead of planting the same species again, try a different species, such as western

It is important to place plants in a location they are best adapted for. In this case, shade-loving hostas thrive in a partially shaded area.

arborvitae (*Thuja plicata*), that is more pest resistant. Instead of sprinkling sprays and dusts on your vegetables because of a few chewed holes on the leaves, perhaps a better approach would be to live with a bit of crop loss and blemishes on fruits and vegetables. Sustainable gardening is all about employing sound gardening practices, building a healthy environment, and sometimes even accepting less-than-perfect conditions.

RIGHT PLANT, RIGHT PLACE

It sounds simple enough, but the idea of using the right plant in the right place has not always been as commonly utilized as one might think. This catch phrase embodies what sustainability, IPM, and sound gardening are all about. I first heard the phrase over twenty years ago from two legendary nurserymen, Fritz Schaefer and Jim Cross. Since then, I have tried to practice that ideal whenever I select or recommend plants for a particular landscape.

Proper plant selection is one of the most important aspects of the sustainability movement. It requires patience, passion, and the ability to research superior species and varieties of plants and their optimal growing conditions. I have met gardeners from all over the world and from all walks of life, and they all have one thing in common. All of them have an insatiable appetite for new, exciting, and superior plants and for growing them to the best of their ability. This phenomenon does not just happen by osmosis but exists because each gardener has a spark that gets ignited every time he or she sets foot in the garden.

Gardening should be fun, satisfying, and educational, and choosing the right location for new plants can be both challenging and exhilarating. While is it always good to experiment and try different plants in different landscape situations, it is also not wise to place plants with reckless abandon. Some thought needs to go into why you purchased the plant in the first place, where it will grow best, and how it will be maintained. Many times gardeners make the mistake of selecting plants based solely on their aesthetic qualities, with the main consideration being: where will the plant look best? The answer to that question is that the plant will look best in the growing conditions it is most suited to grow in. A happy plant will be a productive and attractive plant. Placing a shade-loving plant that prefers moist soil in a hot, dry area of the garden because that's where it is most visible or where there is adequate space is a foolish proposition. Putting plants in areas of the garden where they like to grow will create a lower maintenance, more functional and ornamental landscape feature that will offer long-term benefits. It is true that thanks to extensive plant trials and plant introduction programs, researchers from universities and growers have yielded plants that are more drought-, heat-, shade-, and pest-tolerant than ever before. But basic, sound gardening principles cannot be thrown out the window. Rather, these introduction programs give gardeners the opportunity to create a horticultural showplace with more color, texture, and seasonal interest than ever before with less effort.

EXOTICS VERSUS NATIVES

It is important to mention that the introduction of exotic plant species and their impact on native ecosystems is a hot topic of debate. There is no doubt that many introduced insects, animals, and plants have caused serious harm to our natural environment over the years. But it is also important to point out that a plant that is an exotic species from another country it is not automatically a threat to our ecosystem. In a natural setting, I believe that by all means we should be planting species that are indigenous to that particular area. But in a cultivated garden setting, noninvasive exotic species, natives, and cultivated varieties of natives are perfectly acceptable. Remember, a diversely planted, well-designed garden is a healthy garden. If you are unsure if a particular exotic species is invasive in your area, contact your local nursery or agricultural Extension service.

RAISING THE BAR WITH RAISED BEDS

Once you have chosen plants that will work best for your garden, it's time to find the proper place for them. Raised beds can offer several benefits to creative gardeners who have the time and resources to build them. Raised beds enable gardeners to grow plants on elevated soil mounds in areas where drainage may be a problem. Many gardeners like the ability to have various levels in the garden rather than a totally flat landscape. If done correctly, a series of raised planting beds can give a landscape interesting contours and depth while providing function and improved growing conditions.

Raised beds can be created in a variety of ways, with retaining walls made out of brick, slate, or other flat stone, as well as wood timbers or landscape ties. Stone walls do not have to be held together with cement as long as they are built correctly and are not too high. Wooden ties should be secured using landscape tie nails, which can be secured by predrilling the holes before hammering in the nails.

But a simpler approach is the creation of berms, which is a popular practice of mounding soil to create small, sweeping hills that are then planted. The purpose of a berm is to create height and interest in the landscape while increasing the potential for privacy. For example, berms planted with evergreens can help screen off an unsightly view a bit faster because they raise the trees higher. Adding varying levels to an otherwise flat landscape gives it more character and creative possibilities. You will need to determine if a berm will work for your specific situation. Berms are effective where retaining walls are not necessary. But if you have an area that is too steep, a berm may not be the best idea, and you may have to instead build a secure retaining wall.

You should be careful not to make berms too high. Berms should have a gradual slope rather than a sharp incline. A sharp incline will cause berms to erode even if well planted. A berm should be only a few feet tall and at least five to seven times as long and wide as it is high. This means for every foot high the berm is, it needs to be 5 to 7 feet wide. This ratio will stabilize

Raised beds are easy to care for and are especially useful where there is limited access to soil.

the berm so plants, soil, mulch, and so forth don't slide off after a heavy rainstorm. To ensure that berms blend in with the natural landscape, berms should be visually compatible with their surrounding environment. This can be accomplished by creating gradual transitions in elevation rather than just plopping a bunch of dirt in a pile and putting some plants on it. Creating a berm needs to be a well-thought-out process carried out over a series of steps.

A berm can consist solely of high-quality topsoil, or as a less expensive alternative, use well-drained sandy loam or subsoil underneath with only the top foot of the berm consisting of high-quality topsoil. The volume of soil that the berm consists of really depends on what you are planting on it. If it is just herbaceous plants, they will need a lot less soil than a tree or shrub. Think of a raised planter or berm as a big pot or container. The plant will grow only as much as the volume of soil allows, so the volume needs to be sufficient for what you are growing. *Never* build a berm on top of the roots of large, mature trees or right against the foundation of a house. Building berms over tree roots will greatly impact the health of the trees and possibly cause a hazardous situation over time, while piling soil against a house will cause moisture problems. Below are a few helpful hints on building a berm or raised planting bed.

- Remove lawn, soil, and other material from the area where the berm will be placed, making it level.
- Dig up soil in the area to break up the surface of the soil before bringing in soil to create the berm. This will assist drainage and reduce the profile of compacted soil.
- Bring in well-drained sandy loam, clay loam, or topsoil to create the majority of the berm. This subsoil layer should be shaped exactly as you want it, as it will be the foundation that holds the berm together.

- Spread a layer of topsoil 6 to 12 inches thick on top of the subsoil layer. The two layers should be slightly mixed (2 to 3 inches) to encourage integration of soil types and drainage.
- Rake and tamp the soil down lightly to reduce air pockets and settling.
- The berm can be planted with flowers, groundcovers, trees, or shrubs and should be gently watered each time it is required until the soil has settled and stabilized.

> "Building elevated areas, such as berms and raised beds, will give your garden added interest and character and allow you to grow plants that require good drainage."

WATER CONSERVATION

Although water conservation methods are discussed in-depth in Chapter 5, there is no harm in emphasizing them here. Water is not only essential for all living things to exist but is also an element that makes gardens grow. In many areas of the country, water is scarce, and therefore restrictions limit what home gardeners can do in their gardens. Where I live in the Northeast, the last decade has brought ample water—in some years maybe even too much, due to large, damaging storms—while my friends in the Southwest and the Southeast have suffered through some of the worst droughts in decades. These droughts have not just lasted one year, but have gone on for multiple years. This type of severe weather has been a game changer and has forced all of us as gardeners to rethink how we can grow a garden in a more volatile climate while still conserving the water we need to live a normal everyday life. Meteorologists predict a continued trend of more severe and erratic weather patterns, with many

Berms can be a relatively low-cost, easy way to elevate your landscape.

signs pointing toward climate change as the main cause. While it is hard to predict how long these weather patterns will continue, it is certain to challenge us as gardeners for years to come.

Saving water is a wise thing to do no matter where you live and whether you have adequate water supplies or not. New technologies, such as improved watering equipment, rain harvesting methods, permeable pavers, and utilizing gray water, are all great ways to save and reuse water. But within the garden setting, it is also up to the homeowner to implement simple and effective watering techniques to save water and grow a healthy, lush garden at the same time. For too long we have misused, wasted, and ignored water issues in the garden. With new and improved irrigation equipment and current information on how to properly water the garden, you can cultivate healthy plants that are more resistant to severe weather patterns, pests, and other forces of nature.

Efficient Watering Is Critical

The most responsible way to manage water in your garden is to use new and efficient watering devices such as rotor (rotary) and misting sprinkler heads, soaker hoses, or drip irrigation. While this technology has been around for a while, it is much improved in terms of quality, efficiency, and durability. It's not that pulling a garden hose around the garden with an oscillating or impulse sprinkler won't do the job, but an in-ground sprinkler system will save time and money in the long run. At the very least, water-efficient soaker hoses or drip systems that can be operated by simply turning on a garden hose will make your life a lot easier and save water while delivering the right amount of water to your prized garden plants.

The bottom line, though, is that how you water the garden is totally in your hands and is crucial to creating a beautiful and eco-friendly landscape. I'm going to say this over and over throughout this book: water your garden with the idea that it is does not require water every single day. Gardeners and their automatic irrigation systems both seem to be preprogrammed to repeat the same inefficient watering week after week.

Generally, the majority of the garden should be watered infrequently but deeply. Gardens that get a good soaking for a few hours each time the irrigation goes on but only a few times a week will be much healthier and more efficient than those that are watered lightly every day. To encourage a well-established garden with deep, thick root systems and full, healthy foliage, you must use water wisely. Stick to this general rule, and if you need to water a bit more often during severe heat and drought spells, you can always water more often as needed. If, in a given week, you have adequate rainfall or the garden doesn't need water, turn off the irrigation system until you need it. You should not rely on preprogrammed clocks or irrigation rain sensors, which sometimes malfunction, causing the irrigation system to go on during a rainstorm. Water should be considered a gift that keeps our gardens thriving, and it needs to be respected.

OUR CARBON FOOTPRINT

The main goal of living a more sustainable lifestyle is to reduce the impact that we have on our environment. Human activities—commuting, household consumption, eating, and even gardening—all have an impact on the world around us. These activities contribute to the greenhouse gas emissions that are widely considered the main cause of climate change. The more we waste and the less we reuse, the more energy and resources we need to make new products to consume. This cycle leads to more pollution and a greater impact on our environment. But there are many things we can do to reduce our environmental impact. Each day, the choices we make in our home, at work, and even when we are on vacation all have an influence on the world we live in. Even what we eat and how we dispose of the waste we generate has a significant effect on our carbon footprint. It is important to understand that we must do what we can to protect our natural resources for future generations to enjoy.

Within gardening, daily activities such as mowing, blowing, and using a weed trimmer all impact greenhouse gases (GHGs). Lawn mowing contributes *about 5 percent* of the total GHGs in the United States. Each week, about fifty-four million Americans mow their lawns, using 800 million gallons of fuel, which causes harmful pollutants to be emitted into the atmosphere. It is also estimated that one inefficient gas-powered lawn mower running for eight hours will emit as many pollutants as eight new vehicles driving 55 miles per hour for the same period of time. Since 1995, the EPA has been regulating emissions from lawn mowers. The regulations and improvements to make lawn mowers more eco-friendly have dramatically improved in that time. Before 1995, inefficient lawn mowers introduced about 150 pounds (per mower, per year) of GHGs into the environment, while mowers manufactured after 1995 put out 88 pounds of GHGs every year. While electric mowers put out some emissions when in use, the amount is not nearly as much as that produced by gas-powered mowers. Reel mowers obviously would be the most environmentally friendly, since they put out no emissions when in use.

Here is another scenario that will really hit home, literally. Carbon footprint calculations can help put our impacts on the environment in perspective. For example, a household of four people consisting of three bedrooms with modern efficiencies in place, such as energy-efficient lighting, appliances, heating, and cooling, emits about 18 tons of carbon dioxide (CO_2) per year. The same household with no efficiencies emits 29 tons of CO_2 per year. Clearly there is a great benefit to reducing energy use, waste, and our negative impacts on our environment.

Below are a few other ways to reduce the carbon footprint by following a few simple household initiatives.

- Convert inefficient light fixtures and the light bulbs in them to Energy Star products, and you will help reduce energy costs. Energy Star is an international standard for energy-efficient products that was developed by the EPA and the U.S. Department of Energy. Energy Star light fixtures generate up to 75 percent less heat and use about 75 percent less energy than standard incandescent lighting, while lasting ten to fifty times longer, depending on the type chosen.

- Use other Energy Star products, such as appliances, electronics, and heating and cooling equipment, which can reduce greenhouse gas emissions by about 130,000 pounds annually and save money on energy bills.

- Improving your home's insulation by hiring a licensed contractor and reducing drafts and air leaks with caulking, weather stripping, and insulation can reduce waste and save up to 20 percent on energy costs.

- Besides making free organic fertilizer, composting your household kitchen and yard waste reduces the amount of garbage that ends up in the landfill and reduces GHG emissions. Recycling reduces energy consumption, because it saves on manufacturing new products and disposal of old ones.

- Water conservation is also energy conservation. A lot of energy is needed to power water pumps, heaters, and water treatment systems. Simple water-saving initiatives include not letting the water run while shaving or brushing teeth and fixing a leaky faucet or toilet. A leaky toilet can waste up to 200 gallons of water per day. Also, be sure to run your dishwasher only when there is a full load. That alone can save 100 pounds of CO_2 (per dishwasher, per year) dispersing into the atmosphere.

- Look into powering your home with green power, which is environmentally friendly electricity that is generated from renewable energy sources, such as wind and solar power. This green energy can either be purchased or you can modify your home to make your own green power, such as by installing solar panels. Solar power could also be used to light your garden paths. In fact, solar-powered garden lights have built-in miniature panels that collect sunlight and generate power to keep the garden path lit at night. Although green energy requires an initial investment and a long-term commitment, it reduces pollution. See your local power authority for details on availability of green energy.

> "You can reduce your carbon footprint and the negative effects its has on the environment by using energy-efficient appliances, light bulbs, and garden equipment to your advantage."

HOW TO CREATE THE NEXT GREAT SUSTAINABLE GARDEN

Creating a sustainable garden requires planning, organization, and the ability to follow through and implement the plan. The planning process is critical to success because it sets the foundation upon which you can build the garden. When planning to develop a sustainable garden, it is wise to start simple and gradually add more complex components. Gardeners should not fall into the trap of biting off more than they can chew, especially when resources are limited. Once you have a sound garden design and plan, you can implement goals in priority order. It's okay to think big, but it's prudent to tackle one priority at a time instead of trying to do everything at once.

My recommendation is to design and implement any infrastructure renovations, including walkways, patios, irrigation installation, home improvements, and so on, before moving onto landscaping. Once this infrastructure is in place, you can then site trees, shrubs, hedges, perennial borders, and so on.

When you are designing and planning part or all of your garden, there are several guidelines you should follow. If you are totally renovating your garden, or if you have a blank slate, it is important to lay out the garden to fit your needs. Sketching out where things should go based on the information taken from your site analysis will help you formulate your plan. A well-designed garden should be functional and well balanced, with different components integrated seamlessly. For example, the lawn area should transition into flower beds, shrub borders, and ornamental plantings, while work areas such as vegetable gardens and cutting gardens might be better placed in the rear or side of the house near the compost pile and other related activities. It's just a question of organizing your garden so that related garden features are grouped together. More often than not, gardeners find themselves altering only a portion of the garden, but again, it is important to ensure that whatever elements you are adding are properly placed and integrated well with their surroundings. If you choose to have an open lawn area in the front of the house, with an open view from the kitchen window, you would not want to place a berm of evergreens in the middle of the front yard, as it would look awkward and would eventually hide the view that you are trying to preserve.

SETTING UP A GARDEN SCHEDULE OR PLANNER

Once you have an idea of how you want your garden to look and what features it should offer, it is time to set up a schedule of activities that will help you organize what happens in the garden and when. This garden planner will help guide you in future activities and remind you of past activities that have been performed in the garden. For example, a garden schedule or planner can be used to document when you planted your first crop of warm-season vegetables in the spring or how many daffodil bulbs you planted in the fall. The planner can also remind you when you need to fertilize your trees or herbaceous plantings. One of the advantages of doing this is that it offers a guide on what to do when, and past activities can be referenced for future use. Some gardeners like to use charts, checklists, or even daily garden diaries. Any of these can make your life easier, and you should pick the one that fits your needs the best.

This is a sample chart showing typical garden activities by month. The types of activities that you would want to record are things such as: planting, pruning, fertilizing, mulching, and pesticide applications. This sample chart could be photocopied and used year after year. Schedules like this tend to be a bit more general, while a daily diary can be quite detailed.

Sample Garden Schedule

Activity	Jan.	Feb.	Mar.	Apr.	May	June	July	Aug.	Sep.	Oct.	Nov.	Dec.
PLANTING												
SUMMER VEGETABLES					12 TOMA-TOES							
EVERGREENS				6 AZA-LEAS								
FALL BULBS										100 DAF-FODILS		
FERTILIZATION												
TREES			X	X	X				X	X	X	
HERBACEOUS PLANTS			X	X	X	X			X	X	X	
PRUNING												
SPRING-FLOW-ERING TREES AND SHRUBS (AFTER BLOOM)					X	X	X					
SUMMER-FLOW-ERING TREES AND SHRUBS		X	X	X								
CONIFERS (CANDLE PRUNING)												
BROADLEAF EVERGREENS			X	X	X	X	X					
MULCHING			X	X	X	X	X	X	X	X	X	
PESTICIDE APPLICATIONS												
PRE-EMERGENCE WEED KILLER			X	X								
POST-EMERGENCE WEED KILLER		X	X	X	X	X	X	X	X	X		
FUNGICIDE					X	X						
LAWN MAINTENANCE												
ESTABLISHMENT			X	X	X	X			X	X		
OVERSEEDING									X	X	X	
AERATING			X	X	X	X			X	X		
DETHATCHING		X	X		X	X						

STICKING TO THE PLAN

Everyone has a unique garden plan that is specific to his or her garden, climate, and individual needs. In my garden in the Northeast, the garden plan that I implement is much different from those of my friends in Athens, Georgia. No two garden plans should be the same, because we all garden with different expectations, environmental conditions, and available resources. Gardening is not a contest or race to see who has the best garden. Gardening should be a rewarding and fun adventure that will keep you coming back for more.

One helpful tool is setting up a garden checklist of important things to do to keep you focused. This can be sort of like a grocery list, so you don't forget the major priorities that should be done each year. This list should be flexible and can change as your garden needs do, but it will act as a blueprint for the more important seasonal or annual events that should be done regularly. Here is a checklist of things that I consider at the start of the growing season in the spring and beyond.

Vinnie's Garden Checklist

- ❏ Cut down butterfly bush and other summer-blooming shrubs by March 15.
- ❏ Apply 1 to 2 inches of mulch on all garden beds by May 1.
- ❏ Apply 5-10-5 ratio fertilizer to garden beds and lawn by May 15.
- ❏ Plant tomatoes, peppers, and eggplant by May 30.
- ❏ Prune rhododendron, azalea, camellia, and other spring- and summer-blooming shrubs that bloom on previous season's growth after flowering by June 15.
- ❏ Drain and winterize irrigation system by October 31.
- ❏ Cut down all perennials after November 15.
- ❏ Apply antidesiccant to broadleaved evergreens after November 25.
- ❏ Order seeds for spring season by February 15.

A SAMPLE GARDEN PLAN

Sustainable gardening gives you so many opportunities to retrofit an existing garden or start over completely with fresh new ideas. Whether you decide to partially or totally renovate your landscape, there are many sustainable initiatives you can implement that will make a difference. The beauty of gardening is that every day is a new one with endless possibilities. If something isn't working for you, it can be changed for the better fairly quickly. We love gardens because we get to witness our ideas growing along with the plants themselves and it inspires us. The sustainable garden allows our ideas and hard work to last for many years to come while improving our quality of life.

Home gardeners can design and implement almost any idea that they can dream up, with few exceptions. Time and money are usually the only two limiting factors, since enthusiasm is usually abundant in most home gardens. The key to choosing the right landscape for you is to make sure your garden meets all your needs and you follow sound gardening practices. A well-designed, balanced garden should offer aesthetics, function, and seasonal interest as well as sustainable qualities such as water conservation, drought and pest resistance, and wildlife habitat.

Here (pages 38–39) I offer an example of what I consider an innovative, sustainable garden that features low-maintenance plantings and no lawn. This project was designed by landscape gardener and designer Michael Veracka of New England, and it offers creative ground-cover replacements to a lawn as well as interesting hardscape features that allow for accessibility and proper water runoff. This project is a good example of how native plants used in combination with noninvasive exotic plant species can provide seasonal interest, function, and low-maintenance qualities. The concept of a garden void of a lawn is quite unconventional from most residential landscapes today. This garden incorporates such durable and ornamental groundcovers such as prostrate plum yew (*Cephalotaxus harringtonia* 'Prostrata'), cranesbill (*Geranium sanquineum* 'Album'), Russian arborvitae (*Microbiota decussata*), creeping phlox (*Phlox subulata*), and sweet box (*Sarcococca hookeriana* var. *humilis*). Using these choice ground-hugging perennials and woody plants demonstrates this designer's commitment to the sustainability movement. It also demonstrates an equal and admirable vision by the homeowner to think outside the box. This is an excellent example of why it is important to consult with a landscape professional and of how important it is to have a good working relationship between designer and client.

> "Develop a sound garden plan that considers plant function, existing environmental conditions, and the limitations of your landscape. Setting realistic goals and a time frame to achieve them will ultimately pay off."

GARDENING IN LAYERS

Another interesting concept in garden design is the idea of gardening in layers. Although it sounds complicated, layering your garden with a wide variety of trees, shrubs, herbaceous plants, bulbs, groundcovers, and vines will serve you well in several ways. Layering your garden involves designing it so it offers a wide selection of plant types with varying bloom times, ornamental qualities, shapes, and sizes. First, this type of landscaping will allow for a much more interesting garden with multiple seasons of interest. Various textures, colors, and heights will offer much more interest year-round than having a garden that is dominated by one level of vegetation.

If you look in nature, rarely will you see that a forest is *not* layered. Rather, you will see distinct layers, such as the forest floor, low-growing shrubs, midsize understory trees, and finally the canopy. Layering in a garden setting, besides being attractive, is also very healthy. It provides an environment where plants can live together and benefit from one another, offering one another shade and shelter, not to mention the aesthetic benefit of having complementary plants together on display. And as we know from

sustainability, a diverse ecosystem is far more likely to survive the challenges that the environment can dish out, such as climate change, extreme weather, drought, heat, and pests.

This is a good example of planting in layers with woody plants for structure (crape myrtle), taller flowering plants (foxglove) and lower growing perennials (hosta) in the foreground.

SAMPLE LANDSCAPE DESIGN PLAN

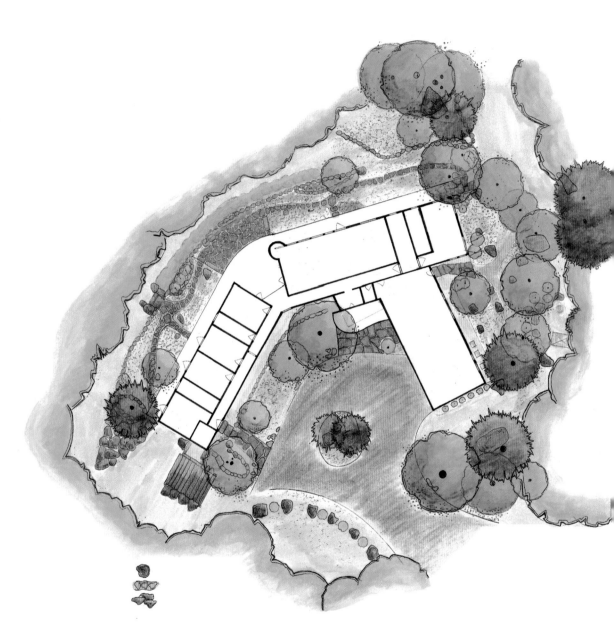

This landscape plan features the creative use of low maintenance groundcovers such as plum yew (Cephalotaxus), cranesbill (Geranium), Russian Arborvitae (Microbiota), creeping phlox (Phlox) and sweet box (Sarcococca), which replace the need for a traditional, high maintenance lawn.

Here is a checklist on how to go about designing you garden in layers:

- Choose a variety of plants that prefer the same or similar growing conditions: soil, light, moisture, and climate.
- Plant the lowest plants in front of the garden beds, with medium-height plantings in the middle and the tallest plants in the back. If the planting can be viewed from all sides, plant the tallest plants in the middle and work down from there with plant heights.
- Do not overcrowd plants, but rather give them their preferred space based on ultimate size.
- Use a balanced combination of tall, medium, and small plants together with a wider variety of blooming times or other ornamental qualities such as fall foliage, fruit, and so on.
- In truly native wooded areas, try to plant only native plants that are indigenous to that area. In a cultivated garden, you can be a lot bolder.

WHEN TO CONSULT WITH A LANDSCAPE DESIGNER

I have met many talented gardeners over the years who were quite capable of designing and maintaining their own gardens. I am often amazed at how effortlessly my gardening friends will know what plants work best where, what colors and textures go together, and how to make everything work together. On the other hand, I have seen inexperienced and novice gardeners who mean well but are less than successful in their garden design endeavors. Landscape design is an art and is not easily absorbed by all of us. Some of us have the knack for knowing what looks good together and what should go where, and others of us do not. I am not suggesting that every homeowner needs to be—or hire—a trained landscape designer in order to have success, but there is a definite benefit from consulting with a landscape design professional at certain times. Knowing when to do it yourself and when to call on a professional is a tricky proposition. It's sometimes difficult to turn your garden over to a landscape professional when you're so passionate about it. There are many factors that affect the decision to bring in a landscape designer to assist in the development of your garden. While the choice is yours, here's a list of scenarios in which you'd want to consult with a landscape design professional:

Top Five Reasons to Hire a Landscape Designer:

1. Your garden is just too large to design yourself, and you need professional help.
2. You are a plant novice, but you know the overall look that you are trying to achieve.
3. You do not have the time to design your garden, but you have the money to pay a professional to do so.
4. You're planning significant installation of infrastructure, such as walkways, arbors, or land clearing, which is outside your scope of ability.
5. You would like a professional landscape designer to give you fresh ideas that you might not otherwise have.

I know many talented landscape architects and landscape designers with whom I consult regularly, and we exchange ideas on horticulture and design concepts. It is a mutually beneficial relationship that brings out the best in me horticulturally and improves my landscape design skills as well. Such synergy will enhance your knowledge of your landscape and allow you to grow intellectually along with your garden.

> "It is wise to hire a professional landscape designer or landscape maintenance professional who can assist you with complex landscape issues and inspire you to reach for new heights in the garden."

Landscape professionals can stimulate new ideas and offer the home gardener many possibilities that would not otherwise be thought of or implemented. The bottom line is: if it is something small you can do yourself, have at it! If you need professional help, whether for maintenance, installation, or design, don't be afraid to seek out the help of a professional.

SUSTAINABLE STRATEGIC PLAN

Gardeners need to know the limitations of their gardens and learn to live within the confines of their resources. I have seen many a gardener who acted like a kid in a candy store, wanting anything and everything to plant in their garden at once. Unfortunately, sound gardening does not work that way, and I have seen real horror shows in which overactive imaginations and well-intentioned enthusiasm went awry. The last thing you want to do is spend a lot of time and money on a garden that is poorly designed, overplanted, and not the least bit sustainable. Besides setting up a garden planner, drawing up a landscape design, and following sound gardening practices, establishing realistic goals is another key piece of the puzzle. As tedious as this might sound, a garden with no plan and no strong set of goals will be extremely difficult to sustain over the long term. The best way to define the goals for your garden is to set up both short-term and long-term sustainable timelines, which will keep you on the right track. Again, home gardens today are typically not designed for the long term, but yours must be if you want it to be more sustainable. Timelines can be appropriately set at intervals of six months, one year, five years, ten years, twenty years, and beyond.

Of course, the guidelines I've outlined on the following pages assume that hardscape features such as walkways, patios, decks, and arbors are already in place or being constructed before garden elements go in. Other elements that should already be in place before planting recommendations are implemented are in-ground irrigation systems, drainage systems, dry wells, and so forth. Installing any of these items after planting has already taken place will just waste time, money, and energy. Any of these initiatives can be moved up the priority list as resources become available.

Six Months

The first six months of transforming your garden into a more sustainable, low-maintenance garden should really be spent on planning and design. This would also be a good time to get organized and begin the process of choosing materials you want to use in the garden. Evaluating the site, sketching and deciding what should go where, and taking photographs of each area to go along with your plan on paper are prudent steps. Life in the garden starts in the soil, so the first six months of developing your new and improved garden should also focus on testing and working the soil to maximize soil health.

Things to Consider for the First Six Months of Garden Development:

- Develop a garden plan on paper.
- Take a soil test and have a complete soil analysis on nutrients and soil pH.
- Develop a compost program and add to soil as an amendment.
- Based on the soil test, start to add lime, fertilizer, and other materials to boost soil fertility.
- Make sure soil is graded properly and address drainage issues.
- Make a checklist of specific plants or garden features you want to acquire.
- Lay out and mark garden features such as new trees, garden beds, berms, rain gardens, lawn, and so on.
- Start collecting and aging compost and mulch for use over the next six months to a year.
- Start to amend and turn over soil in areas designated for vegetables or cut flowers.
- Where you're developing grass meadows or native lawns, kill lawn areas or open spaces by laying down layers of newspapers and compost and plant with a cover crop such as winter rye grass.

Year One

While the first six months should be used to set up and come up with a game plan for the garden, the next six months should be a continuation of those efforts. It should also include implementing some of the infrastructure improvements and developing easy-to-establish plantings such as perennial borders, vegetable garden, lawn, and other landscape features that will establish in a short period of time. If your plan were to reduce an already-too-large lawn and expand garden beds, now would be the time to identify those areas and start to bring in soil, compost, and mulch to make it happen.

Things to Consider for the First Year of Garden Development:
- Continue composting and incorporating compost into the soil.
- Continue enhancing soil pH and nutrient levels.
- Craft garden beds, raised planters, and berms.
- Reduce size of existing lawn or renovate or overseed it; add small lawn area using low-maintenance and/or native grass species.
- Begin planting garden beds with herbaceous plants, native ornamental grasses, and shrubs.
- Begin the process of selecting and placing small and large trees.
- Identify and sculpt area to be used as a rain garden or dry streambed to divert water.
- Eradicate invasive weeds in garden beds, lawn, and natural areas.
- Plant native grass in the area you have been clearing or preparing for meadow planting.

Year Five
Now that the easier-to-establish plantings such as herbaceous planting, lawn, native grasses, shrubs, and smaller trees are in place, it is time to think about the long-range planting plan for the landscape. By year five you should really think about establishing vegetative cover such as evergreen screens and the taller canopy of deciduous trees. These are the plantings that will take the most time to establish and grow to the sizes where they can be of the most value. This is also a good time to continue the

development and long-term maintenance of flowering shrubs that will hopefully help to create the bones, or structure, of the garden.

A green roof can be made up of low-growing groundcovers or even grass.

Things to Consider for the Next Five Years of Garden Development:

- Continue to plant and establish evergreen and deciduous shrub hedges, screens, and woody plantings to create height and depth in the landscape.
- Plant larger deciduous trees for eventual summer shade.
- Start up a management plan for trees and shrubs, including annual pruning, mulching, and pest management.
- Develop a rotation plan to divide and rejuvenate herbaceous plantings on an annual or biannual basis.
- In natural areas, develop tree and shrub plantings such as crabapple, holly, beautyberry, and dogwood as shelter and a food source for wildlife.
- Continue to mow grass meadows once or twice a year or lawns every few weeks, eradicating invasive species as needed.
- Install and manage birdhouses and bat houses in larger trees or vegetated areas.
- Develop a map and inventory of all the more established plantings for future reference.

Year Ten-Plus

The key to a successful sustainability program for your garden is the long-range plans and how they are implemented. It is a lot easier to manage the garden over the short term, but having the foresight and vision to consider ten or more years down the road is both challenging and exhilarating. There are many very positive things that can be done for the first few years to make your garden more sustainable. But it's that ability to continue pushing forward with these successful initiatives for ten or more years that separates the traditional home garden designed for short-term pleasure from the more sustainable, eco-friendly garden that requires less and offers more benefits in the future. For the first decade and beyond, managing the sustainable garden is all about doing less and reaping more benefits. It may take a while to set up and get going, but if done right, your sustainable garden should require less maintenance and interference as time goes by. By this time the priorities should be to continue to plant and manage larger trees and natural habitat, reduce or eliminate the lawn, replace it with groundcovers as larger trees start to cast shade, other low-maintenance initiatives, and refining ideas or initiatives that aren't working as best as they could be.

Things to Consider for the Next Ten Years of Garden Development:

- Manage and continue to plant or replace larger trees, focusing on hardwood species such as oaks (genus *Quercus*).
- As tree canopy begins to shade more of the garden, adjust the types and locations of lower plantings to meet those cultural needs.
- Continue regular selective and rejuvenation pruning on trees and shrubs in both cultivated and natural areas.
- Remove or further reduce the lawn area and replace with native plants, groundcovers, and other plants that require less maintenance and more shade.
- Periodically remove or relocate flower beds or shrub borders to meet the needs of your evolving landscape.
- Continue incorporating mulch and compost to maintain organic matter levels in the soil and to promote a healthy soil environment.
- As native habitat continues to flourish, add or manage bat houses and birdhouses.
- Update your garden map and develop a labeling system for your favorite garden plants.

> "Set short- and long-term timelines for your sustainable garden so that you can stay on track and develop a strong, healthy garden with a purpose."

OTHER GARDENING TRENDS TO CONSIDER
The Green Roof Phenomenon

A green roof is a layer of plants that is grown on a rooftop of a structure such as a building or home. Green roofs have been popular in Europe and other parts of the world for many years and are now gaining in popularity here in the United States. The benefit of green roofs is that they provide shade and have a cooling effect on the roof surface and surrounding area. During the summer months, while the surface temperature of conventional flat roofs can be scorching hot, green roofs will be much cooler. Green roofs also have insulating qualities and are useful in the winter months as well. Now even green walls are becoming popular in commercial uses such as atriums, hotel lobbies, and office buildings. The concept is similar to green roofs, except green walls most often use trailing foliage plants that can grow in a vertical space. This is a great way to add greenery and aesthetics to a public setting.

Many different low-growing plants can be used in green roofs, but the three prevailing qualities required in most cases are a low-growing habit, durability, and adaptability. For example, low-growing groundcovers such as species in the genus *Sedum* (stonecrop) are often used because they can tolerate full sun and hot, dry conditions. New technology even allows stonecrop to be grown and sold in large, flat sheets like sod. It makes planting that much more efficient.

Green roofs have a wide variety of applications but are mostly found on commercial sites and public facilities with expansive flat surfaces. However, there is technology available for green roofs to be installed on private residences as well. Green roofs can be planted with grass, low-growing groundcovers, or even shrubs and trees on larger, commercial applications.

But it is not as simple as pouring some soil on a flat roof and planting it. Green roofs require a lot of planning and technical engineering design, because they are typically heavier than roofs made with conventional materials. For this reason, green roofs are more expensive to construct; however, their long-term durability and environmental benefits will be realized for many years to come. Green roofs not only cool our environment, but also reduce energy costs, absorb and filter pollutants from rainwater and air, and reduce storm water runoff. In addition, green roofs offer aesthetic value and in some cases habitat for wildlife. If you are interested in exploring the option of a green roof, consult with your local architect and engineer to find out more about it. There is no question that your green roof will be the talk of the neighborhood.

DEVELOPING YOUR PLAN

Developing an eco-friendly strategic plan for your garden is essential if you want it to thrive over the long haul. It is the road map that will guide you and keep your ideals and goals on track as you develop your sustainable garden. Gardens without a plan tend to limp along with no clear direction or spiral out of control with too much going on at once. It is clear that humans have a negative impact on the world around us, but we have an opportunity and a responsibility to change that. By planting and planning with decades—not months or a few years—in mind, we can start to impact our environment in a positive way. The art of sustainability is our ability to marry the natural landscape and all its ecological benefits with the beauty and function of the cultivated landscape. Gardening is an active learning experience and a constant reminder that we are in control of the landscape only so much, and then nature must take its course. With the right planning, your landscape will become more sustainable as time goes by.

CHAPTER 2

The Right Plant for the Right Place

Knowing What Plants to Select and How to Use Them

Properly selecting and siting your bulbs, annuals, perennials, shrubs, or trees is easier said than done. It's quite simple to buy some plants at the local nursery and drop them wherever you have room in the garden. It is much more challenging to determine what you are hoping to accomplish or basing your plant purchases on a specific need and then choosing the rights plants for the job. I *know* this has happened to you; it's happened to all of us. Gardeners buy plants on impulse because the plants look good, and then they bring them home looking for room in the garden for them. It is much more prudent to first evaluate your yard and your specific goals and needs, paying close attention to the environmental conditions that your site offers. Once that is done, then a trip to the local nursery can be more focused on what plants will serve your needs and thrive in the soil, light, and overall climate of *your* garden.

The proper selection and siting of plants in the garden is without question one of the most important and sometimes challenging parts of being a good gardener. Sustainable gardening is more than just planting and caring for a bunch of pretty flowers. It is a passionate quest to grow plants that will reach their greatest potential, maximizing their aesthetic value and function in the landscape. Gardeners have an insatiable hunger to strive for a better garden each year; they are never satisfied with the status quo. The ultimate satisfaction for gardeners is to watch the plants that they started from tiny seeds develop into beautiful mature plants, knowing that they had a small part in this growth. It's sort of like the pride parents feel while watching their kids grow up to be successful adults.

SITE ASSESSMENT:
THINK FROM THE GROUND UP!

Before you can determine the right plants for your garden, you need to take a close look at what your garden has to offer. There are many environmental factors that go into the proper growth and cultivation of plants. These factors include soil type and pH, light exposure, wind exposure, surrounding vegetation, wildlife considerations, and so forth. Ask yourself these questions about your site:

- What type of soil do you have? Is it clay, loam, or sand?
- What is the soil pH? Is your soil compacted or in need of amendments?
- Is your garden in full sun, part sun and part shade, deep shade, or a combination?
- Do you live on an exposed site with frequent wind?
- Does your garden have smaller microclimates or areas that are slightly different in temperature than the rest of the garden?

All these questions should be answered before investing a lot of time and money into your garden. By knowing what your garden has to offer, you can determine what plants will grow there. Trying to grow plants that are not suited for your specific climate or environmental conditions will prove to be a frustrating exercise in futility. Many gardeners have tried and failed to retrofit their gardens to suit the needs of plants that are not adapted to grow in that situation. Too much time and money will be wasted trying to get plants to do what we want them to do, rather than what they are adapted to do naturally. I can speak from experience on the trials and tribulations of this dilemma. I have long admired the beautiful spring flowers and undulating, ground-hugging growth habit of spring heath (*Erica carnea*). I have seen this rhododendron relative thrive in the cool climates of Europe and have tried it several times in my garden as well. But because this plant needs absolutely good drainage, and I can offer only heavier clay loam, it does not suceed in my garden. After a third try, I have given up on this spectacular plant and have decided to admire it from afar. This experimentation is in fact a part of the gardening experience. But it is important to realize sooner rather than later that some plants can't be grown in certain situations and time can be better spent concentrating on what you can grow rather than what you cannot. That said, sometimes it is good to experiment with new plants. There is no doubt a wonderful world of new garden plants just waiting to be discovered. As one of my colleagues, Dr. Allan Armitage, often says, "Just shoot the puck!" The key is to try out new plants that are rated to grow in your hardiness zone and soil type.

> "Before you invest a lot of time and money in your garden, pick a day or series of days to check the sun exposure conditions in your landscape. At 8:00 a.m., at noon, and again at 4:00 p.m., go out into the garden and note where the sun hits your flower beds, lawn, and other plantings. It will help to photograph each time so you can remember what you have observed accurately."

Besides assessing the site conditions of your yard, it is also important to seek out well-grown, high-quality plant material. Not that there aren't bargains to be had, but buying plants from a reliable, reputable source is very important. Purchasing plants regularly from sellers who don't know the plants' origins can be risky, since quality control and verifying the source of the material can be an issue. Maybe a better strategy is to buy your plants from a reputable store that specializes in quality nursery stock and garden supplies. It is better to build relationship with a local plant nursery that can focus solely on the growing and selling of plants. Having a personal relationship with a nursery professional who can get you what you need and also keep you updated on new offerings will prove to be invaluable. It is sort of like having your very own plant broker.

WHAT DOES A HEATHY PLANT LOOK LIKE?

In addition to knowing the source of your plant material, knowing what to look for in the quality of that material is equally important. There are physical attributes that well-grown, high-quality plant material should possess, including healthy foliage, a well-established root system, and well-formed branching crowns and trunks with minimal damage. Following is a checklist of items to take into consideration when shopping for high-quality plant material.

- Plants should show good overall health and vigor, with adequate leaf size (leaves that don't look stunted or misshapen) and good leaf color. Leaves should not be wilted.
- Leaves should not be severely scorched (with burned edges), chewed, or otherwise damaged by insects or disease.
- Branches and trunk on trees and shrubs should not have significant scrapes or wounds.
- Rootballs should be evenly balanced and firm, not lopsided or broken.

Nursery plants can come as bare root, in containers, or balled and burlapped.

- Avoid plants that are top-heavy or severely rootbound.
- Containerized plants should be planted firmly in the container and not wobbly. If you are not convinced the root system of the plant is healthy, ask a nursery salesperson to pull the plant out of the pot gently and make sure the root system is healthy, with whitish root tips.

These simple inspection tips will ensure that you are not buying poor-quality plants. While it's okay to tolerate a few bumps and bruises on plants, significant imperfections will only lead to your valuable plants dying before you have a chance to enjoy them. Poor-quality plants are generally stressed, which means that they take longer to establish and are more susceptible to disease, insect infestations, drought, and root rot.

The following chart offers a general guide for rootball sizes of trees and shrubs. This is based on the relationship between the thickness of the main trunk on trees or the height of shrubs. The thickness of the trunk, also called caliper, can be measured by using a ruler or tape measure. The chart clearly illustrates the relationship between size of the plant and appropriate size of the root system. For example, a shade tree with a 1-inch caliper trunk should have a minimum rootball width of 16 inches, and so forth.

Selecting annuals and perennials is a bit different, but the same principles apply. These colorful flowers can be sold in cell packs or plugs,

"Before you spend your hard-earned money on nursery-grown plants, you should make sure you are selecting high-quality plant material. The best way to identify good stock is to check plants visually. Is the plant dried out? Are the leaves deep green, and are the stems strong and free of abrasions? If you are unsure about the health of the root system, ask a nursery salesperson to slip smaller plants out of their pots so you can check for healthy roots. If roots are dried out, brown, or tangled in a circle, pass on the plant and choose another."

may be container, bare-root, or field-grown, and put into pots for transport and sale. In general, container-grown plants should appear healthy and vigorous and not be wilted. Plants should be well rooted and established in the container that they are growing in. This can be determined by gently pulling the plant out of the pot to

Rootball Diameter Examples

Shade Tree		Small Upright and Spreading Trees	
CALIPER	MINIMUM DIAMETER ROOTBALL	HEIGHT (TO 5 FT.) CALIPER (3/4 IN. +)	MINIMUM DIAMETER ROOTBALL
½ IN.	12 IN.	2 FT.	10 IN.
¾ IN.	14 IN.	3 FT.	12 IN.
1 IN.	16 IN.	4 FT.	14 IN.
1 ¼ IN.	18 IN.	5 FT.	16 IN.
1 ½ IN.	20 IN.	¾ IN.	16 IN.
1 ¾ IN.	22 IN.	1 IN.	18 IN.
2 IN.	24 IN.	1 ¼ IN.	19 IN.

inspect the root system. A well-established root system should reach the sides of the container and have a firm rootball but not excessive root growth surrounding the inside of the container (potbound). Potbound plants dry out faster, are generally more stressed, and are harder to acclimate to a new garden environment. One of the best ways to help a potbound plant establish is by taking a hand held cultivator and gently teasing the entire rootball so that the roots are not growing in a circular pattern. This will stimulate the plant roots to grow into the soil rather than continuously growing in a circle.

IT'S ALL ABOUT THE PLANTS

Plants are the backbone of the sustainability movement and are essential to the future of all living things. While this is a pretty bold statement, it is a fact that plants provide food and habitat, prevent erosion, purify air and water, and mitigate climate change. In addition to all these important benefits, plants provide aesthetic value and increase the property value of your home. This is why proper landscaping techniques are so vital to the gardening world. The plants recommended in this chapter are adaptable, durable, and functional additions to the landscape that will serve the garden well.

AND THE WINNERS ARE . . .

This section highlights some of the great garden plants that will enable you to have a more sustainable garden. The selection, siting, and planting of superior varieties of plants for the garden is one of the most important parts of sustainable gardening. Doing all the right things—IPM, composting, watering, recycling, and so on—will be for naught if you misuse plants or select the wrong ones for your specific needs. The key to a successful landscape is to pay careful attention to the proper selection of flowers, shrubs, trees, groundcovers, and vines.

The list provided includes species and varieties of some of my favorite plants for almost any landscape situation. These wonderful plants are durable, adaptable, and reliable performers in the garden. These selections are based on years of observation and admiration for plants that are

of great value to the home garden. Both noninvasive exotic species as well as North American natives have been chosen to provide a complete and diverse offering, and all these plants were selected because of their sustainable qualities.

SHRUBS

Glossy Abelia (*Abelia x grandiflora*)

Ornamental Value

Small, tubular, pale pink to white flowers cover the plant from early summer until the first hard frost in late fall. It is one of the longest-blooming flowering shrubs available. The dark green, glossy leaves turn rich shades of reddish maroon in fall along with rosy pink flower stalks that persist well after the flowers have fallen off. It will be visited often by popular pollinators such as bees and butterflies.

Landscape Value

The upright, rounded, dense growth habit can reach 6 feet tall and equally wide. Glossy abelia is an excellent formal or informal hedge, foundation planting, and companion to perennials, as it plays nicely with its neighbors in a mixed border.

Cultural Requirements

Glossy abelia is heat-, drought-, and pest-tolerant, adapting to a wide variety of soil and light exposure. It prefers well-drained, moist soil and full sun or partial shade. Pruning is not often needed, but glossy abelia can be sheared into a hedge, selectively pruned, or rejuvenated in early spring. This plant is quick to establish, pest-free, and requires minimal care once established, making it a very sustainable addition to the garden. It is hardy from zones 6 to 9.

Cultivars

There are several dwarf forms of glossy abelia that require little or no pruning and not a lot of maintenance. 'Rose Creek' is an outstanding semidwarf variety growing to 3 feet tall and wide. If offers a profusion of blooms and flowers later in the season than most abelia. 'Little Richard' is another compact form growing to 3 feet wide and tall, offering a dense, mounded habit and white flowers. 'Sherwoodii' is a popular variety creeping along the ground and reaching 3 feet tall and spreading to 5 feet.

Related Species

Abelia mosanensis, also known as fragrant abelia, has lustrous, dark green leaves and an upright, arching growth habit to 6 feet. Pinkish white flowers smother the plant in spring and offer an intoxicating sweet fragrance that rivals that of lilac. It is a favorite of butterflies and is also known to be deer-resistant. Fall foliage color can range from orange to red. This plant is hardy from zones 5 to 9.

Bottlebrush Buckeye
(*Aesculus parviflora*)

Ornamental Value

Bottlebrush buckeye is a four-season plant displaying dark green, palmlike foliage; 12-inch-long, frilly white bottlebrush-like flowers in midsummer; golden yellow fall color; and smooth, gray bark in winter. This plant is interesting regardless of the time of year.

Landscape Value

Bottlebrush buckeye can double as a large shrub or a small tree. It does need room and can reach 8 to 12 feet tall and 8 to 15 feet wide. If given the proper room, this amazingly durable plant can be used as a specimen, mass planting, or even a tall screen. It is an excellent plant to use where deer are problematic, since it is highly deer-resistant.

Cultural Requirements

This is a rock-solid plant with very few pest problems or other problems. Bottlebrush buckeye prefers moist, well-drained soil and full sun or partial shade. To keep it inbounds in the landscape, occasional selective pruning can be done in early spring to remove older, mature stems. With the exception of this regular pruning, bottlebrush buckeye is rather adaptable to a wide variety of conditions, making it quite sustainable. Hardy in Zones 4 to 8, and 9 in the shade.

Cultivars

A naturally occurring variety, *serotina*, blooms a few weeks later than the species, and 'Rogers' displays larger blooms to 30 inches long.

Butterfly Bush (*Buddleia davidii*)

Ornamental Value

Butterfly bush offers showy spikes of white, pink, purple, and even yellow flowers all summer. This fast-growing shrub will grow between 5 and 10 feet tall and about half the width. The dark green leaves with silver undersides shimmer in the summer wind.

Landscape Value

As the name suggests, this flowering shrub is a regular stop for butterflies, who love its nectar. Birds will feed on the seed and spread seedlings around the garden. Many environmental experts feel that in some areas of the country butterfly bush should not be planted because it is showing invasive tendencies, often displacing native species that are also important to wildlife. While I would caution the reader to use discretion with this plant, especially near native or natural areas, in a garden setting it should be manageable without a problem. In my observations of this plant, I have only seen it moderately invasive in certain conditions, and I do not believe it warrants waving the white flag to growing it. If butterfly bush is indeed invasive where you live and is on the local invasive species list, by all means use one of the suggested alternatives in this chapter. Butterfly bush has shown rather good deer resistance and is also a durable favorite near the seashore.

Cultural Requirements

Butterfly bush is not too picky about soil type, as long as it is well drained, and it does remarkably well in hot, dry conditions. It does, however, require full sun to look its best. In early spring, while the plant is still dormant, cut your shrubs down to 12 inches to keep them dense and floriferous. Butterfly bush is hardy from zones 5 to 9.

Cultivars

Numerous cultivated varieties are available, but here are a few of my favorites. 'Honeycomb' offers rich, golden yellow flowers. 'Nanho Blue' displays blue flowers and a semidwarf habit 3 to 5 feet tall and wide. 'Pink Delight' has large, pure pink flowers to 12 inches long. 'Silver Frost' is a truly compact form to 5 feet tall and wide, with silvery gray foliage and white flowers.

American Beautyberry (*Callicarpa americana*)

Ornamental Value

This upright, multistemmed shrub can grow 4 to 6 feet tall with an equal width. Plants have a loose, open habit and a coarse appearance with large, serrated leaves to 6 inches long. In summer, pinkish purple flowers give way to spectacular, large bunches of violet magenta fruit. The fruit will persist well into the fall and is a favorite food of many migratory birds.

Landscape Value

This bold plant is an excellent native plant for a woodland setting or in a mixed border in small groupings. It is a great plant to attract wild birds into the garden.

Cultural Requirements

This plant adapts to a wide range of soil, including heavy clay solids. It prefers moist conditions and partial shade or full sun. Plants that are overgrown or leggy can be rejuvenated or selectively pruned in early spring. This shrub is hardy from zones 7 to 10.

Cultivars

'Lactea' is a striking white-fruited form, and 'Welch's Pink' is a wonderful and quite unusual pink variety that is not used often enough in the landscape.

Related Species

An Asian species called common beautyberry (*Callicarpa dichotoma*) is an easy-to-grow beautyberry with a shrubby habit and small but numerous purple fruit in fall. Mature plants can reach 3 to 4 feet tall and 3 to 5 feet wide. This is a fast-growing species that grows from hardiness zones 5 to 8. 'Early Amethyst' is an earlier fruiter with bright amethyst purple fruit that will dazzle the autumn garden. Cutting this plant down to 6 inches like an herbaceous plant every few years will keep it compact and productive.

Summersweet Clethra (*Clethra alnifolia*)

Ornamental Value

Summersweet clethra is called that because it blooms in late summer and provides a rich, potent fragrance in the garden. Spikes of white (or pink) flowers 3 to 5 inches long cover this rounded, medium-sized shrub that can reach 6 to 8 feet tall and 4 to 6 feet wide. Leaves are dark green in summer, turning a pale or rich golden yellow in fall. Flowers will attract bees, hummingbirds, and butterflies. Seedpods will hold on for most of the winter, providing a food source for birds.

Landscape Value

Summersweet clethra is a shrub native to the eastern United States. It grows in a wide variety of landscape situations, from moist woodlands to hot, dry seashores. It is an excellent companion plant to other flowering shrubs and herbaceous plants. It should be used in small groupings or mass plantings.

Cultural Requirements

This tough plant is rather pest-resistant and will tolerate poorly drained, heavy soil or sandy, dry soil. It will also tolerate occasional flooding and salt spray. Summersweet clethra will tolerate full sun or dense shade. It's best grown in partial to full sun and moist, well-drained garden soil. This plant's sustainable qualities include versatility, adaptability, and ability to work well with a wide variety of plants. It is hardy from zones 4 to 9.

Cultivars

Many garden varieties of this plant have been introduced over the years. 'Compacta' is a striking variety with a dense habit to 6 feet tall and wide, very dark green foliage, and 6-inch-long white blooms. 'Hummingbird' is a popular variety that offers a compact habit to 2 or 3 feet tall and a spreading habit. 'Ruby Spice' displays outstanding deep pink flowers with excellent fragrance and dark green foliage.

Southernbush Honeysuckle
(*Diervilla sessilifolia*)

Ornamental Value

This low-growing, suckering shrub offers a graceful spreading habit reaching 3 to 5 feet tall and wide at maturity. In midsummer, clusters of bright sulfur yellow flowers appear that often change to orange-yellow as they age. These delicate, tubular flowers are the perfect shape for visiting butterflies and hummingbirds. New leaves will emerge a bronze color in spring, followed by dark green leaves in summer, which often will have a tinge of reddish purple in fall before they fall.

Landscape Value

This shrub is an excellent choice for erosion control along a steep embankment or on a hill. Southernbush honeysuckle is also effective in a mass planting, foundation planting, or mixed border or as a low-growing shrub in front of taller plants.

Cultural Requirements

This tough shrub native to the southeastern United States is adaptable to most soils and soil pH. It is also drought-, heat-, humidity-, and pest-tolerant. Southernbush honeysuckle will grow best in full sun or partial shade and moist, well-drained soil. Cut plants back in early spring to stimulate flowers the same season. This plant is hardy from zones 4 to 8.

Cultivars

'Butterfly' is a variety that offers deep yellow flowers and dark green, glossy leaves that turn purple in fall.

Seven-Son Flower
(*Heptacodium miconioides*)

Ornamental Value

Seven-son flower can be a large shrub or a small tree growing to 15 to 20 feet tall and 10 to 15 feet wide. This plant is interesting throughout the year, displaying delicate clusters of fragrant white flowers in late summer and lustrous, dark green leaves and bunches of ruby-red flower stalks in fall and early winter. The flowers will attract butterflies and bees to the garden. During the winter the upright, arching branching habit and peeling, tan to slivery-gray bark glistens in the landscape.

Landscape Value

Seven-son flower is effective as a single specimen near the foundation of the house or in a lawn area. It is also an excellent addition to the back of a mixed border as a backdrop to smaller flowering plants.

Cultural Requirements

This adaptable shrub tolerates a wide variety of soil but does best in moist, well-drained soil. It also thrives in full sun and is quite drought-tolerant once established. As the plant matures, it is wise to prune off the lower limbs to expose the striking, exfoliating bark, which gets better with age. What makes this plant so sustainable is that once it's established, you can just leave it alone, because it requires minimal care. It is hardy from zones 5 to 8.

Winterberry Holly (*Ilex verticillata*)

clusters along each stem. In the summer, the fairly generic, nonspiny leaves offer a rich, dark green color and turn bright yellow in autumn before falling. Winterberry holly is a real showpiece in the winter landscape. It grows 6 to 10 feet in height and spread with an upright and arching branching habit.

Landscape Value

Winterberry holly, like most hollies, is dioecious, meaning female plants need a male plant as a pollinator in order to produce berries. So placing a small grouping of female hollies and one male pollinator someplace close by is a good idea. When you buy your plants, you can ask your nursery professional which are male and female. Winterberry is highly valued by birds, and by my observations, it is eaten early in the winter while most evergreen hollies are eaten later in the winter. American robins and north-

Ornamental Value

Winterberry holly is a deciduous holly, meaning it will naturally drop its smooth leaves in the fall and regain them in the spring. Unlike evergreen hollies, winterberry is bare in the winter except for its beautiful, bright red berries in circular

ern cardinals seem most attracted to this plant. Placing this plant near a window or someplace visible from the house will ensure that you get a glimpse of the wildlife enjoying it as much as you do.

Cultural Requirements

Winterberry naturally grows along streams and rivers in wet soils, but it will also thrive in moist, well-drained, acidic soil and either full sun or partial shade. Pruning can be kept to a minimum, since this plant does not typically grow fast, but occasional selective pruning in late winter will keep plants thriving. Because of winterberry's ability to grow in both wet and dry conditions and even near the seashore, and because it requires very little maintenance, it is a great addition to the sustainable garden. It is hardy from zones 3 to 9.

Cultivars

'Red Sprite' is one of my favorites, with noticeable larger, bright red fruit and a semi-compact growth habit. Winter Red™ is a very reliable, heavy fruiting plant. 'Winter Gold' offers large berries that change from green to orange and eventually a golden yellow. 'Autumn Glow' is a hybrid offering a shrubby habit to 10 feet tall, small red fruit that birds love, and yellow fall color. Good male pollinators include 'Jim Dandy' and 'Southern Gentleman'.

Landscape Roses (*Rosa* spp.)

It is important to note that the roses being presented here are not the traditional tea or climbing roses that we know and love so much. Rather, this is a list of landscape roses that offer a shrubby habit, colorful flowers, and most importantly, significant adaptability and disease resistance, unlike tea roses. In short, the landscape roses are quite sustainable in the landscape.

Ornamental Value

Although landscape roses tend not to have quite the same showy, fragrant flowers as tea roses, they still have good color, interesting foliage, and valuable growth habits that can range from low and spreading to upright and hedgelike. Flowers can range from single to semidouble or double and display bright colors, including yellow, orange, red, salmon, and pink.

Landscape Value

Depending on the variety, landscape roses make excellent low, mass plantings and groupings, informal hedges, screens, and companion plants to other flowering shrubs and herbaceous plants. They can even be used in containers in the right situation.

Cultural Requirements

Landscape roses require full sun and well-drained soil. Because they are generally low-maintenance, they do not need regular spraying to keep them free of pests and do not require a high fertilizer diet. Landscape roses are also quite heat- and drought-tolerant once they are established in the landscape. Pruning is not as intense as that done for hybrid tea roses and usually consists of occasional trimming or shearing to keep plants in check or looking tidy. Avoid significant pruning in summer and fall months. Just the facts that these landcape roses require no pesticides to keep them healthy and need less intense pruning than the more traditional roses make these plants a must-have in any eco-friendly garden. Landscape roses are hardy from zones 5 to 9.

Cultivars

Knock Out® roses were developed specifically for landscape function and disease resistance. They come in a wide variety of colors, including Blushing Knock Out®, Double Knock Out®, Pink Knock Out®, Sunny Knockout®, and the original Knock Out®. Established plants can range in size from 3 to 4 feet tall and wide. If plants get too big or are not performing well, they can be pruned down to 12 inches while dormant in later winter or early spring and will bounce right back the same growing season with lush foliage and gorgeous flowers. I have witnessed these roses looking great in many places, including Orlando, Florida; Fort Worth, Texas; Chicago, Illinois; and New York, New York.

But there are other good shrub roses available that can function as groundcovers, foundation plantings, and mass plantings and as companions to herbaceous plants. Flower Carpet® roses are another outstanding series that offer low, ground-hugging roses growing 2 to 2 ½ feet tall and 3 to 4 feet wide. The Flower Carpet® roses have small, showy blooms in clusters and glossy, dark green foliage. They are especially known for their pest resistance and heat and drought tolerance. These plants were even tested in Australia and passed the test for durability and tolerance to extreme heat! They will grow from hardiness zones 5 to 10. In warmer climates it is advisable to grow these roses in part shade. Flower colors include white, light pink, coral, deep rosy pink, yellow, and red. Plants can be cut down in late winter or early spring and rejuvenated, flowering in the same season.

A few other good roses to complement the sustainable garden include the low-growing Drift® Series and the shrubby Carefree Series roses. Both groups offer a wide variety of flower types and colors as well as adaptability in the landscape. Most important, they do not need the regular pesticide applications, fertilizer, or detailed pruning that conventional roses require to keep them looking good.

Littleleaf Lilac
(*Syringa microphylla* 'Superba')

Like roses, one of the most beloved flowering shrubs, lilacs have experienced a renaissance. The common lilac is amazingly fragrant, but once it's finished blooming, it is a rather unattractive plant. By late summer it often gets a white haze on its leaves known as powdery mildew. Several other species and varieties of lilac are more landscape-friendly, offering a smaller, compact habit and much better resistance to diseases. Although not as large and showy, the flowers are still colorful and fragrant. Littleleaf lilac and others are worth including in the landscape as informal hedges, groupings, and foundation plantings.

Ornamental Value
Littleleaf lilac displays rosy pink flowers in spring and often reblooms in late summer or autumn. The shrub has small, delicate leaves and grows to 6 feet tall and 12 feet wide, although it is a slow grower.

Landscape Value
Littleleaf lilac develops into a dense shrub with cascading branches. It is effective as an informal hedge, foundation planting, or backdrop to herbaceous plants and other flowering shrubs. Because of its graceful habit and profuse display of blooms, littleleaf lilac is more user-friendly in a smaller, residential garden than the common lilac is. Your garden will be buzzing with activity during the spring with all the butterflies, bees, and hummingbirds that will visit your lilacs.

Cultural Requirements
Like most lilacs, littleleaf lilac prefers moist, well drained soil and full sun or partial shade. It is very important that the soil drains well, otherwise root rot can be a problem. Pruning needs are minimal, and occasional selective pruning in late winter to remove older, less productive stems will keep plants more compact and floriferous. This species is quite resistant to common problems that typically plague lilacs, such as powdery mildew. These dwarf lilacs need a few years to establish, and then you can just sit back and watch them flourish. This plant is also tolerant of heat and humidity and is also quite cold-tolerant, growing in zones 4 to 8.

Related Species

Meyer lilac (*Syringa meyeri* 'Palibin') is another landscape-friendly lilac with violet-purple flowers; small, glossy leaves; and a compact habit to 4 feet tall and 6 to 7 feet wide. This plant makes a very nice hedge or grouping in areas where you don't have a lot of room. It is hardy from zones 3 to 7.

The Fairytale® Series is a wonderful group of dwarf lilacs that offer various shades of pink flowers, a dense habit, and lustrous foliage. Fairy Dust®, Prince Charming®, Sugar Plum Fairy®, Thumbelina®, and Tinkerbelle® are all unique and beautiful in their own right. They are disease-resistant and are especially good for colder climates, as they will thrive in zones 3 to 7.

VIBURNUM (*VIBURNUM* SPP.)

Asking horticulturists which viburnum they like best is like asking parents which kid is their favorite. Viburnums are so diverse and versatile in the garden, it's impossible to pick just one to use. In fact, you could relandscape your garden just using different species and varieties of viburnum and never be bored. That said, here are a few of my favorites that offer outstanding ornamental value, unrivaled landscape function, and food for wildlife. The flowers of these viburnums will attract bees and butterflies, and the fruit will provide a nutritious feast for birds in winter. For most reliable fruit display, plant viburnums in groups so there is good cross-pollination. Viburnums are like potato chips; you can't just have one! For the gardener who wants to have a more sustainable and beautiful garden, viburnums are a dream come true. Because they provide color all season, provide food for wildlife, and are adaptable to many landscape situations, viburnums are a gardening treasure.

Korean Spicebush Viburnum (*Viburnum carlesii*)

Ornamental Value

Korean spicebush viburnum offers rounded flower clusters that are pink in bud and pure white when open. The flowers are intoxicatingly fragrant and rival the potency of lilac. The entire landscape will smell of the beautiful perfume that this plant offers for several weeks. The fuzzy, dark green leaves turn rich shades of red in fall, and the growth habit is dense and rounded to 4 to 6 feet tall and wide. In late summer and fall, red fruits turn to black and are not conspicuous but certainly edible to birds.

Landscape Value

Korean spicebush viburnum is an excellent informal hedge or small grouping. It is a fine choice to place near the foundation of the house or a walkway, so you can enjoy the fragrance of the flowers. The large, white flowers are beacons to butterflies and other beneficial pollinators.

Cultural Requirements

This flowering shrub prefers moist, well-drained soil and full sun or partial shade but is adaptable. It is fairly care-free and does not require pruning very often. It is hardy from zones 5 to 7 but can grow in zones 4 and 8 with special care.

Cultivars

'Compactum' is a dwarf variety growing only to 3 to 4 feet tall and wide.

Linden Viburnum (*Viburnum dilatatum*)

Ornamental Value

This is another showy viburnum with outstanding floral, foliage, and fruit display. The linden viburnum shows off large, creamy white flowers that look like miniature Queen Anne's lace flowers. They are perfect landing spots for bees, butterflies, and other helpful insects looking for nectar. The rounded, dark green, textured foliage turns brilliant shades of red and maroon in fall alongside clusters of bright red fruit that look like miniature cranberries. At maturity, plants become dense and rounded, growing 8 to 10 feet tall and wide. With judicious pruning in late winter or early spring, plants can be kept smaller, though.

Landscape Value

Linden viburnum will work well in a shaded woodland garden or in a mixed border with herbaceous plants. It is an excellent informal hedge, foundation planting, or single specimen.

Cultural Requirements

Linden viburnum is easy to grow, thriving in full sun or partial shade and moist, well-drained soil. Hardy in Zones 4 to 7, and 8 with some shade.

Cultivars

Cardinal Candy™ is a beautiful form with lush, glossy leaves and large clusters of glossy red fruit. 'Erie' is a vigorous selection with large, 4- to 6-inch-wide flowers and showy red fruit. 'Michael Dodge' offers unusual bright golden yellow fruits that are real eye-catchers in the landscape.

Arrowwood Viburnum (*Viburnum dentatum*)

Ornamental Value

This native viburnum is a tall shrub growing 6 to 8 feet tall and wide, but it can grow larger in ideal situations. The growth habit is upright, dense, and arching, giving this plant a strong and graceful presence in the landscape. The large, flat-topped, white flowers in spring are not at all fragrant but offer a nice display. The sharply serrated, dark green leaves will turn shades of yellow, red, or purple in fall. Bluish black fruit also ripen in fall and offer a tasty treat for birds.

Landscape Value

Arrowwood is most effective in a shaded woodland garden or naturalistic setting. It can be grown in small groupings or as a tall screen or informal hedge it is considered deer-resistant.

Cultural Requirements

Arrowwood thrives in partial shade with plenty of drainage and moisture. It will grow in full sun as long as you provide mulch and water it regularly during drought. This species is particularly susceptible to an insect called viburnum leaf beetle (VLB), which will chew up the leaves. Natural predators such as lady beetles (ladybugs) and lacewings will control VLB. Arrowwood viburnum is hardy from zones 3 to 8 but will grow in zone 2 with protection.

Cultivars

Blue Muffin™ is a semidwarf variety growing 5 to 7 feet tall and displaying bunches of bright blue fruit in fall.

Smooth Witherod Viburnum (*Viburnum nudum*)

Ornamental Value

This native viburnum has showy, creamy white, flat-topped flowers in spring, which attract various species of butterflies. The smooth, lustrous, dark green leaves turn brilliant shades of maroon to reddish purple in fall. The clusters of fall fruit turn from pink to blue to purplish black and are a beautiful complement to the red foliage. This upright growing viburnum can reach 6 to 12 feet in height with a similar spread.

Landscape Value

Witherod viburnum is an excellent choice for a small grouping, woodland garden, or informal hedge or for a low-lying area that collects rainwater, such as a rain garden.

Cultural Requirements

Witherod viburnum can tolerate a wide variety of soil but prefers moist, loamy soil and will also grow in boggy conditions. It will thrive in well-drained, rich garden soil as well. It prefers full sun or partial shade. Selective pruning to remove older stems in late winter or early spring every few years will keep plants dense and vigorous. Hardy in Zones 5 to 9.

Cultivars

'Winterthur', named after the great garden in Delaware, offers abundant blue fruit and red foliage in the fall. The growth habit is semicompact to 6 feet tall and wide. Brandywine™ is a newer selection known as a heavy fruit bearer with a compact habit to 5 feet.

American Cranberry Bush Viburnum (*Viburnum trilobum*)

Ornamental Value

Cranberry bush viburnum is a large, upright shrub with graceful, arching branches growing 8 to 12 feet tall with a similar width. Delicate, white, flat-topped flowers emerge in spring followed by large, translucent, bright red berries in fall and winter. The lush, maplelike leaves transform from dark green to yellow, bright red, or deep maroon. The fruits are a bit stinky as they age, so siting this plant away from a patio or walkway is wise.

Landscape Value

Cranberry bush viburnum works best in small groupings or as an informal hedge or screen. Its sturdy branches are the perfect place to hang a bird feeder.

Cultural Requirements

As with most viburnums, moist, well-drained soil and full sun or partial shade are best for flower and fruit production. Occasional selective pruning to remove old stems in early spring is recommended. Hardy in zones 2 to 7, possibly zone 8 with some extra care.

Cultivars

'Compactum' is a good dwarf form with beautiful flowers and fruit. It grows only to 6 feet tall and wide, making it ideal for smaller home gardens.

Related Species

A European species of cranberry bush viburnum, *Viburnum opulus*, is a bit more commercially available. It typically grows slightly larger but is otherwise very similar in most features.

> "You should really check out some of the new varieties of old-fashioned favorites such as roses, lilacs, and viburnums, which are some of the most landscape-friendly and low-maintenance shrubs available. Go down to your local nursery and pick a few of these beauties to try in a sunny spot in the garden."

TREES

Red Buckeye (*Aesculus pavia*)

Ornamental Value

This southeastern native flowering tree provides quite a floral display in spring with 6-to-10-inch-long spikes of deep red flowers. The individual tubular flowers are great at attracting hummingbirds. The dark green, glossy, palm-shaped leaves and dense, upright habit to 15 to 20 feet tall are also very attractive. In the late summer and fall, fruit capsules open to expose a chestnut-like fruit, but don't be fooled. This fruit is not edible, even for some wildlife.

Landscape Value

Red buckeye is a very useful single-specimen tree in a lawn or in small groupings. It can also work well in a woodland area with naturalistic plantings. Red buckeye can be grown as a single-stemmed tree or multistemmed large shrub.

Cultural Requirements

Red buckeye prefers full sun or partial shade and moist, well-drained soil. It is quite heat- and humidity-tolerant and in hot climates will benefit from afternoon shade. It is hardy from zones 4 to 8.

Shadblow Serviceberry (*Amelanchier canadensis*)

Ornamental Value

Shadblow serviceberry is a tall, upright native tree or large shrub with delicate, small bouquets of white flowers in spring, medium to dark green leaves in summer, and brilliant fall color. Leaves turn various shades of yellow, orange, and red. The smooth, sinuous stems are silvery gray, making them quite noticeable in winter. But probably the most alluring attribute of this plant is the blueberrylike fruits that develop in spring and ripen by early summer. Small fruits change from green to red and eventually blue when they are ripe. If you can beat the birds to them, you'll find that the ripe fruits are sweet and juicy and rival the flavor of blueberries. If not, the birds will feast on them early and often until they are gone. Shadblow serviceberry is usually multistemmed and shrubby, growing between 6 and 20 feet tall, depending on where they are planted and how they are pruned.

Landscape Value

Shadblow serviceberry is very effective in groupings in a shaded woodland garden where there is dappled light and plenty of air circulation or as a single specimen in a mixed border. It fits in best in a naturalistic setting where it can grow freely.

Cultural Requirements

Because shadblow serviceberry is in the rose family, rust, leaf spots, and other diseases common to roses can occur. But if serviceberry is sited in an open, airy location, diseases can be minimized. This is a durable plant that thrives in moist, well-drained soil but also tolerates hot, dry locations in sandy soil. Full sun or partial shade is preferred, and pruning is not required very often. Selective pruning to remove older or damaged stems can be done in later winter or early spring. Serviceberry is hardy from zones 3 to 7 but will grow in zone 8 with protection from the hot afternoon sun.

Cultivars

A related species, *Amelanchier* x *grandiflora*, offers good selections with brilliant fall color and tasty fruit, including 'Autumn Brilliance', 'Autumn Sunset', and 'Ballerina'.

Eastern Redbud
(*Cercis canadensis*)

Ornamental Value

Eastern redbud is an important native tree offering bright pink, pealike flowers in early to mid-spring and lustrous, dark green, heart-shaped leaves all summer. The flowers are not quite red in bud but more of a reddish purple opening to a rosy pink that illuminates the landscape. Even from a distance, this plant is quite noticeable in flower. Flower buds will form in profusion all along the stems and even the main trunk of the tree. The dark green leaves offer a bold texture in the summer but have no significant fall color. Redbud can reach 20 to 35 feet tall with a similar width at maturity.

Landscape Value

Eastern redbud is an excellent single specimen in the lawn or in small groupings in a woodland setting. You will often see it growing along highways and roadsides. Butterflies and bees like the small, pealike flowers of redbud.

Cultural Requirements

Eastern redbud fixes atmospheric nitrogen, meaning it can process nitrogen from the air and make it own fertilizer. That means it will grow in barren or low-fertility soils. Although there are quite a few insects and diseases that bother redbud, it is still worth planting—especially

some of the new and exciting garden varieties. The key to success with redbud is giving it very well-drained soil and either full sun or partial shade. Too much shade, and your plants won't be happy. But overall, because eastern redbud will grow in tough conditions and still flower reliably, it is an excellent addition to a sustainable landscape. Hardy in Zones 4 to 9, and possibly to Zone 3 with some protection.

Cultivars

This plant has so many great varieties, it is hard to pick just a few. 'Appalachian Red' is the closest to a true red, with neon reddish pink flowers; it will stop you in your tracks. 'Forest Pansy' has rich, luxurious, deep purple leaves that are very striking in the summer landscape. After a fresh rain, beads of raindrops glisten from the colorful foliage. Lavender Twist™ is a showstopper with a strongly weeping habit, masses of pink flowers, and large, lush green leaves that look like a waterfall of foliage in summer. 'Royal White' is one of several "white" redbuds that are quite attractive, especially in partial shade. The Rising Sun™ is one of several new yellow-leaf *Cercis* species with new foliage emerging golden orange before fading to chartreuse and finally green.

Flowering Dogwood
(*Cornus florida*)

Ornamental Value

There is nothing quite like a flowering dogwood in full bloom. It doesn't seem like spring officially begins until dogwoods are in full display. The floral display of dogwood is rather complex and is not like many other flowers. The colorful part of each inflorescence, or flower cluster, is called a bract, which is actually a modified leaf. Dogwood blossoms have four white or pink bracts that surround an inconspicuous cluster of flowers. Once pollinated, the flowers eventually transform into beautiful, glossy red clusters of fruit in fall. Dogwood fruits are highly sought after by birds, which will often strip trees clean of their fruit before the onset of winter. In addition, flowering dogwood has brilliant, colorful fall foliage, with leaves typically changing to variations of orange, red, and maroon. The fall color of dogwood rarely disappoints and is consistently showy year after year. Flowering dogwood also develops rough, gray bark like alligator skin. It has a rounded, spreading growth habit reaching 20 to 30 feet tall and wide.

Landscape Value

Flowering dogwood is an excellent specimen tree in a lawn area or in small groupings in a woodland setting. Having an assortment of colors sprinkled across the landscape will liven up any garden. Flowering dogwood is truly a classic native American tree and one of my favorites.

Cultural Requirements

Flowering dogwood is known to be susceptible to several damaging pests, including anthracnose and powdery mildew. But susceptibility can be greatly reduced by siting your dogwoods on the east side of the garden in full sun or partial shade. This will allow plants to enjoy morning sunlight and some protection from the hot summer sun in the afternoon. Moist, organic, well-drained, acidic soil is preferred. Mulching trees with a light layer of wood chips and avoiding overhead watering in the afternoon and evening hours will also reduce stress and alleviate disease problems of this plant. It is hardy from zones 5 to 9.

Cultivars

'Appalachian Spring' is a white variety with good disease resistance and tolerance of heat and humidity. 'Cherokee Princess' offers large, pure white flowers, good vigor, and good disease resistance. 'Cherokee Brave' is a striking variety with deep pink—almost red—flower bracts and excellent red fall color.

Over the past few decades, researchers at Rutgers University in New Jersey have developed hybrid dogwoods that are more disease-resistant than *Cornus florida* but have similar landscape attributes. These hybrids offer large, showy flowers, clean foliage, and slightly later blooming. Aurora®, Celestial™, Ruth Ellen®, Stellar Pink®, and Venus™ are a few selections from the Stellar® Series that are excellent additions to the garden.

Crape Myrtle
(*Lagerstroemia indica*)

Ornamental Value

Crape myrtle is a popular shrub or small- to medium-sized tree used primarily in the southeastern United States, but it is quickly becoming popular in other parts of the country. It displays white, pink, red, or purple flowers, depending on the variety selected, in summer and fall. The large panicles (branched cluster of flowers) of crinkled, crepe paper-like flowers develop into clusters of round seedpods that persist into winter. The foliage is dark green in the summer, changing to brilliant shades of yellow, orange, and red in the fall. But probably the most attractive feature of crape myrtle is its smooth, flaking bark that can range in color from gray to tan or reddish brown. This feature is striking all year but is especially noticeable in winter. Crape myrtle can range in size from a 4- to 6-foot shrub to a 15- to 25-foot tall tree.

Landscape Value

Crape myrtle will be visited by bees and other flying insects but is more known for its aesthetic qualities and durability in the landscape. Shrubby varieties make excellent foundation plantings, small groupings, or companions to other flowering shrubs or herbaceous plants. The large types can be used as hedges, tall screens, or as single specimens in a lawn.

Cultural Requirements

Without question, crape myrtle is one of the most heat- and drought-tolerant plants available to gardeners. It is rather low-maintenance once established and epitomizes the word *sustainability*. Crape myrtles require regular pruning to keep them productive and looking good. Crape myrtles flower on new growth, so pruning is often done in the spring, while plants are still dormant. In warmer climates, pruning right after blooms fade may encourage a second flush of flowers. Pruning large shrubs back to very thick stems or main trunks should be avoided, since this may encourage fleshy, wispy growth to develop. Instead, you can thin out the canopy of the plant, and the tips of the branches can be cut back to branches no thicker than your pinky finger. To train taller-growing crape myrtle varieties as small trees, prune off any young, spindly, or thin branches from the lower part of the plant, leaving several mature main trunks. This will also expose the beautiful exfoliating bark.

Crape myrtles adapt to most soils but thrive in well-drained, moist soil and full sun. Partial shade is acceptable, but too much shade should be avoided. Whether it is an exposed, hot, dry location or a sheltered garden setting, crape myrtles will never disappoint. They are hardy from zones 6 to 9.

Cultivars

There are countless garden varieties of crape myrtle available on the market. 'Pocomoke' is a dwarf variety offering deep pink flowers and a dense growth habit to 3½ feet tall and wide. Similar compact varieties such as the Razzle Dazzle® series only grow 3 to 5 feet wide and tall and require very little maintenance once established. Cherry Dazzle®, Dazzle® Me Pink, and Snow Dazzle® are several good selections. 'Natchez' is a large-growing crape myrtle with white flowers and cinnamon-brown bark that works great as a small tree.

Crabapple (*Malus* spp.)

Ornamental Value

Crabapples, which are close relatives to more commonly eaten apples, are flowering trees with miniature fruit that offer ornamental value to the landscape as well as feed wildlife (and people; they are often used in jellies). The white, pink, or red fragrant flowers of crabapples provide sweet nectar to bees and other pollinators and provide gardeners with a colorful show for several weeks in the spring. The dense, oval to rounded growth habit and dark green leaves also offer aesthetic value in the landscape. The small apples that range in color from yellow and bright red often persist through the late summer, and into the fall and winter months. Juicy crabapple fruits will sustain birds during long, cold winters.

Landscape Value

Crabapples are excellent, durable, adaptable trees that can be grown as single specimens or in groupings. They also work in a lawn area, but I recommend avoiding the placement of crabapples near a walkway, driveway, or patio because of fruit drop.

Cultural Requirements

Crabapples have come a long way from the old-fashioned types that you may be familiar with. Diseases that would distort fruit and leaves and cause plants to defoliate prematurely plagued the old-fashioned types more often than not. But now there are many new cultivated varieties of crabapples that have emerged as tough, disease-resistant, and quite user-friendly in the garden. In general, crabapples prefer moist, well-drained soil and full sun or partial shade, but frankly, they will adapt to a wide variety of environmental situations. Pruning is tricky with crabapples, because they develop vegetative suckers from the roots and water sprouts from the stems that have to be removed regularly in order to keep plants floriferous and looking good. The best time to prune out this pesky, vegetative growth from the ground or cluttering up the canopy of the tree is in midsummer after flowering. Pruning in spring will only stimulate the plant to grow more suckers and water sprouts the next year. Pruning in stages rather than all at once is also recommended. Pruning one-third of your crabapple each year over a three-year period will reduce shock to the plant and also discourage new growth. It is hardy from zones 4 to 7.

Cultivars

So many newer varieties of crabapple now are available on the market. I recommend 'Callaway', which has white flowers and large reddish maroon fruits that are actually tasty to humans. 'Red Jewel' has beautiful white flowers and bright cherry-red fruit. Sugar Tyme® offers masses of pure white flowers and candy apple-red fruits that persist all winter. All these selections offer good resistance to disease and perform well in the landscape. These newer, low-maintetance cultivars make modern day crabapples very sustainable and wildlife-friendly.

Hally Jolivette Cherry (*Prunus* 'Hally Jolivette')

Ornamental Value

Cherries provide the garden with colorful spring flowers, interesting foliage, and wonderfully textured bark. However, many ornamental cherries just get too large and cumbersome for the average residential landscape. A home garden can be quickly consumed by a fast-growing, wide-spreading cherry. But the Hally Jolivette cherry is a small, manageable flowering tree with petite, semi-double, light pink to nearly white flowers in profusion in spring. The dark green, delicate leaves turn shades of orange and red in the fall. The bark on the Hally Jolivette cherry is typically light gray and most noticeable in winter. Plants can be trained as a single stem and are often grafted onto other species of cherry or they can be multistemmed. 'Hally Jolivette' will grow 12 to 15 feet in height with about half the spread, making it ideal for a home garden. Like crabapples, cherries provide sweet nectar for pollinators.

Landscape Value

Hally Jolivette cherry is a nice, small specimen for a home garden and can also be used effectively to line a walkway or driveway or to complement a mixed border.

Cultural Requirements

Moist, well-drained soil and full sun or partial shade are best. Although cherries are susceptible to many pest problems, this cherry is rather durable and relatively easy to grow. It is hardy from zones 5 to 7.

Cultivars and Related Species

'Okame' is another garden hybrid that is also appropriate for the home garden. 'Okame' offers rosy pink flowers in early spring and an upright, vase-shaped growth habit to 20 feet tall. It is hardy from zones 6 to 8. *Prunus mume*, also known as flowering apricot, will bloom as early as midwinter or early spring with bright pink flowers. This tough tree is hardy from zones 6 to 9 and thrives in warm climates. 'Peggy Clarke' is a popular variety with double, deep rose flowers, and 'Matsurabara Red' has striking double, dark red flowers.

Japanese Stewartia
(*Stewartia pseudocamellia*)

Ornamental Value

Japanese stewartia, although an Asian native, is a noninvasive exotic with four seasons of interest. Year-round, this low-maintenance tree will provide continuous ornamental value as few other trees will. The dark green, lush leaves provide a nice backdrop to the large, round flower buds, which look like pearls before they open to pure white circular flowers with yellow centers. Bees will frequent the tree and pollinate the flowers, which will become small brown capsules. This midsummer bloomer will continue to flower for about a month in the landscape. The leaves turn brilliant shades of orange, red, or maroon in the fall. But probably the most identifiable characteristic of this tree is the smooth, multicolored, exfoliating bark, which offers variations of brown, beige, and gray. This beautiful bark feature, along with the tree's strong, upright habit reaching 20 to 35 feet tall with a slightly smaller width, makes this tree a real standout in the winter landscape.

Landscape Value

Japanese stewartia is the quintessential landscape specimen tree. It is ideal in a lawn, mixed border, or woodland garden. This shining star will get better with age and make everything around it look better.

Cultural Requirements

Japanese stewartia is quite adaptable and care-free, but moist, well-drained soil is recommended. Hot, dry, and exposed sites should be avoided. It is a pest-free plant that, once established, requires little pruning, fertilizer, or special care. Japanese stewartia prefers full sun or partial shade. It takes a few years to establish once planted, so be patient. Like a fine wine, your stewartia will only get better with age. It is hardy from zones 5 to 7 and possibly 4 with protection.

Related Species

Stewartia ovata (mountain stewartia) and *Stewartia monadelpha* (tall stewartia) are two species that can offer slightly different qualities in the landscape. Mountain stewartia displays larger white flowers with yellow to purple centers. Mountain stewartia is native to the eastern United States. Tall stewartia, an Asian native, has smaller leaves and white flowers, but the upright habit and cinnamon-brown bark is quite striking. Mountain stewartia is one of the most heat-tolerant species of stewartia available. Both are hardy from zones 5 to 8.

Japanese Tree Lilac
(*Syringa reticulata*)

Ornamental Value

Although related to the shrubby, fragrant lilacs, this small- to medium-sized tree looks quite different and blooms about a month later than common spring-flowering lilacs. The puffy, large, creamy white flower clusters are not quite as fragrant as other lilacs, but the floral display and other ornamental characteristics surely make up for that. Japanese tree lilac also displays lustrous, dark green foliage in summer and striking, dark, reddish brown, cherrylike bark. Even in youth this upright grower displays a vase shape with a single trunk that you will not see in most lilacs. Mature specimens can get 20 to 30 feet tall with about half the spread.

Landscape Value

Japanese tree lilac is excellent as a single specimen or in small groupings. As long as you give this plant the room it needs, it will be a good performer and a carefree addition to the landscape.

Cultural Requirements

Japanese tree lilac is fairly easy to grow, doing best in full sun or partial shade and moist, well-drained soil. However, it is quite tolerant of heat, humidity, drought, and poor soil. It is also resistant to many of the pest problems that plague many other lilac species. It is hardy from zones 3 to 7.

Cultivars

Typically tree lilac needs time to establish before it will flower reliably; however, 'Ivory Silk' is a heavy flowering form that blooms at a young age with silky white flowers.

> "Do not limit yourself as to what you plant in your garden. Use a healthy balance of both native and exotic flowering trees that will provide ornamental value and function in the landscape."

HERBACEOUS PLANTS

Common Yarrow
(Achillea millefolium)

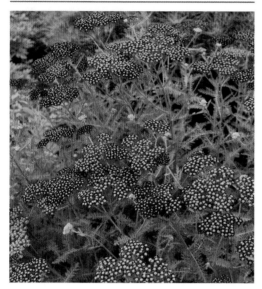

Ornamental Value

Common yarrow is a popular perennial that is grown in many gardens across the world. It has flat-topped flowers that range in color from white to cerise. The fernlike, delicate foliage gives this plant an open, airy look, and flower stalks reach 2 to 3 feet tall in mid- to late summer. The flowers are perfect landing pads for butterflies and bees.

Landscape Value

Common yarrow is rather aggressive, and although it is not native to the United States, it has naturalized along roadsides and in other native habitats. It is best used in areas where it can't spread too far, since it has a thick, matted growth habit. It is usually found in mixed borders planted along with other summer-blooming perennials.

Cultural Requirements

Common yarrow is best grown in well-drained, sandy loam and full sun. It will tolerate poor soil as long as there is good drainage. Yarrow tolerates heat and humidity but will tend to be topheavy and flop in areas where warm, humid nights are common. Cutting back plants in early spring will help keep them compact. They can also be cut back after initial flowering, which will often encourage reblooming. Common yarrow, once established, should be divided every few years to keep the plants vigorous and to check their spread. They will form sustainable colonies in areas where left unchecked. Yarrow is generally hardy from zones 4 to 8.

Cultivars

The Seduction™ Series have shown to be good performers, including 'Peachy Seduction' and 'Sunny Seduction'. 'Pomegranate' offers rich red flowers and gray-green foliage. Two good yellow garden hybrids worth adding to the garden are 'Coronation Gold' and 'Moonshine'.

Japanese Anemone
(Anemone x hybrida)

Ornamental Value

Japanese anemone is an excellent late-season bloomer with white or pink flowers 2 to 3 inches in diameter emerging in late summer and fall. The rich green, dissected leaves and mounded habit are also attractive. The only drawback of this plant is that many selections grow 3 to 4 feet tall and need staking, or they will flop all over the garden. But the pros far outweigh the cons with this plant, and it will add much-needed color late in the season. It will also function as a bee magnet, as pollinators love it.

Landscape Value

Japanese anemone is an excellent addition to a mixed flower border or in groupings. I have seen this plant combined with other earlier season perennials, adding contrast and interest to the garden. Anemones are known to be deer-resistant, which is an added bonus of using these outstanding plants.

Cultural Requirements

Japanese anemone prefers moist, well-drained soil and full sun or partial shade. Avoid wet soil and keep this plant well watered during times of drought. Divide large plants in spring every few years to control their spread. They are hardy from zones 4 to 8.

Cultivars

'Honorine Jobert' is an old-time variety that has been around since the Civil War and is still popular today. It features beautiful white flowers and a 3- to 4-foot-tall robust growth habit. 'Margarete' displays deep pink, semidouble to double flowers and will grow 2 to 3 feet tall. 'Queen Charlotte' displays large, beautiful, pink semidouble flowers and grows to about 3 feet tall. 'Whirlwind' is a tall grower to 4 to 5 feet with large, white semidouble flowers.

Butterfly Weed
(*Asclepias tuberosa*)

Ornamental Value

Butterfly weed, as the name suggests, is a real favorite of many species of butterflies and has vibrant, bright orange flowers in spring and summer. The flowers can also have variations of yellow or even red in the flower. Flowers will give way to ornamental seedpods and silky seeds and are often dried and used in floral arrangements. Adult butterflies value the nectar, and caterpillars will feed on the foliage, giving this useful plant a dual purpose.

Landscape Value

Butterfly weed is found growing extensively in many parts of the United States. It is an excellent choice for a sunny mixed border, meadow, or prairie with other wildflowers or in groupings with other insect-attracting native plants.

Cultural Requirements

Butterfly weed prefers drier soil that drains well, and it tolerates drought quite well due to its tuberous, thick root system. It also thrives in full sun, and it can be often found growing in open fields. It is hardy from zones 3 to 9.

Aster
(*Aster* spp.)

Ornamental Value

Asters are related to chrysanthemums and offer showy, daisylike flowers ranging from white to pink to blue-purple in summer and fall. They typically grow several feet tall with delicate, dark green foliage. For late-season interest, asters are one of the most colorful and floriferous, attracting butterflies, bees, and other pollinators.

Landscape Value

Asters are good in mixed borders with other mid- to late-season perennials and can also be used in groupings or mass plantings. Some species and varieties often need staking in the garden to keep them from flopping.

Cultural Requirements

Asters in general prefer moist, well-drained soil and full sun, although partial shade is also acceptable. Cutting asters down to the ground while they're dormant in winter or early spring will help develop dense and productive plants. The asters mentioned below are hardy from zones 4 to 8.

Cultivars and Related Species

There are many species of asters, but here are a few common ones that will make a good home in your garden. Frikart's aster (*Aster x frikartii*), a garden-friendly hybrid, will get 2 to 3 feet tall by midsummer, flowering through the fall with its bright lavender-blue flowers. New England aster (*Aster novae-angliae*) is a native aster found along the eastern United States. It grows 4 to 6 feet tall with beautiful violet-purple flowers that have bright yellow centers blooming in late summer and fall. New York aster (*Aster novi-belgii*) is a common roadside weed with violet flowers growing 3 to 6 feet high. There are several dwarf cultivars that range from 12 inches to 3 feet tall, including 'Professor Kippenburg', which grows only to 12 inches tall with lavender-blue, semidouble flowers, and 'Ernest Ballard', which grows to 3 feet with semidouble reddish pink flowers.

Threadleaf Coreopsis
(*Coreopsis verticillata*)

Ornamental Value

Threadleaf coreopsis is native to the eastern United States and is one of the most versatile and adaptable perennials for the garden. The lacy, fine foliage and showy yellow flowers in summer make this plant a standout in the landscape. Established plants will grow 18 to 24 inches tall and develop into large clumps in the garden. Threadleaf coreopsis is excellent for attracting pollinators into the garden.

Landscape Value

Threadleaf coreopsis is an excellent companion plant to other summer-blooming perennials and annuals. It works well in groupings in a mixed border as well. Threadleaf coreopsis is known to be a good, reliable deer-resistant plant in the landscape.

Cultural Requirements

Threadleaf coreopsis prefers full sun, but light shade is acceptable as well. Plants will establish rather quickly in the landscape, forming a sizeable clump growing to 2 to 3 feet wide by the end of the summer. These clumps can be divided in fall or early spring. Once the initial flush of flowers subsides, plants can be deadheaded and will often rebloom in the fall. This plant is hardy from zones 3 to 9.

Cultivars

'Moonbeam' is a very popular garden variety with soft yellow flowers. It grows up to 2 feet tall but will flop when it reaches maturity. 'Zagreb' is a more compact variety that tends to stay upright with bright, golden yellow flowers. 'Full Moon' is a hybrid with large bright yellow flowers 2 to 3 inches in diameter. It is a real showpiece in the garden. It is one of several in the Big Bang™ Series.

Purple Coneflower
(*Echinacea purpurea*)

Ornamental Value

Purple coneflower is a very popular perennial with brown to bronze, cone-shaped flowers surrounded by rose-purple petals in summer. The bold, hairy, dark green leaves provide an interesting texture in the landscape as well. Purple coneflower will grow 2 to 3 feet tall with a similar spread. This plant is loved by bees and butterflies that jump from flower to flower to collect its nectar. Even small birds, such as goldfinches, will gravitate to this plant to feed on the seed of the conelike flowers.

Landscape Value

Purple coneflower is excellent when mixed with other summer perennials in a mixed border or in a natural area with other grasses and wildflowers. Coneflower is considered deer-resistant, making it desirable in areas where deer are prevalent.

Cultural Requirements

This carefree perennial prefers moist, well-drained soil and full sun but will tolerate a wide variety of soils and partial shade. Every few years, plants should be divided to keep them vigorous and productive. Purple coneflower is hardy from zones 3 to 8.

Cultivars

'Kim's Knee High' is a shorter variety growing to 1 to 2 feet tall and displaying pink flowers. 'Magnus' offers larger rosy purple flowers and seedheads. 'White Swan' is a beautiful white coneflower with pure white petals that are very striking when combined with traditionally colored purple coneflowers.

Joe-Pye Weed
(*Eupatorium* spp.)

Ornamental Value

Like so many North American native wildflowers, Joe-pye weed is another that has taken the leap into the cultivated garden. There are several species and cultivated varieties that are suitable for the garden setting. Joe-pye weed ranges in size from over

7 feet tall down to just a few feet. The bluish purple, dense, flat-topped flower clusters blooming in late summer and fall and the dark green leaves make Joe-pye weed hard to miss. Bees and butterflies will benefit from the profuse late-blooming flowers as many summer flowers begin to fade. Joe-pye weed tends not to be a favorite food of deer.

Landscape Value

Joe-pye weed can be used in mixed herbaceous borders, and tall varieties can be used in the back of the border to add height to the landscape. It prefers moist soils, so Joe-pye weed can also be used in a rain garden or near the downspout of the house.

Cultural Requirements

Joe-pye weed needs ample moisture and full sun to perform well. This plant should not dry out, and organic soils are best to allow them to reach maximum size. Mature plants can get leggy, so cutting them back a few times earlier in the season will force plants to become bushy. Hardy in Zones 4 to 9.

Related Species and Cultivars

A common species of Joe-pye weed, *Eupatorium purpureum*, is a robust grower to 7 feet or more tall. Give it room, otherwise you will quickly regret how much room it has taken up in your garden. Its flowers are purple, and this rather upright grower is best in zones 4 to 9. *Eupatorium maculatum* 'Gateway', at 5 feet tall, is more compact and bushy with reddish purple flowers. One of the smaller garden varieties is *Eupatorium dubium* 'Baby Joe'. It offers beautiful lavender flowers and grows only 2 to 2½ feet tall, making it ideal amongst lower-growing perennials.

Cranesbill
(*Geranium* spp.)

Ornamental Value

These perennial geraniums should not be confused with the annual bedding plant type known as zonal geraniums (*Pelargonium* spp.) that have white, pink, or bright red flowers. The perennial geraniums, called cranesbill because their fruits look like cranes' beaks, are generally easy to grow and adaptable in the landscape. They range in size and color from a 6-inch low, mounded groundcover to a 4-foot-tall bushy plant displaying a palette of colors that include white, pink, purple, magenta, violet-blue, and red. Perennial geraniums have foliage that is just as interesting as their flowers—often deeply cut and lacey. Perennial geraniums are not considered a regular favorite of deer but are frequented by butterflies.

Landscape Value

Cranesbill can be used in mixed borders and natural areas such as a woodland garden. Even when not in flower, the fine foliage and interesting growth habit make this plant desirable in the landscape. These reliable perennials will gently weave their way into the garden amongst other favorite plants with similar cultural requirements.

Cultural Requirements

In general, cranesbill thrives in moist soil and full sun or partial shade. Some species are rather shade-tolerant, and in warmer climates it is wise to position your plants on an eastern exposure, giving them the cool afternoon shade they desire. Most cranesbills are hardy from zones 3 to8.

Cultivars and Related Species

Grayleaf cranesbill (*Geranium cinereum*) is hardy from zones 5 to 8 and features showy pale purplish pink flowers with pronounced,

dark purple veins. Bigroot geranium (*Geranium macrorrhizum*) is a European species growing to 18 inches tall with a similar spread. It has finely dissected leaves that when crushed have an aromatic fragrance. The plant offers purple-magenta flowers in spring and early summer. It has a spreading root system and will expand in size easily with the proper conditions. It is hardy from zones 3 to 8. A hybrid geranium, 'Rozanne', is an exceptionally good cultivar with violet-blue flowers that have white centers blooming in spring and summer and growing between 12 and 18 inches tall. 'Rozanne' is hardy from zones 5 to 8.

Bee Balm
(*Monarda didyma*)

Ornamental Value

This North American native displays whorled, tight clusters of bright red flowers in summer. The flowers are tubular in shape, making them ideal for bees, butterflies, and hummingbirds. Bee balm grows between 2 and 4 feet tall with upright stems and pointed, aromatic leaves that tend to turn deer off.

Landscape Value

Bee balm is typically used in a mixed border with perennials of similar height and texture. It is also effective in a sunny location near a stream or pond. One ideal use is planting bee balm in a rain garden, where regular moisture is available.

Cultural Requirements

Full sun or partial shade is best for bee balm, and soil must be moist. Rich, organic garden soil is ideal for this attractive garden favorite. Soil that dries out will spell doom for your bee balm. Stressed plants are typically more susceptible to foliar diseases such as powdery mildew. Every few years plants should be divided, as large clumps tend to die out in the center. Deadheading the flowers once they are faded will stimulate new flowers to form. Bee balm is hardy from zones 4 to 9.

Cultivars

New cultivars tend to be more resistant to disease. 'Fireball' has ruby-red flowers and semicompact plants growing about half the size as *Monarda didyma*. 'Marshall's Delight' is another variety that has been rated as good for disease resistance. It provides purplish pink flowers in summer and grows about 3 to 4 feet tall.

Catmint
(*Nepeta* x *faassenii*)

Ornamental Value

Catmint is a vigorous perennial with gray-green foliage and lavender-blue flowers much of the summer. The dense, mounded habit will reach 18 inches tall rather quickly and spread into dense clumps. The aromatic leaves will be cherished by your cat, who will roll in it, but deer will leave this plant alone. Bees and butterflies will also be frequent visitors to these hardy summer bloomers.

Landscape Value

Catmint is a rugged, durable, and adaptable plant working pretty much wherever you use it. It is ideal in mixed perennial borders and groupings and along walkways, rock gardens, and herb gardens. It can be used in a similar way to lavender but will grow where no lavender dares to.

Cultural Requirements

Catmint prefers moist, well-drained soil and full sun or partial shade. It will also adapt quite well to drier, rocky soils and hot, dry locations, but it benefits from afternoon shade in warmer climates. Cutting dead flowers will often encourage reblooming, and dividing large clumps at the end of the season will help keep plants vigorous. Catmint is hardy from zones 3 to 8.

Cultivars

'Six Hills Giant' is a robust grower to 3 feet tall with showy violet-blue flowers that dazzle the summer garden. 'Walker's Low' should not fool you, because its name does not refer to its size. This vigorous grower can reach 18 inches tall and a slightly wider spread. It is an outstanding performer and will rebloom late into the season if cut back and properly cared for.

Black-Eyed Susan or Goldsturm Coneflower (*Rudbeckia fulgida* 'Goldsturm')

Cultural Requirements

Goldsturm coneflower is a particularly vigorous variety with few demands. It thrives in well-drained, moist soil but is remarkably adaptable to a wide range of soils. It will also perform well in partial shade. It is drought-tolerant and is not prone to pest problems. Occasional dividing in the fall will keep large clumps in check and of a reasonable size. This plant is hardy from zones 3 to 9.

Related Species

Rudbeckia hirta 'Herbstonne' ('Autumn Sun') is a big, bold cultivated variety with long, drooping sulphur-yellow flowers that have green centers and a tall, upright growth habit to 5 feet tall. It is hardy from zones 4 to 10.

Autumn Joy Stonecrop (*Sedum* x 'Autumn Joy')

Ornamental Value

The Goldsturm coneflower, sometimes called black-eyed Susan, blooms profusely in summer and fall with bright, golden yellow flower petals surrounding dark brown to black centers. The 18- to 24-inch plants with thick, dark green leaves form large masses within a few years. This plant will serve as a magnet for bees and butterflies.

Landscape Value

Goldsturm coneflower is a showy, colorful plant that is quick to establish as a standalone mass planting or in groups with companion plants such as purple coneflower, ornamental grasses, and summer-flowering shrubs. Not much can beat it for late-season color in the garden.

Ornamental Value

This tried-and-true succulent perennial is one of the best at attracting bees, butterflies, and gardeners alike because of its vivid flat-topped pink flowers that age to a rich reddish bronze. Autumn Joy stonecrop flowers from late summer into the fall, and the seedheads will persist through the winter. The fleshy, thick green leaves will emerge from the base in spring, eventually forming dense clumps of foliage reaching 1 to 2 feet in height.

Landscape Value

Autumn Joy stonecrop is excellent when mixed with other late-season bloomers such as asters, goldenrod, and ornamental grasses. There is nothing quite like a mass planting of stonecrop fluttering with the activity of butterflies in the late summer.

Cultural Requirements

This plant prefers well-drained soil and full sun. It is adaptable, but too much shade will cause weak, unhappy plants that will topple over. If sited in partial shade, cutting back your plants in early summer will keep them dense and less likely to flop. This may also cause smaller but more numerous flowers. Clumps can be divided in spring and will also keep mature plants from becoming too large. Hardy in Zones 3 to 10.

Goldenrod (*Solidago* spp.)

Ornamental Value

Goldenrod is often maligned as a problem plant. It is accused of being invasive and causing hay fever (other species actually trigger hay fever) for people who have pollen allergies. But true goldenrods are excellent wildflowers and are important to wildlife such as bees, butterflies, and birds. The feathery, bright golden yellow flowers are unmistakable in the late summer and autumn garden. *Solidago canadensis* is found in prairies and native meadows across North America. Frankly, unless they are already growing in a nearby meadow or natural area, I would recommend sticking with a few good garden varieties of goldenrod. Goldenrods are also known to be reliably deer-resistant.

Landscape Value

Goldenrods are showy, upright perennials with soft plumes of flowers, making them ideal companions for late-season plants such as ornamental grasses, black-eyed Susan, and stonecrop in a mixed border. Or goldenrod can be used in wildflower meadow or amongst native grasses in an open field. They are often admired from afar along roadsides.

Cultural Requirements

Rich, organic soil and full sun are best for goldenrods, and well-drained, loamy garden soil works just fine.

Cultivars

Solidago rugosa 'Fireworks' is an outstanding cultivar growing to 3 feet tall with a dense, upright habit. The dense clusters of blazing yellow flowers look like streams of fireworks cascading off the plant. This variety is hardy from zones 4 to 8.

Solidago sphacelata 'Golden Fleece' offers tight plumes of bright yellow flowers and a fairly compact growth habit to 18 inches tall. This variety is also hardy from zones 4 to 8. *Solidago shortii* 'Solar Cascade' is similar in size to 'Fireworks', with beautiful arching branches loaded with showy yellow flowers, but it is a bit more hardy to zone 3.

ANNUALS

A few good low-maintenance annuals to add color and attract pollinators to the garden are:
- Beggarticks (*Bidens*)
- Million bells (*Calibrachoa*)
- Cosmos (*Cosmos*)
- Dahlias (*Dahlia*)
- Heliotrope (*Heliotropium*)
- Hummingbird mint (*Agastache*)
- Lantana (*Lantana*)
- Marigolds (*Tagetes*)
- Tobacco plant (*Nicotiana*)
- Salvia (*Salvia*)
- Verbena (*Verbena*)
- Zinnia (*Zinnia*)

"When you select your herbaceous plants from a local nursery or even a mail-order catalogue, make sure they are useful to pollinators and wildlife. When you are deciding what flowers to purchase, you should ask the salesperson which ones are bird- and insect-friendly. Often plant labels that are attached to the plant or in the pot will identify the plant for those qualities."

THINKING OUTSIDE THE BOX: USING NATIVE GRASSES IN A CULTIVATED GARDEN

Ornamental grasses have been a part of the cultivated garden for many years. Ornamental grasses began their meteoric rise in popularity in the 1980s when Wolfgang Oehme, a German-born landscape architect, and American James Van Sweden began to incorporate ornamental grasses into their landscape design projects in the United States. For the past three decades, ornamental grasses have become a staple in well-designed perennial gardens across North America and the rest of the world. Ornamental grasses provide professional garden designers with a soft, flowing texture and natural look as well as versatility and adaptability in the landscape. Home gardeners love ornamental grasses because they are relatively easy to grow and complement other flowering plants in the landscape.

But some of these ornamental grasses, several of which are exotic species, have been overused. Some, such as Japanese blood grass (*Imperata cylindrica*), maiden grass (*Miscanthus sinensis*), and fountain grass (*Pennisetum alopecuroides*), have even become invasive in some areas. Luckily, over the past few years, along with the sustainability movement, there has been a real push by ecologists, horticulturists, and nursery professionals to introduce and breed some of our great American native grasses for inclusion in the

cultivated landscape. There is no doubt that ornamental grasses are still very important to garden design, it is just that now natives play a much bigger role in designing and enhancing the American landscape. The advantages of using native grasses are that they are adaptable to our climate, noninvasive, and provide added benefits for birds and insects, such as meeting specific shelter and food requirements. But not all wildlife like them. Most ornamental grasses are quite resistant to deer.

Here are a few of my favorite native grasses that are quickly becoming much more than just grasses you see in a meadow. Native grasses today have credibility as useful and ornamental plants with multiple uses. What makes these grasses more desirable is their clumping growth habit, meaning they won't spread very far in the landscape. The idea that native plants, while better for the environment, are boring compared to their exotic counterparts is false. It is important to note that these grasses are mostly native to North America. A few nonnative species that are not considered invasive are offered as well.

NATIVE GRASSES WITH SOME PIZZAZZ
Appalachian Sedge
(*Carex appalachia*)

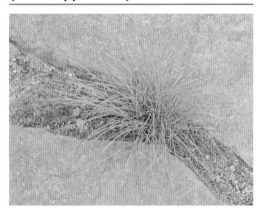

Ornamental Value
This beautifully fine-textured native sedge forms tight clumps to 12 inches tall with a graceful, flowing habit. It blooms in early spring, producing small, somewhat inconspicuous flowers and seedheads.

Landscape Value
This low-maintenance sedge is ideal in groupings, as an edging plant, in containers, and even in dry shade.

Cultural Requirements
Appalachian sedge prefers moist, well-drained soil and partial shade but is quite adaptable to a wide range of soils, including dry conditions. Partial or full shade is tolerable to this plant. Morning sunlight and afternoon shade are recommended. This plant is hardy from zones 3 to 7.

Cultivars
Ice dance sedge (*Carex morrowii* 'Ice Dance'), a noninvasive Japanese counterpart, offers variegated clumps of foliage to 12 inches tall. This plant is a carefree groundcover that will also work in a wide variety of landscape situations. It looks similar to the commonly used and sometimes overused liriope. Cut back damaged foliage in early spring to tidy up plants. This plant is hardy from zones 5 to 9.

Big Bluestem
(*Andropogon gerardii*)

Ornamental Value

Big bluestem is truly the grand poobah of native grass species. It exhibits silvery gray to blue-green foliage that turns to a coppery red in fall. The plant seems to glow in the winter landscape against a blanket of snow. The flower stalks turn a beautiful a purplish color late in the growing season. Big bluestem can reach 4 to 6 feet tall with about half the spread.

Landscape Value

This magnificent native is often found in meadows and prairies along roadsides. It can be used in natural areas and in groupings, where it will naturalize.

Cultural Requirements

Big bluestem prefers full sun and well-drained soil but is very tolerant of heavy clay soil and drought conditions. It is hardy from zones 4 to 9.

Feather Reedgrass
(*Calamagrostis* x *acutiflora* 'Karl Foerster')

Ornamental Value

Feather reedgrass is an upright, narrow-growing grass that ranges in height from 2 to 4 feet. Its foliage changes from green in summer to to beautiful golden yellow in the fall. Pinkish flowers are borne on erect stalks in early summer and change to golden brown by late summer. Another attractive related species is Korean feather reedgrass (*Calamagrostis brachytricha*), which forms clumps of dense, rich foliage and large, bushy plumes of flowers reaching 3 to 4 feet high.

Landscape Value

Because of its upright habit, this grass can be used as a standalone plant or in groupings. It is effective in combination with other sustainable plants such as purple coneflower, black-eyed Susan, and Joe-pye weed. Feather reedgrass can also be used in rain gardens, because it likes moisture.

Cultural Requirements

Feather reedgrass prefers full sun and moist soils that do not dry out. It is tolerant of clay soil and grows in zones 5 to 9.

Little Bluestem
(*Schizachyrium scoparium*)

Ornamental Value

Little bluestem is easily one of my favorite native grasses. It forms upright clumps of blue-green foliage in summer with purplish bronze flower heads and clusters of fluffy, silvery white seedheads, which are striking. Plants will reach 2 to 3 feet or more by the end of the summer. The foliage turns brilliant shades of golden yellow to reddish bronze and glows in the winter landscape.

Huge masses of little bluestem resemble ambers waves of grain as they sway in the wind.

Landscape Value

Little bluestem is most effective in groups and masses in natural, open areas of the garden. Some new varieties can be effective when used in combination with late-season perennials, but I prefer my little bluestem on its own in an open area of the garden.

Cultural Requirements

This tough, adaptable grass tolerates dry or moist soil and thrives in moist, well-drained soil and full sun. It is remarkably drought-tolerant and requires very little to succeed. It does not need fertilizer and may flop late in the season in fertile, rich soils. In the early spring, cut plants down in preparation for a new batch of foliage. This is no doubt one of the most sustainable grasses out there, because it only has to be mowed once a year and can survive in a wide variety of conditions. It is hardy from zones 3 to 9.

Cultivars

'The Blues' has distinct blue-green foliage changing to shades of reddish bronze in fall, while 'Blaze' is grown for its vivid red fall and winter color. 'Standing Ovation' is an upright form that is less likely to flop in a garden setting.

Pink Muhly Grass
(*Muhlenbergia capillaris*)

Ornamental Value

Pink muhly grass looks like any other grass when not in bloom, growing between 1 to 3 feet in height. But in fall, big clouds of puffy pink flowers develop, creating an unbelievable show that is nothing short of stunning.

Landscape Value

Pink muhly grass is very effective in large masses or smaller groupings mixed with other fall-interest plants.

Cultural Requirements

Pink muhly grass prefers full sun or partial shade and thrives in soils with good drainage. It is rather heat- and drought-tolerant and will also tolerate windy sites. It is hardy from zones 7 to 10 and is probably an annual in zone 6.

Cultivars

'White Cloud' displays masses of white flowers in fall. While it is not as heart-stopping as its pink relative, it is still a handsome grass for the landscape.

Prairie Dropseed
(*Sporobolus heterolepis*)

Ornamental Value

This native meadow grass can also serve as a specimen plant in the garden. It forms soft-textured mounds of foliage with open, airy flower clusters in fall, reaching 2 to 3 feet tall. The flowers have a subtle fragrance similar to that of coriander. The foliage turns rich shades of golden yellow to orange in autumn.

Landscape Value

Prairie dropseed is excellent in small groupings or in large masses. It can also be used in open natural areas and in rain gardens.

Cultural Requirements

Prairie dropseed prefers dry to moderately moist, well-drained soils but adapts to many soil types. It is also quite heat- and drought-tolerant. It is hardy from zones 3 to 8.

Switchgrass
(*Panicum virgatum*)

Ornamental Value

Switchgrass forms dense, upright tufts of growth. The olive-green to blue-green foliage and profusion of loose, airy flower heads make this grass very desirable. Flower heads turn from pink to beige as they age. In the fall, plants will turn yellow and eventually tan for the winter. Switchgrass will eventually reach 3 to 6 feet tall, making it a possible replacement for maiden grass (*Miscanthus*).

Landscape Value

Switchgrass likes moisture and can be used in groupings or mass plantings by itself or with flowering herbaceous plants. It can be used in natural areas and rain gardens as well.

Cultural Requirements

Switchgrass adapts to a wide variety of soils, from dry to moist. It will thrive in moist, well-drained soil and full sun or partial shade. It is hardy from zones 4 to 9.

Cultivars

'Dallas Blues' is a distinct variety of switchgrass with wide, blue foliage and large flower heads that are tinged with purple. 'Heavy Metal' emerges in the spring with a striking metallic blue color, which changes to a golden yellow in the fall. 'Northwind' is a distinctly vertical form with a compact habit to 4 to 5 feet. The showy yellow flower heads will develop in late summer, making this fine-textured plant nearly 6 feet tall by the end of the season. 'Shenandoah' offers reddish pink flower clusters and a beautiful burgundy-red fall color that is sure to brighten up the autumn garden. Mature plants with foliage and flower heads will reach 4 feet tall.

A FEW GREAT NONNATIVE CLUMP TYPE GRASSES
Japanese Forest Grass or Hakone Grass (*Hakonechloa macra* 'Aureola')

Ornamental Value

Japanese forest grass is a rather well-behaved exotic species with a spreading, graceful habit and two-tone green-and-yellow leaves. Only growing 12 to 18 inches tall and wide, this grass turns a beautiful yellow-bronze color in fall.

Landscape Value

Japanese forest grass makes an excellent groundcover or edging plant and can be mixed with other ornamental grasses and perennials. It is especially effective as an accent plant in a shade garden. It will brighten up any dark spot in the garden.

Cultural Requirements

This plant does best in moist, well-drained soil and partial shade. It will tolerate full shade but will often lose some of its bright and variegated color. Japanese forest grass should not be allowed to dry out, as it will not perform well. It is hardy from zones 5 to 9.

Cultivars

'All Gold' is a brightly colored variety with leaves that are completely golden yellow.

Mexican Feather Grass (*Nasella tenuissima, Stipa tenuissima*)

Ornamental Value

This beautiful grass has fine-textured, feathery foliage forming clumps and growing up to 2 feet tall. The fine green foliage is covered by silky, soft flower heads that form in early to midsummer before they change to a striking light golden blond color. It is a sight to behold when this plant gently sways in the summer wind.

Landscape Value

Mexican feather grass is quite striking in masses along a walkway or edge of a path. I have seen it used very effectively with tall species of verbena (*Verbena bonariensis*) and in combination with other ornamental grasses.

Cultural Requirements

Mexican feather grass prefers moist, well-drained soil and full sun. It is fairly drought-resistant once established. Cut back plants in early spring to remove old foliage. This plant is hardy from zones 7 to 10.

"Native grasses are quickly emerging as some of the most interesting and useful plants in a sustainable landscape. These species, which were once limited to the great American prairies and meadows, are now infiltrating the cultivated garden as well. You should selelct an area of the garden that you don't mind being a bit more wild and try some of these lesser-known but fabulous native grass species."

Letting a field, pasture area, or part of the lawn grow long for the summer months is very eco-friendly.

CREATING SUSTAINABLE GRASS MEADOWS: NO-MOW ALTERNATIVES TO THE SAME OLD LAWN

For some time now, I have been observing and admiring grass meadows. I continue to be amazed by their complexity and sheer beauty when they are done right. Of course, I think nature creates grass meadows better than humans ever could, but if you have the time and inclination, why not try? Grass meadows are among the most eco-friendly and sustainable ecosystems in the landscape. They support a delicate and important relationship between plant life, wildlife, and soil organisms that all depend on one another. Our role is to preserve and protect these ecosystems—and sit back and enjoy them!

I used to think that creating meadows was easy; just sprinkle some seed on an open area or stop mowing a grass field, and—voilà!—instant grass meadow. This, however, is far from the truth. It takes time and effort to create grass meadows right. Once the initial planning and preparation are done, and the meadow is established, then you can sit back and admire them. Unfortunately, all too often, outside factors such as invasive species can cause challenges when establishing a grass meadow. But grass meadows are gaining in popularity, and in some cases they are replacing the traditional manicured lawns found in so many American landscapes.

Grass meadows offer many benefits. Over time, grass meadows can support a diversity of plants rather than the monoculture that exists in a traditional mowed lawn. The combination of grass species and occasional wildflowers can add interest most of the year. In addition, grass meadows will attract and sustain a wide variety of birds, mammals, and insects that benefit the garden. Although grass meadows require a lot of planning and preparation, once established, they are far easier to take care of than mowed grass. Meadows do not require regular watering or fertilizer and get mowed only once a year as opposed to once a week. After a grass meadow is established, regular monitoring to keep out invasive weeds is required. But think of how much time and maintenance you will save, not to mention fuel for your mower. Is week after week of back-breaking work to keep your lawn mowed, edged, and weed-free really worth it? There is more to be discussed about this issue, but if you decide to plant a grass meadow, it will probably need to be in the backyard or in areas along the fringe of the property. Many communities have specific ordinances prohibiting grass meadows or "weedy" plantings in the front yard and up to the sidewalk. Don't worry, though; there are many solutions to this problem.

Site Selection and Preparation

My best advice if you're planning to convert your lawn or garden to a grass meadow is start small. Select a 5x5 foot area of the garden and use it as a test plot. This will ensure you truly like the meadow concept and work out any kinks before you invest in a bigger section of the garden. Choose a site that is in full sun or at least partial shade with a good amount of light. Dig in the soil and determine what type of soil and drainage you have. This will help you determine what types of native meadow grass species will grow on your site. Choose the types of grasses that you want to grow and try to find a reliable source for seed or small plants. There are two categories of grasses: cool-season and warm-season. Cool-season grasses grow in the spring and early summer, when the weather is cooler, while warm-season grasses thrive during the summer, when the air and soil temperatures are warm. The grasses mentioned above are warm-season grasses, while native fescue and ryes tend to be considered cool-season grasses. It is wise to have a combination of both in a meadow planting, provided they will not compete with one another.

The second step in creating a sustainable grass meadow is to get rid of your lawn or undesirable vegetation growing in the area where you want your meadow to be. This can be done by cutting out the grass or plants with a shovel into smaller sod strips. Another way to get rid of unwanted vegetation is to cover it for a few months with black plastic or plywood. I have also seen gardeners use a generous layer of newspaper covered with a thick layer of wood chips to hold it down. These methods could be used in the fall or very early spring to ensure that the plot of land you are using is free of vegetation—most importantly, weeds. Although nonselective herbicides can be used in spring to clear an area effectively, why not use nonchemical methods? I would recommend using herbicides only if the area you are planning to convert to a grass meadow is very large. Whatever method you choose, your site must be smooth and free of weeds before the meadow is planted.

Native meadows are beautiful and sustain a wide variety of wildlife.

Planting Your Meadow

Spring is an excellent time of year to plant your grass meadow, especially for warm-season grasses. Fall planting is acceptable for cool-season grasses, and often a cover crop of annual rye grass helps protect the bare soil. Rototill or plow under the soil and smooth it out with a garden rake. Remove any large clumps of dead vegetation or roots, large rocks, and so on before planting. Seed can be spread by hand or with a broadcast spreader. You should read the directions carefully when sowing your grass seed. After sowing, apply a light layer of sifted compost or fine mulch and water the seed well. Native meadow grass germination and establishment can take some time, so be patient. If your area is small enough, and you choose to plant small plants instead of seed, establishment of your meadow will be quicker and controlling invasives a bit easier.

After your new grass meadow has germinated and started growing, it is important to patrol it regularly for invasive weeds. There is nothing as frustrating as doing all this hard work only to have your meadow overtaken by invasive species. The first few years are most critical to your new and vulnerable meadow. Spot weeding by hand and eliminating weeds before they go to seed is important. Spot herbicide applications can be done on noxious, hard-to-eradicate weeds. The first year, you can mow your meadow to about 4 inches high to reduce the likelihood of weed plants going to seed. In the second year, you can reduce mowing to once a year in the late fall or early spring. I prefer mowing in spring to give birds and other wildlife winter cover.

HARDINESS ZONES: WHAT ARE THEY, AND WHY ARE THEY SO IMPORTANT?

The USDA Cold Hardiness Map (pages 13) is designed to illustrate the average minimum temperatures in eleven separate zones throughout the United States. The map was updated in 2012 from weather data that was collected between 1976 to 2005. This update is significant because it shows how most of the areas of the United States have become warmer over the past three decades. That means we can grow things that we never thought we could before (conversely, this can also mean we can no longer grow things we did before). This map is the standard by which gardeners and growers can determine which plants are most likely to survive and thrive in their area. The map divides the United States into zones based on average annual minimum winter temperatures. Each zone represents a 5-degree Fahrenheit increment of temperature. Zone 1a is the coldest zone, with an average annual minimum temperature of -60 to -55 degrees-Fahrenheit. Zone 13b is the warmest zone, with

an average annual minimum termperature of 65 to 70 degrees Fahrenheit. Although the USDA Cold Hardiness Map is considered the best way to determine where a plant will grow successfully, there are other environmental factors that impact plant survival, too, such as heat, humidity, and rainfall.

To use the map, identify the area on the map where you live. There will be a zone number followed by a letter assigned to that region of the country. For example, the hardiness zone for Atlanta, Georgia, is zone 8a. In the map legend, the temperature range for your hardiness zone lies to the left (Fahrenheit) and right (Celsius) of your zone number. It is important to identify the zone where you live to ensure that the plants you select will survive in that climate. Selecting plants that are not adapted to grow in your hardiness zone may result in poor performance or death of the plant. Of course, every self-respecting gardener pushes the envelope on hardiness at some point, trying to defy the laws of nature and grow things that are not supposed to grow in a particular zone. Throw caution to the wind when you see fit, but also

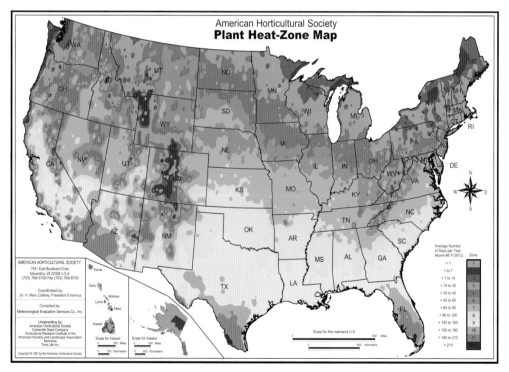

Reproduced with permission of the American Horticultural Society (www.ahs.org)

realize that you will only get away with that type of reckless abandon some of the time. In this chapter, the plant hardiness zone range for each species is listed under "Cultural Requirements."

CAN'T TAKE THE HEAT!

Plant survival depends on a lot of factors, including soil, annual rainfall, cold, heat, and humidity. We usually spend a lot of time worrying whether our plants will make it through the winter, but we hardly consider whether they will make it through a long, hot summer. So, in addition to cold hardiness, we must consider heat index data. Heat index measures the average [annual] maximum temperature for a given area. Just as the hardiness zone in Texas is different from that of New York, so is the heat index. The heat index in Houston, Texas, may be 96 degrees Fahrenheit, while the heat index in New York City is 82 degrees Fahrenheit. This difference should be considered because it is a factor in plant growth and survival. Excessive heat can cause stress and negatively affect plants as much as excessive cold can. Heat index data can be found on the National Weather Service (NWS) website at www.nws.noaa.gov/os/heat/index.shtml.

The American Horticultural Society (AHS) recently updated its own AHS Plant Heat Zone Map to go along with the USDA Cold Hardiness Map (at left). The AHS can be found at www.ahs.org/gardening-resources/gardening-maps/heat-zone-map. It works similarly to the USDA Cold Hardiness Map but instead considers maximum temperatures. This data was complied and published by analyzing NWS daily high temperatures within the contiguous forty-eight states between 1974 and 1995. NWS data collection stations that recorded maximum daily temperatures for at least twelve years were the only ones included in this project. There are twelve zones represented on the map, which indicate the average number of days that a given area of the country experiences temperatures over 86 degrees Fahrenheit in a given year. The zones range from zone 1, representing less than one heat day, to zone 12, which represents more than 210 heat days. This information will make its way into literature and will likely be incorporated into care information you receive at local plant nurseries and garden centers along with cold hardiness information.

In addition to heat stress, another issue that you must be concerned with as gardeners is the relative drought tolerance of plants. Plants that are inherently drought-tolerant will adapt to rising mean temperatures better than those that are not. Certain species, like junipers and juniper relatives, are likely to adapt better than ericaceous plants in the rhododendron family. For this reason, it is more important than ever to site plants in the proper location with the environmental conditions to which they have adapted. Putting plants where they are not adapted to grow will just add unwanted stress and increase the likelihood of failure. A big part of sustainability is putting plants where they want to grow and creating an environment that will sustain plant life for the long term. I suspect that plants that are able to tolerate heat and drought stress will be more sought after than ever before in the near future.

ONE GARDEN AT A TIME

The debate about global warming and whether it exists continues among scientists, environmentalists, and gardeners alike. While data support the belief that the average mean temperature across the United States has risen over the past few decades, the debate over whether this is a short-term phenomenon or will have longer-lasting consequences continues. Whether you agree or disagree with the idea that the Earth is getting warmer, there is no denying the fact that sustainability is crucial to our future. By putting the right plant in the right place and following sound gardening principles, we can help the environment in which we live be a better place. All we can do is improve the world around us one garden at a time. My hope and belief is that over time, the global warming trend will reverse course, and weather will return to historic patterns. Regardless, climate change is affecting where we grow plants and in some cases, that we are able to grow certain plants in areas we never thought possible. On the other hand, we need plants to regulate and hopefully mitigate the effects of climate change as well.

CHAPTER 3

Attracting Wildlife to Ensure a Sustainable Garden

Putting Out the Welcome Mat for Helpful Critters

It is important for us, as gardeners, to understand that we are not alone in our quest to develop more sustainable ways of living. Conventional thinking would have us believe that humans are at the top of the food chain, and all other living things are secondary. History has shown over and over that humans have taken from the Earth more than they have given back. But the sustainability movement has surely demonstrated that humans are only part of a bigger picture within our global ecosystem. Humans, animals, plants, and *all* living organisms need one another to survive.

Some of the earliest civilizations have shown that the best way to survive and thrive is to respect the land and all its creatures. Native American cultures are good examples of societies that survived by respecting the land and taking from it only what they needed. In modern times, hunters and fishermen who take only what they need, rather than all that they can, employ some of the best sustainability practices. They know that by preserving nature and protecting animals, they can continue to enjoy the sport that they admire so much.

This same principle can be applied to the sustainability of your landscape. By protecting your natural resources and native habitats, and by reusing and recycling, you too can invest in our future and the long-term management of our environment.

WILDLIFE MATTERS

Wildlife is a very important component of a sustainable garden. Sustainability is not only about reducing waste and not overburdening our resources; it is also about how animals play an important role in our environment. Frankly, sustainability only works if we realize that we cannot do it alone. Animals such as insects, frogs, lizards, snakes, birds, foxes, and so forth complete the sustainability cycle. Without them, we are kidding ourselves that we can save the planet. Animals are our protectors, pollinators, seed dispersers, and planters. They do a much better job at all those things than we can, so we shouldn't take them for granted.

> "You should do everything humanly possible to develop a healthy and attractive habitat for pollinators, because they help produce fruit and vegetable crops and support plant diversity. This is easily done by selecting some trees, shrubs, and flowers that provide food and shelter for beneficial insects."

INSECTS THAT SPREAD THE WEALTH

Beneficial insects come in many shapes, colors, and sizes and serve different functions in the garden. Insects such as butterflies, bees, and lady beetles all play a valuable role in our natural world. One of the main reasons to avoid using pesticides indiscriminately is because by using them, you are likely to kill off more beneficial insects than bad bugs. That is why when pesticides are needed, they are used to target a specific pest. Butterflies and bees are particularly sensitive to insecticide applications. By reducing unneeded hazards and providing a safe and desirable habitat for wildlife, the sustainability process will thrive. Following are several

groups of beneficial insects, their functions, and how to keep them coming back for more!

Butterflies

There is nothing quite like a warm, sunny day when the garden is busy with the fluttering of colorful butterflies. Butterflies not only come in a wide variety of colors and sizes, but they are among the best plant pollinators, along with bees. Pollinating your plants is very important to the survival of the landscape. Pollination allows plants to develop seeds and fruit; it is estimated that about one-third of food you eat depends on pollination. Most important, pollination facilitates plant diversity.

Butterflies have four basic requirements in order to thrive in the garden. They need full sun at least part of the day, shelter from wind and heavy rain, a source of water, and food. In order for butterflies to survive in your garden, you need to provide plants that are a food source for butterfly larvae (caterpillars) as well plants that provide nectar and pollen for adults. Because caterpillars do eat plants, you must be willing to allow some damage to your ornamentals, and you must be willing to avoid using insecticides regularly, as they harm both caterpillars and adults. Accept some damage to ornamental plant hosts. To alleviate this issue, you can site plants that caterpillars feed on in a less visible area of the garden while placing plants that provide nectar and pollen for adult butterflies in a more prominent location.

In addition, having a healthy mix of both native and exotic plants in mass plantings that

Monarch butterflies and other native species are excellent pollinators.

offer blooms from spring until fall will support healthy butterfly populations. The types of flowers that are attractive to butterflies are also important to consider. Flat-topped or clustered flowers will provide convenient landing platforms for butterflies in pursuit of nectar. Brightly colored flowers offering a wide range of colors such as white, pink, purple, yellow, orange, and red will do the job.

> "In addition to colorful, flat-topped flowers, provide a variety of flat rocks, which will offer an easy landing platform and will make your garden a friendly destination for butterflies."

With butterflies, it is important to remember that they have several stages of their life cycle, including the larval (caterpillar) and adult stages. Because of that, different food sources are needed to attract and help butterflies thrive in the garden. The ever-popular monarch butterfly caterpillars prefer swamp milkweed and butterfly weed (*Asclepias* spp.) while adults like milkweed, butterfly bush, Joe-pye weed, and goldenrod. Black swallowtails feed on parsley, carrot, dill, fennel, and Queen Anne's lace as caterpillars and on butterfly weed, clover, and phlox as adults.

It is important for butterflies to bask in sunlight to regulate their body temperature. One way to encourage basking is by scattering flat stones or other landing surfaces throughout the garden, where butterflies can rest and absorb sun and heat. A water source is also important for butterflies, and using items you already have around the garden can easily provide this. Take a small saucer from a potted plant and put a few flat or round river rocks in it. Then fill the saucer with water and watch the butterflies flock to it to rest and have a drink. Gardeners can also provide a container of wet sand or pour water on bare soil to create a muddy puddle, where butterflies can obtain salts and minerals. Check out this list of recommendations for food, water, and shelter to attract butterflies into the garden.

- Plant a wide diversity of plants in masses with bright colors and flat-topped or tubular flowers.
- Milkweed, butterfly weed, goldenrod, butterfly bush, and Joe-pye weed are all excellent sources of nectar for butterflies.
- Provide flat rocks and other landing surfaces so butterflies can sun themselves.
- Provide water dishes, muddy puddles, and wet sand so butterflies can drink and absorb vital minerals and salts.

> "There are very important native bees, such as the bumblebee, carpenter bee, and miner bee, that may not be as popular as the honeybee, but work just as efficiently in the garden. Plant brightly colored flowers and flat-topped flowers, such as yarrow and Queen Anne's lace, to encourage these unsung pollinator heroes."

The Garden Is Abuzz

Bees are all too often considered pests in the garden and are lumped under the same category as hornets and wasps. This couldn't be further than

Coneflowers are excellent attractors of pollinators.

the truth, as true bees are vital to plant life and the entire ecosystem. Although native bees and their European and Asian cousin, the honeybee, can sting, they usually do so only in defense, if threatened. Generally bees are social but nonaggressive, often too busy at work in the garden to care much if we are present. Some wasp (nonparasitic) and hornet species can be more aggressive and can be a risk to animals and humans if provoked. Yellow jackets are a good example of a rather aggressive wasp with potent venom that can wreak havoc in the summer landscape. Not all wasps are aggressive, though. Mud wasps and cicada killers tend to be nonaggressive and are usually harmless to humans.

Both native bees and nonnative honeybees are rather valuable pollinators, transporting pollen from flower to flower and fertilizing plants. This fertilization process in turn allows seed production and the reproduction and diversification of vegetables, flowers, trees, and shrubs. While honeybees are far more popular, native bees are also very important in the pollination of plants. There are about four thousand known species of native bees in North America, including bumblebees, carpenter bees, sweat bees, mining bees, and leafcutter bees.

Native bees thrive in an environment where certain plants provide plentiful nectar. The plants that are particularly attractive to bees are clovers, sunflowers, Queen Anne's lace, yarrow, Joe-pye weed, apple, blueberry, and cherry, as well as vegetables such as melons, squash, cucumber, and tomatoes.

Native bees often nest in the ground and prefer undisturbed areas of the garden such as native wetlands, untilled garden plots, or unmowed fields. This habitat will provide a source of food, water, and shelter for these resourceful insects. Below is a list of considerations for habitat, food, and shelter for bees.

- Introduce masses (usually groupings of five or more plants) of native plants with overlapping bloom times.
- Provide undisturbed soil areas, wet or muddy areas, unmowed areas, stone or sand piles, windbreaks, or logs in and around the cultivated garden for nesting and shelter.

- Nearby streams, ponds, or ditches can provide a reliable source of water.
- Plants such as apples, cherry, and clovers, as well as flat-topped flowers such as yarrow and Queen Anne's lace, are excellent sources of nectar for bees.

Lady Beetles to the Rescue! What's Crawling Around Your Garden?

Lady beetles, also called ladybugs, are not all alike, and there are actually more than 450 species just in North America. Lady beetles may make us feel warm and fuzzy, but if you are a soft-bodied insect such as an aphid, soft scale, or a mite, you don't stand a chance. Lady beetles are voracious eaters, quickly devouring everything in their path. It is estimated that one lady beetle can consume five thousand aphids in its life cycle. Both

Ladybugs are voracious eaters and will control several species of soft-bodied insects.

the adult and larval stage will feed on pests in your garden. The larval stage is spiny and alligatorlike, and will eventually transform into an adult beetle with spots. Some species of lady beetles will also feed on pollen and nectar from plants.

These tiny wrecking machines can provide excellent pest control in the garden, provided there is a food source and shelter to keep them happy. It sounds sort of counterproductive to attract pests into your garden for lady beetles to eat, but without some insects to munch on, there is no reason for these good guys to be there. The key is to have a healthy balance, so that the lady beetles will sustain themselves without the pest population getting too large and taking over. That is all done as part of your monitoring of the garden on a regular basis. Many garden centers, nurseries, and mail-order catalogs offer lady beetles for purchase and release in the garden. If you decide to buy them, remember to keep your lady beetles in a cool place until you release them in the early evening around dusk. Mist your plants with a spray bottle of water before you release the lady beetles. This will allow your beetles to take a drink and will encourage them to settle into their new home and not fly away to the neighbor's yard. Within a few days, these released insects may migrate to a different area depending on their food source and habitat. Here are a few key ingredients to make lady beetles happy:

- Lady beetles live wherever their food sources are active but mainly on crops such as vegetables, grain crops, legumes, and grass fields and on trees and shrubs.
- Lady beetles will eat nectar and pollen, so planting flowering herbaceous plants is beneficial.
- Release lady beetles in the evening and mist your plants with water to attract the lady beetles.
- Do not spray insecticides in the garden at the same time that you are releasing lady beetles or other beneficial insects.

"Lady beetles are voracious eaters that control small, soft bodied insects and typically do not stay in one place for very long. If you release lady beetles into your garden, you should do that in the evening, when it is cool, and gently spray down the foliage of your plants with water."

It is important to note that in addition to many native species of lady beetles, there are Asian species as well. The common Japanese lady beetle, while beneficial to humans, can also be a nuisance, because in autumn they often look for warm buildings and structures to overwinter in. Hundreds of lady beetles can be found clustering on south-facing windows and walls in a house. Make sure no windows are left open without screens and that any cracks or openings are sealed before the onset of cold autumn weather.

THOSE AWESOME AMPHIBIANS

There are over 5,600 species of frogs and toads known worldwide, and about 100 of these are native to the United States. Across the North American continent there are a wide variety of frogs and toads, and while many live primarily in water, some live in trees or burrow into the ground for much of their life. Some common species found in the United States are tree frogs, true frogs, true toads, spadefoot toads, microhylid frogs, neotropical frogs, tailed frogs, burrowing toads, and tongueless frogs. The following shows each group, its preferred habitat, and its diet.

The American Bullfrog is a hardy, adaptable creature that will consume a large variety of insects and other small animals.

It should be noted the American bullfrog is the largest and probably the most aggressive of any frog or toad. It will consume anything it can catch including insects, snakes, smaller frogs, fish, and even small mammals. But in general, these amphibians are beneficial to the environment and

Frogs and Toads Native to the United States

Group Name	Habitat	Diet
TREE FROGS (INCLUDING PEEPERS)	TREES, GRASSES, AND LOW VEGETATION	FLIES, MOSQUITOES, CRICKETS, AND OTHER SMALL INSECTS
TRUE FROGS	PONDS, STREAMS, AND OTHER WATERWAYS	FISH, INSECTS, SMALL FROGS, AND SMALL MAMMALS
TRUE TOADS	UNDER ROCKS AND IN BURROWS, WOODPILES, AND VEGETATION	MAINLY INSECTS
SPADEFOOT TOADS	BURROWS ON LAND	FLIES, CRICKETS, CATERPILLARS, MOTHS, SPIDERS, CENTIPEDES, MILLIPEDES, EARTHWORMS, AND SNAILS
MICROHYLID FROGS	LAND, TREES, OR NEAR WATER	INSECTS, TERMITES, ANTS
TAILED FROGS	LAND AND IN COLD STREAMS WITH FAST-MOVING WATER	LARVAL AND ADULT INSECTS, SPIDERS, AND SNAILS

your own backyard because they control a wide variety of pests. Whether you provide an artificial water source as a small backyard pond or are lucky enough to have a natural stream or pond in on your property, frogs and toads are certainly an important component of the natural landscape and its sustainability.

> "Frogs and toads will eat a variety of insects, slugs, millipedes, and other crawling creatures in the garden. If you have a water feature in the garden, such as a stream or pond, make sure it is well planted and offers logs, rocks, and other areas for frogs and toads to sun themselves or hide."

REPTILES UNDER THE RADAR
Smooth, Slithering Snakes

I know a lot of gardeners, myself included, who are leery of snakes. They seem to sneak around the garden and pop up when you least expect them. But as many nature lovers and wildlife experts have assured me, snakes are very beneficial to the environment because they eat a wide variety of insects, rodents, and other creatures we don't want invading our gardens. Most species of snakes are nonvenomous and pose no threat to humans. While there are many species of snakes native to the United States, a few common species include the common garter snake, milk snake, corn snake, king snake, ribbon snake, and rat snake. All of these nonvenomous snakes control pests, such as field mice, moles, insects, and so forth, that would otherwise wreak havoc in your garden. There is nothing more frustrating than planting a new crop of vegetables or

A garter snake patrols the garden in search of food.

planting a new bed of perennials that cost a small fortune only to discover the next morning that rodents or insects have destroyed them. Snakes are guardians of our gardens and help minimize these frustrations. If you think about it, it is far scarier to lose a plant you love than to run into a harmless little snake occasionally.

Unlike many other wildlife discussed, snakes don't really need to be enticed to come into your garden. They will find it on their own as long as the conditions and the habitat are right. Most snakes like quiet areas where they will not be disturbed, like heavily vegetated areas; woodpiles and rock piles; cool, damp underground spaces such as cold frames; under sheds, and so on. A well-established garden with masses of trees, shrubs, flowers, grasses, small ponds, and places to sun themselves, like rock walls, is conducive to these elusive creatures. Here are some tips on attracting snakes into the garden:

- Snakes are attracted to hiding places, such as woodpiles and rock walls, and cool, damp places.
- Ponds make excellent places for snakes to hunt for insects and mammals. They provide a water source as well.
- Heavily planted areas of the garden, as well as unmowed grass, provide a cool, secluded habitat for snakes.

Slow but Steady Turtles

Another very beneficial group of reptiles are turtles. These hard-shelled helpers are excellent at controlling a wide variety of pests, including slugs, snails, insects, millipedes, and so forth. Turtles are built for the long haul; they have been on the planet for over two hundred million years. Many species can live to over one hundred years old. Today there are about 260 species of turtles worldwide. About 50 of these are native to North America.

Turtles can be land dwellers or aquatic, living in freshwater ponds and streams. While there are many species indigenous to the United States, I will feature two—one aquatic dweller and one terrestrial—that are widespread across the country.

The eastern box turtle eats slugs and other harmful garden pests.

> "Both snakes and turtles are shy animals that prefer secluded, quiet areas of the garden."

The eastern box turtle is a docile, shy creature that is found in most states. Its habitat can vary, but generally it is found in hardwood forests and woodlands. Box turtles have distinct orange, yellow, and black markings and a dome-shaped shell. These placid animals can be found plodding through the garden and sunning themselves on a rock or patio. Box turtles like shaded, wooded areas with a lot of leaf litter, where they can hide and overwinter. Most important, box turtles eat insects, and they also have a taste for slugs, which are quite harmful to plants, especially hostas and other large-leafed plants. Like snakes, box turtles cannot be bribed. They usually just find your garden rather than you offering the invitation. If you have a well-balanced, shady garden with natural areas, though, a box turtle is sure to pay you a visit.

Another common species that can be found in slow-moving freshwater is the painted turtle. This turtle is unmistakable in appearance, because it has a distinct smooth, oval shell and skin that can range from olive to black with red, orange, or yellow stripes on its legs and neck. Painted turtles are quite stealthy, zipping quickly into the water if they feel threatened. Painted turtles can be found floating on logs or sunning themselves on rocks in and around water. They generally eat algae, insects, and fish, and unlike the box turtle, often are found in groups. If you have a natural or artificial pond big enough to sustain these fascinating animals, painted turtles can be entertaining and beneficial visitors to the garden. Some helpful turtle tips are:

- Although not aquatic, box turtles need a water source, and they will often be found at the edges of streams and ponds.
- Box turtles will eat a wide variety of plants, fruits, and insects, and they prefer slugs.
- Painted turtles have a varied diet and are nature's cleaners. They eat fish, insects, snails, plants, algae, and dead animal matter.

BIRDS OF A FEATHER

It is hard to imagine a garden without the sweet chatter of birds. A garden is not complete without the song and dance of birds as they glide across the landscape in search of food and shelter. Our feathered friends are not only

The northern cardinal will forage for fruit and seed all year.

Garden-Friendly Bird Species

Name	Habitat	Beneficial Food Plants
AMERICAN ROBIN	LOWER HALF OF TREES, BUILDINGS, LIGHT FIXTURES	DOGWOOD, HOLLY, JUNIPER, SUMAC
BALTIMORE ORIOLE	SHADE TREES	BLACKBERRY, CHERRY, SERVICEBERRY
EASTERN BLUEBIRD	NEST IN TREE CAVITIES, NEST BOXES	ELDERBERRY, HOLLY, DOGWOOD, JUNIPER
CHICKADEES	NEST BOXES, NATURAL CAVITIES	SEEDS AND BERRIES
DOWNY WOODPECKER	NEST IN CAVITIES OF TREES	DOGWOOD, SERVICEBERRY, ACORNS, GRAINS
HOUSE WREN	NESTING BOXES, LOW SHRUBS, BUILDING CREVICES	DOES NOT EAT PLANTS; EATS MOSTLY INSECTS
HUMMINGBIRDS	NESTS IN SMALL TREES OR SHRUBS	NECTAR FROM PLANTS SUCH AS BUTTERFLY BUSH, HONEYSUCKLE, LANTANA, TRUMPET VINE, COLUMBINE
NORTHERN CARDINAL	NEST IN SMALL TREES AND SHRUBS	DOGWOOD, HOLLY, MULBERRY, SUMAC, GRASSES
NORTHERN MOCKINGBIRD	SMALL TREES AND SHRUBS	HOLLY, BLACKBERRY, DOGWOOD, SUMAC
PHOEBES	NESTING PLATFORM, EAVES OF BUILDINGS AND OTHER STRUCTURES	HACKBERRY, SERVICEBERRY, SUMAC
PURPLE MARTIN	TREE CAVITIES, NESTING BOXES, HOLLOW GOURDS	DOES NOT EAT PLANTS; EATS MOSTLY INSECTS
TITMICE	NATURAL CAVITIES, FENCES POSTS, PIPES, NESTING BOXES	VARIOUS SEEDS AND BERRIES, ACORNS, BEECHNUTS
YELLOW WARBLER	NEST IN SMALL TREES	VARIOUS BERRIES

entertaining, bringing the garden to life, but they also provide many benefits, including eating damaging pests that would otherwise run amuck in the garden. A garden can provide a rich sanctuary for birds, as many plants provide them seeds, fruit, and nectar as well as protection from predators. In return, birds are the ultimate watchdogs of the landscape as they patrol the land for sustenance.

With over eight hundred known species of birds found across the United States, bird watching in your garden can be a full-time job. Many wild bird species are beneficial to the garden, but I offer a few specific ones to look out for. It is in a gardener's best interest to consider specific types of plants that will attract birds, because birds require a diverse diet, which cannot be provided solely by what you put in the bird feeder. When not feasting on the plants you provide them or food from the bird feeder, your feathered friends will feed on a wide range of insects, including caterpillars, beetles, flies, mosquitoes, and more. The chart on the facing page offers some exceptionally garden-friendly bird species to watch out for.

As with all living things, there are three basic requirements birds have in order to attract them and keep them in the garden: food, shelter, and water. Food can be provided by planting the plants listed in the chart. Plants that provide important edible fruit include serviceberry (*Amelanchier* spp.), beautyberry (*Callicarpa* spp.), dogwood, (*Cornus* spp.), holly (*Ilex* spp.), juniper (*Juniperus* spp.), sumac (*Rhus* spp.), and viburnum (*Viburnum* spp.), to name a few. Planting a wide variety of trees, shrubs, annuals, and perennials will ensure that the neighborhood birds have a plentiful food supply most of the year. Birds may also eat different types of fruit and seed at different times of the year. Early in the season, breeding parents may select sweet fruits such as mulberry, cherry, serviceberry, and blackberry for energy, while in the fall before migrating, they tend to feed on fruit higher in protein and fat such as dogwood, holly, and viburnum. The fruit from juniper, bayberry, crabapple, and sumac also help sustain birds during cold winters.

"Birds require a variety of food such as flower nectar, insects, fruit, and seeds, which can be supplemented by bird seed."

There are a wide variety of bird feeders that will help supplement the diet of many bird species.

To supplement a bird's diet of insects and fruit or seeds, bird feeders can also attract a wide variety of birds into the garden. Materials such as sunflower seeds, peanut kernels, safflower seeds, and nyjer (thistle) are excellent foods for many birds. Suet feeders are pressed birdseed cakes, which are made from beef fat, nuts, and seeds. These cakes are typically surrounded by a small cage that can be hung from a tree branch and are enjoyed by woodpeckers, cardinals, wrens, bluebirds, and many other species of birds. Providing birdseed to birds is especially beneficial in winter, when food is scarce.

Water and Shelter

A clean water source is also an important ingredient to offer birds in your garden. A birdbath should have a durable, rough surface so it does not become slippery when wet. The depth of your birdbath should be less than 3 inches, since birds need just enough water to drink and bathe

Creating bird nesting areas is important to keep birds coming back to the area.

themselves. Your birdbath does not have to be fancy, and often homemade birdbaths, such as a garbage can lid or a shallow pan, will do just fine. It is important to keep your birdbath clean, changing the water regularly to prevent algae from developing or mosquitoes from breeding. Also, in order to ensure birds will visit year-round, birdbaths should be filled more often during the winter in northern climates to prevent the water from freezing. Fancy birdbaths can also be outfitted with heaters so that the water doesn't freeze. Having a bird water fountain with constantly moving water will save time since it will prevent the need to clean or heat your water.

There are several ways to provide adequate shelter for birds. A bird-friendly landscape is one that offers different layers of plants for a variety of birds to utilize. Since many species of birds typically live in the same areas, the garden should be as accommodating as possible to birds. Some birds may forage on the ground, while others may nest in the high canopy of large trees, while still others may eat the fruit of lower-growing shrubs. It is equally important to note that even the same species of bird may choose different layers in the landscape to feed, roost, or seek shelter.

> "The best way to attract a wide variety of birds in the garden is to offer them a wide selection of plants, bird feeders, a clean water source, and safe nesting areas."

One major key to developing a sustainable garden is to create a diverse and adaptable landscape. This includes a varied plant palette that can offer multiple seasons of interest and also provide vegetative cover and a food source for wildlife throughout the seasons. To provide layers of vegetation in your garden, you should choose a variety of plants with varying heights to create a balanced, tiered effect in the garden. This will not only be aesthetically pleasing but also will provide a suitable environment for all types of wildlife, including birds. For example, having a healthy, balanced combination of tall trees to provide shade and overhead cover, intermediate shrubs and smaller trees to fill the understory, and low-growing shrubs, flowers, grasses, and groundcovers to complete all the layers will greatly benefit all creatures that visit the garden.

Two tips on keeping birds healthy and happy are to reduce lawn areas, which offer little benefit to birds and other wildlife, and to refrain from using pesticides, which can cause health issues for some species of birds.

Birds will find many areas to nest, including in the dense canopy of trees and shrubs, natural cavities of trees, under eaves of buildings, and in other artificial structures. Providing nesting boxes can be beneficial to certain types of birds, including bluebirds, purple martins, chickadees, and wrens. There are a wide variety of birdhouses that can be purchased to accommodate various species of birds. However, you may also want to purchase a birdhouse for a specific species. For example, a bluebird house, which houses a single family, is different from a purple martin birdhouse, which usually accommodates multiple birds.

Location, Location, Location

Putting your birdhouses in the right location is another important consideration. Birdhouses should not be placed too close to the house or too low to the ground so that predators can have easy access to them. Placing your bird house at least 10 feet high on a sturdy tree branch or strong post will work well. Some bird species are very picky as to where they will nest in the garden. Birdhouses placed in the woods with cover will often be occupied by chickadees and titmice. Boxes placed on the forest edge are likely to be visited by wrens, and boxes placed in an open field on a metal or wooden pole, 5 to 6 feet above the ground, will often be the ideal location for bluebirds.

> "Bats are shy creatures and bat boxes should be kept at a safe distance from the house and patio."

GOING BATTY IN THE GARDEN

Bats are often considered creepy creatures that sneak up on us in the dark of night, when we least expect it. But that's just an old wive's tale. However, bats are an important part of the ecosystem, and the amount of insects they eat is staggering. Bats can consume thousands of insects in one night, including beetles, moths, mosquitoes, and other flying insects. There are about forty-five species of bats known in the United States and Canada.

Bat boxes mounted about 15 feet high in a tree will help attract bats to your garden.

Two important and well-known species are the little brown bat (*Myotis lucifugus*) and the big brown bat (*Eptesicus fuscus*). Unfortunately, a recent fungal outbreak known as white-nose syndrome (WNS) has decimated bat populations. This devastating disease was first documented in a cave visited by thousands of tourists each year. It is important to point out that humans and bats should not interact closely in any way, and viewing bats from afar is sound advice. The best way to help bats is to provide

Little brown bats and other bat species eat thousands of insects.

the proper habitat for them to live in. Several night-blooming plants, such as evening primrose, phlox, goldenrod, and moonflower will attract insects such as moths that are active at night, which bats feed on.

Bats also need a clean, abundant water supply. If you are fortunate enough to have a pond or lake in your backyard, that will suffice. If not, a birdbath will also work well as a water source for bats.

Lastly, bats need trees for roosting. In addition to large living trees, dead trees that have been left standing in natural areas of the garden make great habitat for bats. Bats will roost in cavities and crevices of trees.

Bat houses can also attract bats into the garden. It is important to place these wooden houses away from your home, preferably in a wooded area and near a source of water. The bat house can be placed on a large tree or mounted on a pole at least 15 feet above the ground. Your bat box should be 24 inches tall, 14 inches wide, and at least 4 inches deep. Bat boxes typically have several chambers to accommodate many bats and an extension at the bottom to allow for easier landing and entry into the box. Bat boxes can be purchased preassembled or as kits for easy assembly and installation.

A truly sustainable landscape requires many factors to work in unison. As humans, we control the destiny of our landscapes, but we cannot do it alone. Sustainable landscapes require help from animals, plants, and many other living organisms. All creatures, big and small, make an impact on their environment and other living things around them. There is a delicate and natural balance that is essential to the survival and long-term sustainability of the landscape. By allowing nature to do most of the heavy lifting, more often than not the landscape will take care of itself.

CHAPTER 4

Integrated Pest Management

Incorporating a Variety of Controls to Manage Garden Pests Safely

Since the 1960s, there has been tremendous public outcry to ban pesticide use in the United States. In 1962, Rachel Carson's book *Silent Spring* brought to the forefront the negative effects pesticide use had on the environment. Popular pesticides like DDT and their effects on bird populations were highlighted in the book. *Silent Spring* is credited with inspiring the American environmental movement. This movement led to the ban of DDT in 1972, which is believed to be the main reason why the American bald eagle has come back from near-extinction. Since 1970, when the first Earth Day was celebrated, protecting the environment has become much more of a popular public issue.

Out of the environmental movement a very important and sustainable idea was born: integrated pest management, or IPM. Although IPM has been part of national legislation since 1972, it was in the mid-1980s that it became a common term in horticulture, arboriculture, agriculture, and related industries. IPM was created in response to the continuing overuse and abuse of pesticides in the United States and in Europe. The conventional practices of using pesticides without regard for the environment have spurred criticism from legislators, environmentalists, and health officials. In the past, it was common for home gardeners to apply pesticides regardless of whether a problem existed. It was not at all uncommon to see garden pesticides applied as *preventatives* in case pest problems arose or in response to a past problem that homeowners were afraid would recur. Too often our hearts are in the right place, but our minds are on autopilot about the use of pesticides, chemical fertilizers, and other potentially harmful products.

WHAT IS INTEGRATED PEST MANAGEMENT?

IPM is an approach to pest control that utilizes regular monitoring to determine if and when treatments are needed. IPM incorporates various forms of pest control, such as physical or mechanical removal of pests, cultural practices, crop rotation, biological controls, and even plant selection to keep pest numbers low enough to prevent intolerable damage or annoyance. IPM uses information about crops, pests, and the environment to plan and implement effective management strategies. The first line of defense in any IPM program is to manage your landscape and address pest issues before they become a problem.

IPM is not about just seeing a pest and spraying it with a chemical. IPM is more about taking responsible steps to first evaluate if you even need a chemical; maybe another alternative is more appropriate. The use of chemical controls such as pesticides is usually considered a last resort under the guidelines of IPM. If a pesticide is needed, often a gardener will use the least toxic pesticide possible to do the job. By integrating many forms of pest control rather than just one, you can effectively and efficiently control pests while reducing the risks of pesticide exposure. The key to a successful IPM program is monitoring pest populations to aid in the decision-making process. The overall intent of IPM is to identify and reduce factors causing pest problems. So getting to the root of the problem and addressing it before it becomes an issue is your best line of defense against pests. The true essence of IPM is to choose a treatment method based on your observations and then implement this treatment in the manner least disruptive to the natural environment.

It is estimated that over 5.1 billion pounds of pesticides are used in the United States each year. With the increasing concern that pesticides pose serious threats to human health, IPM has become more accepted by professionals, and that has trickled down to homeowners as well. The overall belief is that an effective IPM program will encourage better environmental management techniques and ultimately the reduction of toxic pesticide use. With proper monitoring and implementation of sound pest management practices, landscapes can be managed more efficiently and effectively. This creates a productive, safe, and aesthetically pleasing environment for all to enjoy.

IPM was originally developed in row-crop agriculture but has evolved to include the management of ornamentals and turf as well. With the ever-changing threats that pests pose, IPM has become an effective strategy, because the fundamentals still work even though pest threats may change from season to season. Pests such as insects, diseases, and weeds can significantly damage or kill valuable garden plants. On a larger scale, pests cause millions of dollars in damage to crops, forests, golf courses, and parks.

Since the fundamental philosophy of IPM has always been to integrate many pest control strategies to control or eliminate pests, it is no surprise that this allows gardeners to look for alternatives to pesticides. The implementation of IPM strategies often results in the reduction of pesticide use because the resourceful gardener has found another way to manage the pest problem. While pesticides are one of several pest management tools that are available, they are usually considered a last resort. Due to environmental and health concerns, the reduction of pesticide use has come to the forefront of many public debates, and IPM has been credited with easing these concerns. However, it should be noted that IPM does not mean that pesticides are off-limits completely but rather they are one of several options that gardeners can use.

Pests can cause various degrees of harm to plants, including economic and aesthetic ones, and health risks in humans. For example, high pest populations can cause crop failure at a farm, which can have serious economic impact by causing rising prices at the grocery store. Pest damage can also significantly reduce a homeowner's property value by damaging valuable landscape plantings. Finally, pests can cause medical problems, such as West Nile virus (spread by mosquitoes) or Lyme disease (caused by deer ticks). So, when implemented correctly, IPM has great value beyond just helping you maintain a beautiful garden.

> "Integrated pest management allows gardeners the opportunity to incorporate a variety of pest control methods to keep harmful pests at bay."

Regular monitoring of your garden for insect and disease problems will reduce the chances of a serious infestation.

MANAGING INVASIVE SPECIES

Within the realm of insects and plants, there are good guys and bad guys and in nature, there is a delicate balance between invasive exotics and native species. In the garden setting, with a constant influx of new and exciting plant species and varieties being introduced, keeping this balance is even more difficult. Invasive insects and plants have become a serious issue worldwide, and the environmental and economic impacts are significant. For example, according to the U.S. Forest Service, the Asian longhorn beetle (ALB) and the emerald ash borer, both exotic, wood-boring insects, cause an estimated $1.7 billion in local government expenditures annually and approximately $830 million in lost residential property values every year. Norway maple (*Acer platanoides*) is an exotic shade tree from Europe that is on the invasive species list in several states. It is a very fast-growing, weak-wooded tree that produces heavy shade and propagates readily by seed. In spring you will observe a carpet of tiny green seedlings germinating on the surface of the soil. Because of this invasive characteristic, Norway maples are able to crowd out native species, such as sugar maple (*Acer saccharum*). Since many animals rely on the sugar maple as a food source and it is also a very important species to the maple syrup industry, it is easy to understand why the Norway maple presents a problem both to native and cultivated landscapes.

Monitoring is a key element of any successful IPM program. Regularly inspecting the landscape is critical because it will help identify potential problems before they become an issue. A gardener must know what is going on in his or her own backyard in order to properly manage it. The occurrence of pests on landscape plants varies from year to year and in different locations within the garden. But at the same time, patterns or cycles may form allowing you to be better prepared the next time a similar issue arises. In addition, monitoring allows gardeners to anticipate proper timing of control methods. In the past, conventional pest management programs incorporated cover sprays—regular use of pesticides to control pests, whether there was a pest present at the time or not. These cover sprays were aimed at protecting plants without truly knowing if there was a problem or what the consequences would be for beneficial wildlife. Pest levels were generally unknown, and often more harm than good was done. This ultimately resulted in overuse or waste of pesticides and reduction in beneficial insect populations, which typically help keep pest populations in check. Cover sprays and lack of knowledge about what is going on in your garden are counterproductive to both sustainability and IPM.

Monitoring the landscape and regularly observing pest levels allow well-informed gardeners to make responsible decisions about pest management. In many cases, pesticides may not be the best option, or no action may be needed.

In conjunction with monitoring procedures, setting thresholds is also desirable in an IPM program. Thresholds, also known as tolerance levels, are the point at which gardeners may need to take some form of action to protect their plants.

If a pest problem is bad enough and is now at the point where it will harm your plants, it's time to implement some form of control. Every property has a different set of thresholds with no one site being the same as the next. Even within one site, tolerance levels may be different in certain areas. For example, insect problems in your vegetable garden may be less tolerated than in your backyard lawn. While IPM implies that some level of pest populations must be tolerated, since it is impossible to completely wipe out all pests, the concept of setting thresholds is important. A threshold is simply how much pest damage you are willing to tolerate before taking action. Each person and situation may have a different threshold, but ultimately once plant health is at risk or irreversible damage is a reality, it is time to take some form of action.

To implement an effective monitoring program, home gardeners need to be food scouts. As a scout you will need tools to perform monitoring of the landscape. These tools include a 10X hand lens, pocketknife, pruners, and small trowel or soil probe. One helpful way to monitor your landscape is to use indicator traps or pheromone devices. These devices can be purchased from the online garden supply companies listed in the "Resources" section of this book. Pheromone traps draw insects by using chemical compounds that are excreted by insects. These traps can allow you to capture and observe what types of insects are crawling and flying around the garden.

KEEPING ACCURATE RECORDS

Once you have evaluated your landscape and have collected information based on your observations, put this information into a usable form. Gardeners should be well organized and prepared to deal with ongoing pest problems in the garden. Sustainability does not reduce your risk of pest occurrences, but it does enable gardeners to be more prepared to address the problem when it happens. Keeping a garden journal or daily logbook is a great way to stay focused and organized. While pertinent information such as planting and harvest dates, composting schedules, and watering schedules are all important to note, pest activity is also important to record. The following chart shows an example of the type of information that can be recorded in a daily logbook. This information can be handwritten, or charts like the one below can be created.

Note that the information collected is pertinent to a gardener's ability to make responsible pest management decisions. Information such as plant type, identification of pest, date observed, and treatments made are all recorded. This information should be kept in a safe, accessible location in the toolshed or the house and referred to year after year. This will allow gardeners to keep accurate records of past history in their garden. Since pest infestations often run in cycles, gardeners can anticipate problems before they occur.

IPM Record Keeper

Plant Name	Location	Problem	Date Monitored	Treat- ment	Treatment Date	Comments
ROSE	NORTH SIDE OF HOUSE	BLACKSPOT	6/12/2012	NEEM OIL	6/18/2012	MODERATE INFESTATION
N/A	NEXT TO FRONT DOOR	CANADIAN THISTLE WEED	7/3/2012	HAND PULL	7/5/2012	NOXIOUS WEED REMOVED MANUALLY
ZINNIA	NEXT TO POOL	POWDERY MILDEW	8/2/2012	FUNGICIDE	8/10/2012	MONITORING EFFECTIVENESS OF TREATMENT
N/A	SOUTHEAST CORNER OF DECK	POISON IVY	8/12/2012	ROUNDUP HERBICIDE	8/15/2012	WEED CONTROLLED WITHIN TWO WEEKS

> "Keep a daily log of pest activity so you can keep close tabs on pests before they take hold in your garden."

COMPONENTS OF IPM

Remember that the beauty of IPM is that it integrates many different forms of pest control measures to create an efficient, effective, and safe pest management plan. These measures include chemical, biological, bio-rational, physical, mechanical, and cultural practices, as well as plant selection. One of these practices alone would be less effective, but collectively they are much more effective.

Chemical Controls

Chemical controls include any pesticides or other synthetic materials that kill or have other negative effects on pests. (Some pesticides act as poisons or growth retardants.) Pesticides have been highly publicized in the news over the past few years in a negative way. Many states have passed legislation requiring professional pesticide applicators to notify homeowners and property owners prior to the application of any pesticides. Initially many experts worried that this would impede the effectiveness of a true IPM program, since monitoring would be difficult if prior notification was needed to alert landowners. For example, if a professional landscaper had one hundred clients, people thought it was unlikely he or she would have the resources available to effectively monitor pest levels at each property and notify all clients and their neighbors, especially since pest problems arise quickly and very often need to be dealt with quickly. The fear was that requiring prior notification would drive professionals to use more cover sprays and conventional methods that offer quick results rather than less harmful IPM alternatives. But the reality is that professionals and home gardeners alike have risen to the challenge and embraced the principles of

IPM that make it so effective. Whether a homeowner applies pesticides or hires a landscape professional, IPM allows for flexibility and a commonsense approach to garden maintenance. Pesticides should not be viewed as the enemy; rather, they are one of many options a gardener has to control pests. The responsible use of pesticides when needed is still a viable option. Hiring a landscape professional to make necessary but strategic pesticide applications is an excellent option for homeowners.

Biological Controls

Biological controls have become very popular, since they encourage the use of beneficial organisms to control pests. This is a way for gardeners to wage biological warfare on harmful pests safely and sustainably. A good example of biological control is releasing ladybugs or other predatory insects into the landscape to take a

A praying mantis waits patiently to capture its next meal.

bite out of damaging pest populations. Other beneficial insects include predatory wasps and praying mantises, or biological controls such as *B.t.* (*Bacillus thuringiensis*) and milky spore disease. Several companies raise beneficial insects for sale. These organisms can be purchased and released into the environment as needed.

Beneficial organisms are a favorite of environmentalists because they are the least harmful to air, water, and soil. These beneficials will be discussed in greater detail later in this chapter, but here's one good example of releasing beneficial organisms to control harmful pests. *B.t.* is a beneficial bacteria that is very host-specific, attacking only caterpillars, and is not toxic to humans. Gypsy moth caterpillars, which can devastate entire forests, can be controlled by applying liquid products that contain *B.t.* As the soft-bodied caterpillar ingests the leaves, it also absorbs the bacteria, causing death within a few days. You can accomplish your goal without having to use hazardous chemicals. If environmental conditions are right and cool, wet weather persists; *B.t.* will cause the caterpillar population to collapse rather quickly. Like the beneficial insects, environmental conditions must be optimum for *B.t.* to remain effective.

Carefully removing weeds by hand is necessary around your favorite garden plants.

Biorationals

Biorationals are a group of pest controls that are relatively nontoxic and ecologically safe. These control methods can be chemical or naturally occurring. Low-toxicity chemicals, such as horticultural oils, soaps, Neem oil, *B.t.*, and milky spore disease, are all good examples of biorationals that are effective and break down rather quickly in the environment, leaving no lingering effects, unlike conventional pesticides. Beneficial insects and microorganisms are also considered effective biorational control methods.

Physical Controls

Physical controls provide a nontoxic means of pest control and are quite simple to implement. Harmful pests can be removed or killed by physically removing them from your plants. For example, pests such as scale can be wiped off plants very easily with a cloth and rubbing alcohol. Although this is very time-consuming, it is also very safe. Or whitefly and spider mites can be suppressed by regularly dousing the plants they are on with plenty of cold water.

Mechanical Control

Mechanical control is similar to physical control, but it usually involves some type of machinery. The use of tillers or plows to manage weed crops in an agricultural field is one good example of mechanical control. Gardeners can effectively use small, motorized soil cultivators to control weeds in garden beds or vegetable gardens. For larger-scale problems, often professionals use brush chippers and stump grinders to eliminate the breeding ground for pests when sanitation is the best means of control.

Cultural Practices

Cultural practices refer to sanitation to reduce disease or insect problems. Cultural practices also relate to creating optimum environmental conditions and reducing plant stress. This in turn will reduce the likelihood of plants being vulnerable to pest problems. For example, pruning and destroying diseased limbs from a shrub to reduce the chance that diseases will spread to healthy plants is a type of cultural control. Roses that have blackspot or other leaf diseases can be maintained this way. In vegetable gardening, crop rotation with unrelated species will prevent pests from establishing in a garden.

A motorized dethatcher can help revive dead grass and maintain a healthy lawn.

Plant Selection

Among the various kinds of pest control available, none are more important or effective than proper plant selection. Using the right plant in the right place and following sound gardening practices, such as planting procedures and watering, will go a long way to achieving success in the garden. The reality is that plants thrive in the conditions they have adapted to, not necessarily where we think they look best. Using plants in the type of soil, light, and conditions they were meant to grow in naturally will no doubt make the difference between the life and death of those plants. Common sense should prevail when choosing and siting plants in the garden. For example, don't plant your junipers in dense shade when they thrive in hot, dry sunny conditions, and don't plant your rhododendrons in the blazing sun when they do best in moist, shady conditions.

"A treasure trove of new plant selections are available each year to enhance the landscape and reduce garden maintenance. Don't be afraid to try new things. Be sure to go out to your local nursery or garden catalogue to see what's new. Try to buy at least one new plant each year that you are interested in and don't already have."

In addition to using the right plant in the right place, many new and exciting varieties of landscape plants and agricultural crops are regularly being developed. Using superior species and varieties of plants is one of the most important components of IPM and garden sustainability. Like the use of sound gardening techniques and good cultural practices, the use of new, genetically superior, or pest-resistant plants is essential. These plants are bred for pest resistance, drought tolerance, and aesthetic values. Experts feel the use of these superior plants in the appropriate location will significantly reduce pest problems and the need for pesticides. Many universities have plant evaluation and selection programs to evaluate plants for this purpose. At the University of Georgia, the plant selection program evaluates plants for heat, drought, and pest tolerance. Many universities, such as Cornell, Penn State, and the University of Michigan, have similar programs. The results from these programs are filtered down to farmers, nursery professionals, retailers, and eventually to you.

INVASIVE SPECIES AND IPM

Although there are many invasive and noxious weeds, insects, and diseases that can impact your garden, it is unlikely that gardeners are going to know what to do in every instance. But IPM gives gardeners the tools to apply proper pest management practices and employ the best control methods available to them. Following are two charts that name several insect and weed species that are widely considered among the most damaging and invasive in the United States.

Invasive Insects

There are several good examples illustrated here of invasive species that can be controlled with methods other than pesticides. Asian longhorn beetle arrived in the United States in 1996 from China and has caused serious damage to trees in New York and Chicago. There are no known effective predators or insecticides registered to control ALB. This wood-boring insect is best controlled by removing infected trees, grinding the wood and debris, and replanting with a nonhost species.

Another good example is controlling grubs in your lawn or garden beds. Japanese beetle larvae feed on the roots of plants, and in the adult stage they feed on foliage of garden ornamentals. While grubs are most vulnerable in the larvae stage and insecticides can be effective if applied at the right time, hand picking, trapping adults, or using a biological control in the form of a beneficial bacteria known as milky spore disease are nontoxic control methods. Like *B.t.*, milky spore disease is a biological control that can be applied to turf and garden beds to naturally control grubs.

Common Invasive Insects

Insect	Damage	Crops Affected	Treatment	Other IPM Considerations
ASIAN LONGHORNED BEETLE	WOOD BORING	MAPLE, WILLOW, ELM, POPLAR, ASH	NONE	SANITATION: REMOVAL OF INFECTED TREES, REPLACEMENT
EMERALD ASH BORER	WOOD BORING	ASH	SYSTEMIC INSECTICIDES	SANITATION, BIOLOGICAL CONTROLS
GRUBS	ROOT FEEDING	TURF	INSECTICIDES	HAND PICKING OR TRAPPING ADULTS, MILKY SPORE DISEASE
GYPSY MOTH	DEFOLIATION	OAK, APPLE, BIRCH, LINDEN	INSECTICIDES, *BACILLUS THURINGIENSIS*	PHYSICAL REMOVAL
WOOLLY ADELGID	SAP SUCKING	HEMLOCK	HORTICUL-TURAL OILS AND SOAPS, SYSTEMIC INSECTICIDES	PLANTING ALTERNATE SPECIES, POTENTIAL FOR BENEFICIAL INSECT CONTROL
JAPANESE BEETLE ADULT	CHEWING FOLIAGE	ROSES	NO CHEMICALS USED	HAND PICKING

The adult Japanese beetle feeds on leaves of roses and other ornamental plants.

But there are other situations where pesticides may be the best or only course of action for a particular pest. Hemlock woolly adelgid is an aphidlike insect that sucks the sap from hemlocks. Canadian hemlock is one of the great American native evergreens in forests and landscapes across the East Coast, and thousands of plants have been killed by this lethal insect infestation. If the infestations are severe enough, it eventually weakens the tree, and if left untreated, large specimens will succumb. It is called woolly adelgid because of the fuzzy white appearance of the insect on the leaves of the plant. In this case, pesticides are the best form of control known now. Use of predatory beetles to control this pest is still in the developmental stage, and the only other alternative is planting a different species to replace hemlock. So the use of low-toxicity insecticides, such as horticultural oils and soaps, once or twice a season will effectively control this pest and save your beautiful hemlocks from the compost pile. While IPM encourages alternatives to pesticides, pesticides are still appropriate in specific situations.

Invasive Plants

Weeds can be just as damaging and troublesome as insects and diseases in the landscape. In fact, the majority of a gardener's time is spent patrolling the lawn, flower beds, and shrub borders for uninvited leafy guests. In the past, the first line of defense against weeds was to reach for a weedkiller to solve our problems. Reaching for an herbicide is usually easier and can provide faster results than mechanical removal or removing weeds by hand. Now, more than ever, IPM allows us more flexibility to look at more sustainable ways to manage pesky weeds. This chart on the next page highlights a few invasive weeds that are commonly encountered in gardens and the IPM considerations that be used to effectively control them.

Weeds such as kudzu, garlic mustard, and Norway maple pose serious threats to our ecosystem. It is estimated that kudzu vine, most prevalent in the southern states, can cover up to 100,000 acres per year across the United States. It covers shrubs, trees, structures, and anything it can grab onto, smothering its victim. While chemical controls are available, removing vines by hand or with machinery has also proved effective in large areas.

> "Invasive pests can be controlled by using low-toxicity chemicals such as oils or soaps or nonchemical means such as sanitation, physical removal, or planting alternate species. You should use these environmentally friendly pest control measures whenever possible."

Garlic mustard is a biennial weed that completes its lifecycle in two years. At the end of the second growing season, it flowers and produces seed. Removing or cutting down the plant before it has a chance to disperse seed can be a very

Kudzu is one of many invasive species that impacts the landscape.

effective way to keep this plant in check. Using weedkiller on garlic mustard is usually done only when populations are out of control.

The Norway maple is one of the most challenging and ecologically destructive invasive trees in the United States. It grows very rapidly, disperses *thousands* of seedlings once a tree is mature, and survives in a wide variety of environmental conditions, all key elements that define invasive species. Although great efforts have been made to ban this exotic tree from the nursery trade and limit its distributions, it is still prevalent in many communities. While weedkillers are potentially effective on young plants, removal of seedlings or young trees by hand or with machinery is most effective in the control of Norway maple. Although it's more time consuming, a nonchemical control of Norway maple is the most practical and eco-friendly management of this pest.

I must emphasize that there is an important difference between invasive plants and exotic species. Just because a plant is imported from another country does not necessarily mean it is going to be invasive in your garden. There are many great landscape plants that are noninvasive exotics adding ornamental value and function to the garden. Exotic species such as paperbark maple (*Acer griseum*), katsura tree (*Cercidiphyllum japonicum*), ginkgo (*Ginkgo biloba*), and Japanese stewartia (*Stewartia pseudocamellia*) are a few good

Common Invasive Weeds

Weed	Type	Damage	Treatment	Other IPM Considerations
GARLIC MUSTARD	BIENNIAL	CROWDS OUT NATIVES	SYSTEMIC HERBICIDES	HAND PICKING, CUTTING DOWN WITH MOWER BEFORE GOING TO SEED
PURPLE LOOSESTRIFE	PERENNIAL	OVERTAKES WATERWAYS	HERBICIDES	HAND PICKING, BIOLOGICAL CONTROL, MECHANICAL REMOVAL, NOT PLANTING IN WET AREAS
KUDZU	VINE	CHOKES OUT VEGETATION	SYSTEMIC HERBICIDES	HAND PICKING, MECHANICAL REMOVAL
BITTERSWEET	VINE	CHOKES OUT VEGETATION	SYSTEMIC HERBICIDES	HAND PICKING, MECHANICAL REMOVAL
NORWAY MAPLE	TREE	SHADES OUT NATIVES	SYSTEMIC HERBICIDES	HAND PICKING SEEDLINGS
WILD ONION	PERENNIAL	LOOKS UNSIGHTLY IN LAWN AND GARDEN BEDS	SYSTEMIC HERBICIDES	HAND DIGGING AND DISCARDING

examples of such plants. On the other hand, one can easily make the argument that some North American natives are far more problematic in the garden than their Asian counterparts are. These natives include American sweet gum (*Liquidambar styraciflua*), Virginia creeper (*Pathenocissus quinquefolia*), black locust (*Robinia pseudoacacia*), and sassafras (*Sassafras albidum*). While all these plants can provide an important presence in natural settings, they can also be difficult to manage in a cultivated garden. Now more than ever I believe that it is less important to pit natives versus exotics and more important to encourage plant diversity in the landscape. A garden that encompasses a wide variety of species and varieties will likely be much more sustainable than one that consists of only a few species of plants.

> "Many natives and noninvasive exotic species can add variety and beauty to the garden without invading it."

WEED-SUPPRESSING GROUNDCOVERS

One way to combat troublesome weeds in the garden is by covering the ground with groundcovers. The idea is to choose low-growing

Lady's mantle is a carefree groundcover that helps suppress weed growth.

Weed-Suppressing Groundcovers

Plant	Habit	Height	Ornamental Value	Culture
CORAL BELLS (*HEUCHERA* SPP.)	CLUMP	18–24 IN.	LUSH FOLIAGE OF VARYING COLORS, SPIKES OF PINK FLOWERS	MOIST, WELL-DRAINED SOIL, SUN OR PART SUN
MOSS PHLOX (*PHLOX SUBULATA*)	MATTING	4–6 IN.	GLOSSY GREEN FOLIAGE; WHITE, PINK, OR BLUE FLOWERS EARLY IN THE SEASON	MOIST, WELL-DRAINED SOIL AND SUN OR PART SUN
LILY TURF (*LIRIOPE SPICATA*)	CLUMP	8–12 IN.	GRASSLIKE FOLIAGE; WHITE, PINK, OR BLUE SPIKES OF FLOWERS	MOIST, WELL-DRAINED SOIL AND SUN OR PART SUN, TOLERATES DRY SOIL
LADY'S MANTLE (*ALCHEMELLIA MOLLIS*)	CLUMP	12–18 IN.	LARGE, GREEN LEAVES GLISTENING AS THEY HOLD DROPLETS OF WATER, CHARTREUSE FLOWERS IN SUMMER	MOIST, WELL-DRAINED SOIL, SUN OR PART SUN
LEADWORT (*CERATOSTIGMA PLUMBAGINOIDES*)	MATTING	8–12 IN.	SMALL, LIGHT GREEN LEAVES WITH DEEP BLUE FLOWERS	TOLERATES DRY SOIL, SUN OR PART SUN

plants that provide a thick, matted growth habit to prevent weeds from establishing in the garden. Planting groundcover with dense foliage is far better than leaving bare ground and even better than using some types of mulch. In addition to function, these groundcovers also offer nice flowers and a variety of foliage colors and textures. These groundcovers can develop into either a matting type or clumping type plant. Matting type groundcovers tend to spread and root into soil as they grow, while clumping type groundcovers generally stay in one area without spreading too far. For this reason, clumping type plants should be planted closer together to ensure the ground is thoroughly covered quickly. This practice will ultimately reduce maintenance and weeding of the garden as well as the need for weedkillers and other chemicals. The chart below shows a few easy-to-grow, weed-suppressing groundcovers. There are a few more selelctions available in Chapter 6.

Lily turf is a rather durable, low-maintenance groundcover that tolerates shade and reduces weeds.

"Weed-suppressing groundcovers will add beauty and function to the landscape and with their dense habit will reduce hand pulling of weeds. Find a few groundcovers that will grow in your hardiness zone and try them in a few areas of the garden where weeds have typically been a problem."

THE GOOD GUYS

Plants and insects have a mutually beneficial relationship that is essential to their survival. Plants provide food and shelter for insects, birds, amphibians, and other animals. Animals return the favor to plants by serving as pollinators, seed distributors, and pest reducers. Adding plants that attract these beneficial animals into the garden will encourage a more sustainable, self-maintaining environment.

There are a host of plants that not only offer beautiful flowers and colorful fruit and foliage but also act as insect attractors. The simple fact is that the only way to attract and keep these good guys in the garden is to offer them a regular source of food, water, and shelter. These plants can be natives or noninvasive exotics and can easily be incorporated into a cultivated or more natural garden setting. The following chart illustrates some common garden plants and the desirable insects that they attract. These plants represent a sample of annuals, perennials, and woody plants that support healthy populations of beneficial insects, such as butterflies, bees, flies, and lady beetles, as well as bird species.

In addition to incorporating into the garden plant species that attract beneficial insects and birds, it is important to understand what role these animal good guys play. The chart on the next page offers a sampling of some garden-friendly animal species and the benefits they provide to your landscape.

Helpful insects such as bees, butterflies, and lady beetles are near and dear to our hearts as they flutter around the garden. Honeybees, although not native to the United States, are important pollinators. They are social, nonaggressive, and resourceful insects that create large colonies in the landscape. Not only do they benefit the garden as pollinators, but honeybees also provide us with honey, beeswax, and royal jelly. Beeswax can be used for cosmetic products, lip balm, candles, lubricants, and much more. Royal jelly is also used in skin care products and is high in amino acids, vitamins, and minerals.

Native North American bees, such as bumblebees, carpenter bees, miner bees, and sweat bees, just to name a few, are also excellent pollinators and offer benefits similar to those that honeybees provide. However, some experts say that bee for bee, native bees pollinate fruits and vegetable crops far more effectively than honeybees do. This is because many native bee species forage earlier or later in the day than honeybees do, and native bees will often visit flowers in wet or cold conditions, while honeybees remain in the hive. Native bees are also less susceptible to colony collapse disorder, a drastic reduction in beehive populations generally attributed to mites, pesticide use, environmental stresses, and malnutrition.

You can supplement these insect populations not only by attracting insects into your garden, but also by releasing additional insects such as lady

Incorporating a wide variety of flowering plants will attract butterflies to your garden.

Asters are excellent late season bloomers that are prized by pollinators.

Plants That Attract Wildlife in the Garden

Plant	Bloom Time	Insects and Birds Attracted	Hardiness Zone	Type
BUTTERFLY WEED (ASCLEPIAS TUBEROSA)	SUMMER, FALL	BUTTERFLIES, BEES, HUMMINGBIRDS	3–9	PERENNIAL
YARROW (ACHILLEA MILLEFOLIUM)	SUMMER	LADY BEETLES, PARASITIC WASPS, BEES	3–9	PERENNIAL
SUNFLOWER (HELIANTHUS ANNUUS)	SUMMER, FALL	BUTTERFLIES, BEES	N/A	ANNUAL
ASTER (ASTER NOVAE-ANGLIAE)	SUMMER, FALL	BUTTERFLIES, BEES, FLIES	3–9	PERENNIAL
CONEFLOWER (ECHINACEA PURPUREA)	SUMMER, FALL	BUTTERFLIES, BEES, BIRDS	3–8	PERENNIAL
GOLDENROD (SOLIDAGO CANADENSIS)	SUMMER, FALL	BUTTERFLIES, BEES, FLIES, BEETLES	3–9	PERENNIAL
JOE-PYE WEED (EUPATORIUM PURPUREUM)	SUMMER, FALL	BUTTERFLIES, BEES	4–9	PERENNIAL
TRUMPET HONEYSUCKLE (LONICERA SEMPERVIRENS)	SUMMER	HUMMINGBIRDS, BUTTERFLIES	4–9	WOODY VINE
BUTTERFLY BUSH (BUDDLEIA DAVIDII)	SUMMER	BUTTERFLIES, BEES, HUMMINGBIRDS	5–9	SHRUB

beetles, praying mantises, and lacewings into your garden as needed. Several companies sell beneficial insects and deliver them by mail. Upon receiving your insects, you should read the instructions carefully. In most cases, it is best to release your insects in the morning, when it is cooler. Praying mantises are shipped as egg cases and can be released after they hatch. It is important to understand that if you choose to release beneficial insects, there must be a pest population to support them. If there is no food source, your insects will quickly die or migrate to another location that has a plentiful food source. It's important to do your homework. Research where these insects are coming from and know what types of insects you are releasing in your garden. Having a reliable and safe source of beneficial insects is extremely important.

One insect that is usually most prevalent near ponds, streams, or other small bodies of water is the dragonfly. As dragonflies dart through the air, they catch crawling and flying insects, effectively controlling pests naturally. Dragonflies may look and sound intimidating, but they are harmless to people and should be left alone to do their work.

Beneficial nematodes are microscopic, unsegmented roundworms that live in the soil. There are many species of nematodes, most of which are harmful to plants, but a few nematodes are in fact helpful in protecting plants. These tiny worms can also be added to the soil to control pests in ornamentals and turf areas. Beneficial nematodes can control root-feeding insects such as grubs, weevils, and cutworms. These fast-acting organisms can also infect insect pests with bacteria that help kill them. Beneficial nematodes are typically released in a liquid solution under certain ideal environmental conditions. These ideal conditions consist of high relative humidity, no

Animals and Their Function in the Landscape

Species	Benefits	Pests Controlled
HONEYBEE, NATIVE BEES	POLLINATORS	N/A
BUTTERFLIES	POLLINATORS	N/A
LADY BEETLES (LADYBUGS)		APHIDS, SCALE, MITES
LACEWINGS		APHIDS, SCALE, WHITEFLIES, MEALY BUGS, CATERPILLARS
PRAYING MANTIS		MOTHS, CRICKETS, GRASSHOPPERS, FLIES
PARASITIC WASPS		APHIDS, BEETLES, CATERPILLARS, FLIES, SAWFLIES, SCALE INSECTS
DRAGONFLIES		MOSQUITOES, ANTS, WASPS, FLIES
BENEFICIAL NEMATODES (WORMS)		GRUBS, FLEAS, WEEVILS, CUTWORMS
BATS		MOSQUITOES, MOTHS, WASPS, BEETLES
BIRDS		CATERPILLARS, MOTHS, FLIES, BEETLES, AND SO ON
SNAKES		RODENTS, VARIETY OF INSECTS
LIZARDS		VARIETY OF INSECTS
TURTLES		SLUGS, SNAILS, WORMS, INSECTS
FROGS AND TOADS		INSECTS, SNAILS, SPIDERS, WORMS, SMALL FISH

direct sunlight, moderate air temperatures with no extreme fluctuations, and moist soil ranging from 55 to 90 degrees Fahrenheit on average.

As for mammals, bats are among a gardener's best friends. Bats control a large quantity of insects, such as mosquitoes, moths, beetles, and more. While there are many bat species

Native bees and other pollinators are extremely important for fruit production.

native to North America, two of the most common are the little brown bat (*Myotis lucifugus*) and the big brown bat (*Eptesicus fuscus*). These flying marvels are capable of consuming thousands of insects in one night. Bats are most active during dusk and dawn and can be encouraged to stay nearby by putting up bat houses. Bat houses should be placed away from the house, patio, or garage.

While there are a wide variety of birds that control harmful insects in the garden, some of the most effective are barn swallows, bluebirds, chickadees, purple martins, robins, meadowlarks, mockingbirds, phoebes, and woodpeckers. Like bats, these bird species can eat thousands of insects in a day without harming the environment they live in. How many birds, what types, and how long they stay around the garden all depend on the food and habitat you are offering. With the proper selection

Dragonflies live near ponds and streams and will snatch harmful insects.

of plants on the menu, birds will keep coming back without the enticement of a bird feeder.

The last group of good guys that help provide balance in the natural landscape includes snakes, lizards, frogs, toads, and turtles. These beneficial reptiles and amphibians will find you on their own, provided they have a naturally welcoming environment with habitat and food. These somewhat shy creatures should be left alone to forage for pests in your garden. Although there are a wide variety of reptile and amphibian species indigenous to the United States, you may want to identify specific inhabitants in your garden as you observe them. Chapter 3 covers in more detail how to create a suitable habitat for these helpful garden creatures.

THE PROS AND CONS OF GOING ORGANIC

IPM and sustainability are complementary philosophies that both support the idea of living a healthy, lower-maintenance, and organic lifestyle. IPM strengthens the practice of going organic, since the main goal of IPM is to use chemicals as a last resort and not as a first line of defense. There are advantages and disadvantages to caring for your garden in an organic way. Here are a few pros and cons to consider as part of a sound sustainability program.

Pros

- Organic gardening protects our environment, including soil, water, air, and the health of our families and pets.
- Although debated, studies suggest organically grown food is richer in nutrients and antioxidants and is not contaminated with harmful chemicals, making it safer. (Or, at least, less contaminated since it's difficult to completely control pesticide "creep" through the air and soil.)
- Gardening organically will save money, because you will not have to rely on expensive store-bought fertilizers and pesticides.
- Conventional garden maintenance techniques tend to work for a short period of time and often involve the use of chemicals that offer a quick fix, while organic techniques offer long-term care and enhancement of soil, water, and overall health of the garden.

Cons

- Maintaining your garden organically with less or no use of chemicals is more labor-intensive and time-consuming.
- Without the use of chemicals, lower yields may be experienced because of increased pest infestations and slow-acting organic fertilizers.

> "Having an organic garden may take more hard work to maintain but in the long term will equal more savings and a healthier landscape."

Besides the obvious and important value of gardening organically to save our planet, there are also economic benefits and costs associated

Organic produce may be more expensive, but it can also be tastier and healthier.

with organic gardening. IPM and less chemical dependency certainly saves money on expensive chemical fertilizers, weedkillers, fungicides, insecticides, and other pest-control products. But these organic methods also come at a cost. First, organically grown produce and ornamentals are typically more expensive to purchase, since they require more costly methods to grow. Because there is less reliance on chemicals, there is generally more crop loss and more culling out of damaged crops, so it takes more resources to produce the same amount of sellable crops in commercial organic gardening. Since organic farmers do not rely on chemicals, more labor is required for weeding and spreading of organic fertilizer like manures. Produce that is certified organic from the USDA is not easy or inexpensive to obtain. As with agriculture, home gardens that are maintained organically that don't rely on pesticides tend to be more vulnerable to disease and insect damage. But by creating the right environment for beneficial insects and mammals and using organic products such as horticultural oils, this damage can be minimized.

Organic produce can cost as much as 50 to 100 percent more than nonorganic alternatives. This is directly related to the fact that commerically grown organic products are more costly to produce. So while there are some savings associated with going organic, such as through making

your own organic fertilizer by composting and through purchasing less conventional products, buying truly green products will cost more.

Besides the monetary costs, another factor to consider when going organic is the availability of resources. Sustainability is all about maximizing the resources around you. A gardener who does this will no doubt create a more sustainable landscape that is less expensive to maintain. Common sense should prevail when making the most of your natural resources. If you live in an area of the country where pine straw is in great quantity, then you should use that material as mulch in the garden. Why purchase wood chips or another form of processed mulch that is foreign to your neck of the woods when you have an abundant natural form of mulch right under your nose? Or if you have a pond, stream, or even a sump (low spot that collects water) in your backyard, why not landscape it with native plants that attract beneficial insects such as butterflies, dragonflies, and lady beetles so this healthy environment will sustain their presence for the long term? Sustainability gives gardeners an opportunity to reuse, recycle, and maximize available resources. It takes a commitment of time and an investment of money to get the program up and running, but it pays dividends for years to come. The amount and types of resources that are available to you are essential to the long-term viability of any sustainability program.

Chemical Pesticides: To Use or Not to Use

Chemical pesticides, fertilizers, and other products can be expensive and harmful if used improperly. IPM doesn't offer alternatives to pesticides with the objective to abolish their use, but rather to reduce their misuse and our landscape's dependency on them.

Pesticides can be a useful tool to gardeners if needed, but they are not a silver bullet that one should go to every time there is a problem in the landscape. While going organic means not using chemicals, IPM means just using them with discretion and only when absolutely necessary.

For example, aphids are tiny green-and-black insects that suck the sap out of a wide variety of plants. If an infestation is really serious, organic pest control may not be effective. In this case, it would be to your advantage to spray the aphids with a pesticide such as horticultural oil or soap, which will reduce the population greatly. Once the insect population is manageable, you could release lady beetles a few weeks later if needed to control any remaining aphids. This would be the most effective, efficient, and eco-friendly use of your resources. Such in-field decisions are critical to the long-term care and sustainability of the garden. Use pesticides only if you have to and follow the label on the container or bag. If you are not sure what to do, consult with your local agricultural extension service or landscape professional.

OTHER IMPORTANT ADVANTAGES OF IPM

IPM has many short-term and long-term benefits. The most important advantage of IPM is the ability to make responsible, safe, and effective decisions about managing pests. The overuse of pesticides can result in increased pesticide resistance and the reduction of beneficial insect and bird populations. IPM minimizes ecosystem disruption through an ecologically based management approach.

However, IPM can also have significant economic impact as well as environmental benefits. In addition to effectively controlling pests that would otherwise cause serious damage to crops,

IPM offers a cost benefit, because in the long run, it helps us save money and encourages the most economically sound approach to pest management. IPM can create an efficient, cost-saving management plan that is also effective, especially for the home gardener.

In a three-year study from 1982 to 1984 at the University of Maryland, a cost-benefit analysis was performed in three separate locations. Conventional pesticide spray programs were used in 1982 and compared with IPM practices implemented in 1983 and 1984. The results showed an overall cost savings of 63 percent in 1983 and 47 percent in 1984 by using IPM methods rather than pesticides. Although labor costs did increase during this time, this example illustrates the efficiency that IPM can offer everyone, from a professional to a home gardener.

Although IPM started as a tool used by professionals, home gardeners can use it to reduce pest damage more naturally. IPM encourages us as gardeners to make responsible, informed decisions on managing pests in the landscape by using sound gardening practices. By closely monitoring the landscape and knowing what to look for and when, pests can be managed effectively before they become a problem. Although sustaining an organic garden takes time, patience, and an initial economic investment, a well-balanced, healthy and manageable landscape are the fruits of that labor. It is inconceivable to think that a sustainable garden can be successful without some form of IPM incorporated into the overall management of the garden.

IPM offers an opportunity to better manage damaging invasive species while supporting a sustainable landscape. IPM and sustainability are closely aligned, with similar goals and principles. This is why IPM is such an important component of a sustainable landscape. The strength of a successful IPM program lies in your ability to manage your landscape with a variety of control measures, not just with chemicals. If you utilize nature's resources, create a desirable habitat for wildlife, and keep a watchful eye on your garden, pests won't have a chance.

CHAPTER 5

Water Conservation

Making the Most of Every Drop

Water—and its role in our lives—is all too often taken for granted. We go about our lives day after day never really considering what would happen if we one day didn't have fresh, clean water at our fingertips. Let's face it: compared to people living in other parts of the world, Americans are fortunate to have an abundance of water for drinking, bathing, recreation, and irrigating our lawns and gardens.

Since ancient times, when humans adopted agriculture as a way of life, water has been a vital component of society. Ancient civilizations knew that without a steady and reliable water supply, they could not survive. The ancient Romans and Greeks built aqueducts and cisterns to move and store water. In more recent history, the twentieth century has produced an interesting tale about water consumption in the United States. Between 1950 and 1980, there was a steady increase in water use in the United States. The main theory behind this rise in water consumption was that as the population increased, so did the need for water. But contrary to that theory, water use has remained relatively stable over the past few decades even though there has been a steady increase in population in the United States. Technological advances, improved equipment and regulations, and increased awareness of the need for water conservation have all resulted in more efficient use of water.

It is estimated that in 2005, about 410 billion gallons per day (Bgal/d) of water were used in the United States. This total has varied very little since 1985, as usage has been consistent in the two largest areas of water consumption: thermoelectric power and irrigation. It is estimated that irrigation represents about one-third of water use in the United States. Irrigation water use includes water used for agriculture and farming, frost protection, chemical applications such as weed control, and for maintaining large public facilities such as parks and golf courses. Historically, surface water has composed about 80 percent of the total water used, and 20 percent was taken from groundwater. But from 1950 to 2000, the use of groundwater nearly doubled. This has become a problem, because chemicals such as pesticides and fertilizers can leach into the groundwater, contaminating it for public use. For this reason, there have been restrictions put on certain chemical uses to reduce the likelihood of compromising groundwater.

Since 1950, irrigation has represented about 65 percent of total water use. The number of acres irrigated with sprinkler and micro-irrigation systems has continued to increase and now makes up more than half the total irrigated acreage in the United States. Although homeowners, farmers, golf courses, and so forth are using improved, more efficient irrigation systems that save water, with so many people using water, there is still a strain on public water supplies. But thanks to new technology each year, homeowners and professionals alike have an opportunity to save water and reduce costs.

WATER RESTRICTIONS: A NATIONAL DILEMMA

It's easy to think that our water supply is endless and that surface water and groundwater can be pumped whenever we need it. But that is not the case, and Americans are starting to realize that conserving water is not just a nice thing to do; it's a necessity. Many communities are experiencing firsthand the reality that water is not an infinite resource to be used or misused without consequences. Water restrictions frequently start as voluntary programs, and during times of severe drought or high water usage periods, water restrictions will often become mandatory. In many cases, not complying with these mandates can result in substantial fines. For example, states like Georgia, Florida, Texas, and Arizona have strict water regulations that require compliance as determined by the municipal water authority. In Atlanta, Georgia, water restrictions include watering only between the hours of 4:00 p.m. to 10:00 a.m. and odd-even schedules for certain types of water usage. This odd-even schedule requires odd-numbered addresses to water only on Tuesdays, Thursdays, or Sundays and even-numbered addresses to water on Mondays, Wednesdays, or Saturdays, with no watering on Fridays. Interestingly, newly planted landscapes can be watered at any time of the day during the week, but only during their first thirty days. There are certain exemptions to these regulations—most notably the use of drip irrigation or soaker hoses, which use much smaller amounts of water than traditional sprinkler systems use.

In Austin, Texas, complex water schedules are divided among public schools, commercial uses, and residential uses. These uses are further broken down between automatic irrigation and hose-end sprinklers. For example, under residential restrictions, hose-end sprinklers must be used before 10:00 a.m. or after 7:00 p.m. on Saturdays (odd addresses) or Sundays (even addresses). Automatic irrigation systems may be used before 5:00 a.m. or after 7:00 p.m. on Thursdays (even addresses) or Wednesdays (odd addresses). Again, low-volume systems such as drip irrigation and soaker hoses are exempt from these regulations.

In 2012, the city of Tucson, Arizona, prohibited the use of irrigation except for those areas where reclaimed water is being used. The city reserves the right to implement a similar irrigation schedule in place of the tight restrictions if it is deemed appropriate. In 2012, in Safford, Arizona, residents were forced to implement tight water restrictions, such as watering lawns only on certain days of the week and only for a maximum of two hours on those days. Residents were asked to refrain from planting new sod or ornamental grass.

MORE RESTRICTIONS COMING? MAYBE, MAYBE NOT!

All these scenarios are serious, and they are more than just an inconvenience for the folks who live in these communities. As average temperatures get warmer each year, and droughts become more persistent, these types of water restrictions will become more common. Many climate experts predict that the Earth's surface will continue to get warmer, causing more extreme weather patterns. These weather patterns include drought and heat, which affect water consumption. Even in areas that do not experience heat, drought, and water restrictions regularly, water conservation should be encouraged.

Why? Because it is the sustainable thing to do! Overirrigating a landscape can cause as much damage as underirrigating it. In the Northeast, where I live, I have witnessed countless scenarios in which homeowners water the lawn whether it needs it or not and program automatic irrigation systems to either under- or overwater the landscape. Over the past few years, this region has experienced adequate rainfall; overwatering at these times not only wastes valuable water, but also puts unneeded stress on your plants. Root-borne diseases are more prevalent during periods when rainfall is consistent and regular irrigation still occurs. In addition, many experts feel that overwatering coupled with saturated soil compromises trees during times of high winds or natural disasters such as hurricanes. While this is just a theory, it makes perfect sense that a tree with possible root rot in soft, waterlogged soil can blow over easier than a healthy tree in drier soil.

Rain barrels are a great way to harvest and reuse rainwater.

> "In some areas of the country, water restrictions are a way of everyday life. Wherever you live, you should always try to conserve water and check local regulations from your water authority."

DIVERTING WATER AND THE LAW

Harvesting rainwater is an often-debated issue in certain western states, such as Arizona, Colorado, New Mexico, and Utah. Believe it or not, some states have enacted laws restricting water diversion, or the collection of rainfall. The theory behind such restriction is that when people capture rainwater provided by Mother Nature, less water flows into streams, lakes, and aquifers, where it is needed for wells and springs. In other words, by harvesting precipitation, you are stealing water that would otherwise be available to others downstream, who are legally entitled to the same water. Prior appropriation water rights have dominated water use law in the western states since the nineteenth century. In general, water rights are unrelated to land rights and can be sold or financed like other property. Under these water rights, the first person to use water from a water source for a beneficial use has the right to continue to use that water for that intended purpose. Subsequent users of that water can use the remaining water for their own beneficial purposes provided that they do not impact the rights of the previous water users. Each state has its own unique stance on water rights concerning rainfall. The legal details vary among states.

But others see the harvesting of rainwater as a practical, commonsense answer to ongoing water shortages and storm water runoff, which can cause serious erosion issues. They wonder: how could we put restrictions on resources that are created by nature: water, air, sunlight, and so on? Now many western states are loosening their restrictions on rain harvesting, especially for homeowners and residential sites. In Europe, rain harvesting has been a common practice for quite some time. Many gardeners attach their drainage leaders to 50-gallon drums or barrels that catch the water coming off the roof. This water is then used later to water houseplants or containers plants by a hose bib located at the bottom of the barrel.

In the United States, this practice has not been as popular. Even though some western states have passed legislation restricting the collection of rainwater, in areas where there are no restrictions, rainwater harvesting has not taken off the way one might expect. But with loosening restrictions and new efforts by home gardeners to become more sustainable, rain harvesting and other water conservation techniques are ready to flourish. Following is a chart illustrating various states and their stance on rain harvesting. While some states have had strict regulations in place on this issue, recent amendments have allowed for some flexibility and even incentives for homeowners to collect and use rainwater wisely.

BEING PROACTIVE: SAVING WATER BEFORE YOU LOSE IT

It is no secret that most Americans don't consider water a scarce resource. I don't think any of us intentionally waste water, but the reality is that many of our everyday watering practices are wasteful. How many times do you see irrigation systems running during rainstorms, toilets that leak slightly, leaky garden hoses, or sprinklers that are left on all night accidentally? It happens more than you think, and it wastes thousands of gallons of water. This water can be saved by each of us if we follow a few simple measures.

This is a book about sustainability in the garden, but water conservation must extend inside the home too. One way to save water and reduce costs is to check your household equipment for breaks, loose connections, or wear that might cause leaks. For example, your bathroom faucet might drip water. This could be due to a loose faucet tip, worn washer, or some other equipment within the faucet. Repairing or replacing this equipment can make a big difference in how much water you use.

Some Significant Rain Harvesting Legislation

State	Legislation
ARIZONA	ARIZONA OFFERED A TAX CREDIT FOR THE COLLECTION OF RAINWATER, BUT THE CREDIT EXPIRED IN 2012. THE STATE ESTABLISHED A JOINT LEGISLATIVE STUDY COMMITTEE ON MACRO-HARVESTED WATER, WHICH STUDIES ISSUES ARISING FROM THE LARGE-SCALE COLLECTION AND RECOVERY OF RAINWATER.
COLORADO	COLORADO HAD SOME OF THE STRICTEST RAINWATER HARVEST LAWS, PROHIBITING THE PRACTICE FOR THE MOST PART. IN 2009, TWO LAWS WERE PASSED THAT LOOSENED RESTRICTIONS ON RESIDENTIAL PROPERTY OWNERS WHO OWN CERTAIN TYPES OF WELLS FOR COLLECTING AND USING RAINWATER.
UTAH	UTAH ALLOWS THE DIRECT CAPTURE AND STORAGE OF RAINWATER ON LAND OWNED OR LEASED BY THE PERSON RESPONSIBLE FOR THE RAINWATER COLLECTION. THE MAXIMUM CAPACITY OF AN UNDERGROUND STORAGE CONTAINER MUST BE NO MORE THAN 2,500 GALLONS, AND FOR ABOVEGROUND COVERED STORAGE CONTAINERS, NO MORE THAN TWO CONTAINERS GREATER THAN 100 GALLONS.
WASHINGTON	STATE LAW ALLOWS COUNTIES TO REDUCE RATES FOR STORM WATER CONTROL FACILITIES THAT UTILIZE RAINWATER HARVESTING TECHNIQUES. RATES MAY BE REDUCED BY A MINIMUM OF TEN PERCENT FOR ANY NEW OR REMODELED COMMERCIAL BUILDING.

Even one drip of water per minute can add up to a significant amount. An average home with three sinks that leak at a rate of one drip per minute will waste 104 gallons a year. Showers and toilets can leak just as easily and should be checked and maintained regularly. Often the internal parts of a toilet tank, such as the fill valve and flapper, which fill and hold water in the tank, will leak unnoticed. Checking external plumbing connections regularly in the bathroom, kitchen, and basement, such as on boilers and hot water heaters, will save you time and money.

IRRIGATION
Irrigation Methods

One main issue you need to consider when deciding on the type of irrigation system for your garden is the types of plants you will be watering regularly. Gardens typically have a diversity of plants, including lawn, herbaceous and woody plants, evergreens, and tropical plants, all of which require different amounts of water. For this reason, it is important to diversify your irrigation methods to meet the needs of your landscape. That means selecting and installing an irrigating system with a combination of features for irrigation your lawn, flowers, trees, and shrubs, and other select plants in the garden.

Irrigation systems can be as simple or as complex as you desire. They can range from low-tech, manual systems to more automated systems.

Strategic placement of drip irrigation emitters can lower your water use.

There are advantages and disadvantages to both, and your choice really depends on your specific situation and budget. Manual systems tend to be more economical and easier to maintain and repair but require more labor to operate. Automatic irrigation systems are more expensive to install and maintain but require less labor to operate.

A manual system can be a series of hoses and sprinklers that are moved around the garden or an in-ground system that is turned on and off as needed. Either way, manual systems give you the most control and are the most labor-intensive. I have seen entire gardens watered using hoses and hose bibs, which are typically available in ½-inch and ¾-inch sizes. If not monitored closely, manual irrigation systems can become inefficient and wasteful.

In-ground irrigation systems make life a lot easier because all the piping and irrigation equipment is underground and always in place. In-ground irrigation systems can be manual or automatic. The equipment is the same for both; the only difference is that automated systems have preprogrammed controllers that operate the system.

Polyethylene tubing and piping can be used for drip irrigation systems and underground sprinkler systems.

Irrigation equipment for residential sites can vary, but they use two main types of piping: polyethylene (PE) and polyvinyl chloride (PVC). PE is generally black tubing generally ¼ inch or greater in diameter. It is used because it is easy to work with, flexible yet durable, and economical. PVC typically comes in ¼ inch or more diameter and is usually white or gray in color. While both types of piping can crack and leak over time, PVC usually has a longer life span. Whichever type of pipe is used, over time both can crack and leak. You should check your irrigation system regularly, especially when it is running, to make sure there are no excessive leaks or puddles. Repairs should be done as soon as possible, as lingering water leaks are not only costly but can affect the long-term health of plants that do not appreciate wet soil. If you have a water leak, and plants that generally grow in well-drained soil are now subjected to soggy, poorly drained soil, root rot or some other disease is sure to take them out. With both PVC and PE, repairs are rather easy and can be done by an irrigation professional or by you with the right tools, clamps, and couplings. Either way, don't wait to fix leaky pipes, or it will cost more in the long run than just a higher water bill.

Proper irrigation techniques are another very important part of watering your garden. An improperly watered garden full of stressed, poorly developed plants is more likely to fall victim to an infestation of invasive plants or pests. Following proper watering techniques is a huge part of creating a sustainable garden. Using common sense and following a few simple rules will go a long way toward reaching plant nirvana.

I see landscape after landscape either over- or underwatered. It pains me to see how much water, time, and money is wasted by homeowners who water improperly. One of the biggest culprits in this madness is the automatic irrigation system with an irrigation timer or controller. This is a device that can be programmed to water your garden automatically according to whatever information you input. I am not a big fan of automated systems, because they are often programmed incorrectly and give you less control of watering. There are so many variables that help determine proper watering, such as sun and shade, soil drainage, temperature, and so on. An automatic irrigation system takes very little of this into consideration. Although manual irrigation systems are more time-consuming, I prefer them, because you have complete control and can water as needed with more attention to details. Many automatic irrigation timers have manual overrides, so you can operate them in both modes.

Of course, if your garden is truly sustainable and low-maintenance, over time you should be able to rely less and less on your irrigation system. If you must use an automatic irrigation system, make sure you consider the following guidelines.

The basic rule amongst professionals is that when you're irrigating your garden, whether automatically or manually, watering should be less frequently and more deeply. For example, many residential irrigation systems will run five to seven days a week for an average of thirty to forty-five minutes each day. This is considered frequent, shallow watering, which wastes water and promotes poorly developed, shallow root systems. I do not recommend this type of watering. Watering in this manner, especially on a hot sunny day, will only moisten the surface of the soil and will not penetrate down to the roots of your plants. Much of the water will evaporate as soon as it hits the surface of the soil or grass. By contrast, an example of good watering practices would be watering two or three days a week as needed for hours at a time. (I say "as needed" because it's important for you to learn to check soil moisture regularly and water when plants need it, not take an autopilot approach to watering. If your plants don't need watering, then don't water them.) This will make the best use of your water, because it will penetrate the soil and encourage the development of a deep root system. Of course, the exact amount of water your garden needs will vary depending on soil type, drainage, heat and humidity, light exposure, and most importantly, the types of plants you are watering.

Another important rule of thumb is to water early in the morning, avoiding midafternoon and evening watering whenever possible. Watering in the morning, when it is cooler, reduces the evaporation of the water. It also reduces the likelihood of widespread development of disease, because the plants' foliage has a chance to dry off during the day, unlike plants that are watered in the evening. Watering in the heat of the day is not ideal, because much of the water will evaporate before being absorbed by the soil. This type of watering is okay if you have stressed or wilted plants that must get cooled down quickly, a technique sometimes called syringing. This type of watering is often done to reduce heat stress on lawns. Evening is the worst time to water, because foliage stays wet for too long, promoting diseases.

So as a recap, here are a few helpful hints to follow when watering your garden.

- Check soil moisture by gently digging down a few inches in areas of the garden where your plants are growing.
- If watering is needed, turn on your irrigation system and give your garden a thorough, deep watering.
- Water thoroughly a few times a week rather than a little every day.
- Pay close attention to puddling or flooded areas and reduce watering as needed.
- Water in the early morning, before the heat of the day, and never water in the evening if you can avoid it.

> "To save water and encourage deep-rooted, drought-tolerant plants, water your garden less frequently but more thoroughly during each watering."

Irrigation Equipment: A World of Possibilities

There is a wide variety of irrigation equipment available to gardeners today. Now more than ever, irrigation equipment is efficient and effective. Today systems require less water volume and pressure then they did in the past. These efficient methods of distributing water save both money and water, and they are relatively easy to operate and repair.

Drip Irrigation

Drip irrigation, or micro-irrigation, has been used since ancient times but was refined during the twentieth century. Today's drip irrigation systems are among the most efficient and effective ways to supply plants with water. Drip irrigation is a method by which small volumes of water slowly drip to plant roots through a system of pipes, tubing, valves, and emitters, which lie on or just below the surface of the soil. The system can be hooked up to a faucet or other water source and comes with filters, pressure control valves, and backflow preventers. Drip irrigation kits can be purchased and are fairly easy to install. This effective water distribution method, which has been used in agriculture and growing of horticultural crops for many years, is now a viable option for home gardeners as well. Drip irrigation can be used in flower beds, vegetable gardens, shrub borders, containers, and hanging baskets.

Pros: durable, long-lasting, good on slopes, moderately priced

Cons: assembly and regular maintenance of equipment required

Soaker Hoses

Soaker hoses are porous hoses that can be attached to a garden hose or faucet to evenly distribute water to the soil. There are no emitters or other equipment to worry about, and they are simply installed by laying them evenly spaced on the ground about 12 to 18 inches apart. Soaker hoses range in length from 50 to 100 feet or more, but connecting hoses longer than 100 feet may reduce effectiveness (unless you have excellent

water pressure). The beauty of soaker hoses is that they can be placed on the surface of the soil and left exposed or hidden with a thin layer of mulch. Just be careful that you do not slice the soaker hose when digging in the garden. Soaker hoses have many applications, such as in vegetable gardens and flower beds and around trees and shrubs.

Pros: inexpensive, easy to install and operate

Cons: fragile as they age, can look unsightly unless hidden

Rotary and Mister (Spray-Type) Sprinklers

With new technology, in-ground sprinkler heads have become much more efficient and effective then they were twenty or thirty years ago. There are several types of sprinkler heads that automatically pop up when activated.

The first type is known as a rotary sprinkler, and it sprays a stream of water to a desired width and length as it rotates. The type of rotation, angle, and application of water depends on the adjustment and size of the head. These are designed to use lower volumes of water while providing uniform watering. Rotary sprinkler heads are made primarily of lightweight plastic and/or stainless steel. Rotary type sprinklers can either be recessed in the ground and pop up when the water is turned on, or for applications where taller perennials or shrubs are obstructing the stream of water, taller rotary sprinklers can be installed in beds.

Soaker hoses are an inexpensive way to distribute low volumes of water where you need it.

New types of sprinklers like this impulse sprinkler can save water and provide more uniform coverage.

Misters will also pop up or can be installed aboveground to water taller plants, but they deliver a finer spray of water than rotary types do, and they do not rotate. They also do not typically spray water as far as rotary types do and are better for areas where shorter applications of water are needed. Misters are excellent in flower beds, along narrow strips of grass or ornamental plants, and in mixed borders with shrubs and trees.

Pros: efficient, convenient, uniform watering

Cons: can be expensive to install, must be maintained and in cold climates, winterized

Irrigation Controller

Advances in technology have made irrigation systems much more efficient, requiring less water volume and pressure and saving water. But the irrigation controller, also known as an irrigation timer, is still an important piece of equipment. Whether you decide to manually control your irrigation system or program it to operate automatically, installing an irrigation controller is important. Irrigation controllers require only low voltage to operate. They can be controlled manually by turning them on or off or automatically by presetting times, dates, and durations. Most gardens will have to be separated into zones, because it will usually be impossible to water your entire garden all at once. Even if you decide to water manually by turning on a zone when you like, irrigation controllers will save you time, because they will automatically turn off the irrigation after the cycle that you have preset is finished. If you program your system to run automatically, you can preset different durations of watering for each zone to accommodate specific needs. For example, zone 1 may be a lawn area in full, blazing sun and sandy soil requiring two hours of water each time, while zone 4 may require only one hour because it is a shady area with moist, organic soil that dries out less often. These types of custom adjustments will save water and create a much healthier, more sustainable landscape.

Irrigation Bags

Irrigation bags, also known by the brand name Treegators, are plastic or rubber bags with weep holes at the bottom that are specifically designed to slowly water trees and shrubs in the landscape. They come in several styles and are wrapped around the base of the plant and then filled with water. Over the course of a few days, the water slowly leaks out, evenly watering the plant. Irrigation bags are especially effective with new transplants and in times of drought.

Pros: inexpensive, easy to install and maintain

Cons: need to be filled regularly to be effective, when empty must be secured so they don't blow away

> "Make sure you are using the latest irrigation technology, because new sprinkler systems are most efficient, saving time, money, and most important, water."

PERMEABLE PAVERS: WHERE IS YOUR WATER GOING?

Permeable pavers are the next big innovation in the landscape world. They are paving blocks that can withstand vehicular and foot traffic and can be used in place of asphalt, cement, and other commonly used materials for driveways, walkways, and patios. Permeable pavers are installed similarly to brick or slate, but the material used under the pavers is various grades and sizes of gravel, which provides both support and drainage. When the pavers get wet from rain or irrigation, the water doesn't run off in every direction is it does with nonpermeable surfaces. Instead, the water seeps through the joints of the pavers and penetrates the ground and the soil. This is a significant innovation, because in many landscapes, too much water runs away from the garden, down the driveway or patio, and into the street or into drains. This often creates erosion problems and is a total loss of water that could be used for your landscape. Permeable pavers allow water to penetrate the ground, reducing erosion and flooding, and letting water impurities get filtered through the soil. This process greatly reduces pollutants getting into local water supplies and allows water to get to the water table more effectively. Permeable pavers come in a variety of colors and sizes and can be creatively designed to enhance the landscape. In large applications, such as driveways and large patios, it is best to have a mason or landscape professional install permeable pavers. In smaller applications, such as a walkway, small patio, or border for flower beds, home gardeners can install permeable pavers by following these instructions:

1. Dig and level the area where you want to lay permeable pavers.
2. Lay nonwoven separation fabric and drainage pipes if needed.
3. Lay 6 inches of number 2 gravel (1 ¼-inch or more), moisten, and compact. (You can use a handheld tamper, push roller, or gas powered tamper to compact gravel.)
4. Spread, moisten, and compact a 4-inch layer of number 57 (½- to ¾-inch) gravel, which has a medium texture.
5. The last layer is a 2-inch layer of number 8 (¼-inch or less) bedding gravel, which is finely crushed stone that the pavers sit in. This gravel is also put in between the pavers to ensure small gaps where water can penetrate. Be sure to leave ½ inch of space between pavers for this purpose.
6. Make sure that you again compact the entire area, filling in any openings or cracks in the joints between pavers with fine bedding gravel.
7. Make sure the surface is smooth and level, with no tripping hazards or uneven areas.

If this sounds like a lot to take on, have a professional do it. It will require an investment of money, but permeable pavers will last longer and require less maintenance in the long run than asphalt and cement. They also look a lot nicer, and you will be the envy of the neighborhood. Most important, you will be able to keep the water that falls on your property in your property without unintentionally sharing it with the neighbors or letting it run off into storm sewers. There is no question that permeable pavers are a great way to manage storm water runoff.

> "Permeable pavers are attractive yet functional masonry that help keep rainwater in your garden. Before you replace your ashphalt driveway, cement walkway, or patio, check into the cost of a permeable surface."

HARVESTING RAINWATER
Rain Gardens

There are several ways to harvest rainwater and maximize the benefits of one of nature's most valuable resources. Creating a rain garden is one great way. The creation of rain gardens has really started to gain momentum over the last few years, and rain gardens are now common in both commercial and residential sites. This technique is a bit different from harvesting rainwater and collecting it in barrels or cisterns, because rain gardens divert water back to underground water supplies rather than saving it for future irrigation. In fact, rain gardens have much in common with the goals and benefits of permeable pavers. The concept behind rain gardening is quite simple and ingenious; let nature do the work. Rain gardens are low-lying areas that collect rainwater from roofs, walkways, driveways, and other waterproof surfaces. These water collection areas are landscaped with plants that are adapted to regular or occasional flooding. These are typically plants that like "wet feet" but do not like standing water all the time.

The idea of a rain garden is that as this water accumulates and seeps into the ground, the plants, roots, and soil will help filter out impurities in the water before the water makes its way into an aquifer or other groundwater supply. Rain gardens are very beneficial because they reduce storm water runoff and erosion, reduce pollution, and replenish freshwater supplies. When properly installed, they are also very beautiful, lush plantings that can be attractive features in the landscape.

Permeable pavers can have small gaps and be installed like brick or they can have larger gaps where grass can grow through.

The installation of a rain garden takes careful planning but can be a fun and rewarding project.

Rain gardens can be used as valuable green spaces in parking lots.

There are some basic requirements you must consider when developing a rain garden for your own landscape. It is not always as simple as selecting a site in your garden that tends to flood during rainstorms and planting some shrubs and perennials in that area. Believe it or not, rain gardens require drainage. Water that stands for too long—several days, for instance—is not a rain garden. It's a pool of stagnant water. Gardeners should be wary of rainwater collecting and standing for too long, as still water allows mosquitoes and other nasty pests to breed. A properly functioning rain garden should drain rather quickly, certainly within a day. Rain garden sites can be areas that naturally collect water after a rainstorm, or you can help the process along by digging out an area that is convenient for you. Here are a few quick tips to follow when selecting and designing a rain garden.

- Select area of the garden where water naturally flows or collects. Rainwater can be directed to this area by using drainpipes connected to your house's downspouts. Rain gardens should be placed at least 10 feet from the house and away from the septic system.
- Dig out the area with a shovel to ensure that the subsoil is well drained. If needed, remove heavy soil and replace it with coarse sand or gravel. The sides of the rain garden should be gradually graded toward the middle. Rain gardens are shallow depressions and do not need to be any deeper than 6 to 12 inches.
- On top of the well-drained subsoil layer, spread a 6-inch layer of topsoil for growing plants.
- Before planting, let the area sit for a few weeks. Observe if the soil is collecting water and draining properly.

- Once you are satisfied with the function of your rain garden, plant groupings of ornamental plants that will grow in this low, wet area.
- Plants such as native grasses, ferns, butterfly weed (*Asclepias* spp.), joe-pye weed (*Eupatorium* spp.), summersweet clethra (*Clethra alnifolia*), and winterberry holly (*Ilex verticillata*) are good examples of plants adapted for this use.

Another factor that you should consider when creating a rain garden is the size needed to accommodate the runoff generated by a given area. A good formula to follow is that a rain garden should be at least one-sixth the size of the area draining into it. If your roof or patio is 20 x 30 feet (600 square feet), you divide that by six to get the proper size for your rain garden. That means that your rain garden needs to be at least 100 square feet or 10 x 10 feet.

If you do not have adequate room for a full-sized rain garden, do not fret. You can create a miniature rain garden by using a big planter or container filled with water-loving plants. Put the container at the base of your downspout, and it will absorb and deflect the water from running all over the garden. If you choose this route, make sure your container is large enough and heavy enough to accommodate dousing. Small, undersized containers will fall over, and plants will become potbound too quickly to serve a long-term function in the garden. Clay, ceramic, or cement pots are excellent materials for a miniature rain garden.

"The next time it rains, observe where water naturally collects, dig that area out, and plant it with water-loving plants. Make sure your rain garden drains within twenty-four hours and the water does not become stagnant."

Storing Water for Future Use

In areas of the country where collecting rainwater and using it is unrestricted, there are a variety of opportunities for homeowners to "cache" in. Rain barrels, which are popular in European gardens, are also available to us in the United States. They generally range in size from 30 to 50 gallons and up, and they can be made of durable plastic or wood. There are advantages and disadvantages to both styles of barrel. Wooden barrels look more natural but are generally more expensive and deteriorate over time. Plastic barrels offer more options in color, shape, and size. They are generally less expensive and longer-lasting but can appear more artificial in the garden.

Whichever type you choose, rain barrels can be handy gardening tools to help save and better utilize water. A rain barrel is tied into the downspout of the house by placing it under the pipe and removing the bottom half of the pipe so it fits directly into the top of the barrel. When it rains, the water that accumulates and flows into the gutters makes it way to the downspout and eventually the barrel. Barrels usually come with a faucet at the base, so water can be used as needed. A garden hose can be attached to the faucet. The water can be gravity-fed, or there are pumps available to efficiently distribute the water from the barrel to the garden. The water in the barrel should be used regularly so it does not become stagnant. Rain barrels are ideal for watering outdoor annual containers, flower beds, vegetable gardens, houseplants, trees, and shrubs.

Cisterns are essentially larger versions of rain barrels, serving a similar function but designed to hold larger volumes of rainwater—anywhere from 100 to 10,000 gallons. Cisterns are typically made of steel, concrete, or heavy-duty plastic and can be placed on the surface or underground. Cisterns should be watertight and are often used for irrigation, washing machines, and other household needs for which nonpotable water is appropriate.

There are many benefits to using cisterns, including the obvious benefit of saving water. Cisterns reduce energy costs, because they relieve a burden from your domestic water supply. By

Larger rainwater harvesting systems can be designed to collect the maximum amount of water possible.

catching and collecting rainwater, you are also reducing runoff and erosion.

But cisterns and rain barrels do need regular maintenance. You should regularly inspect your collection devices to ensure they are free of debris and leaks. Cleaning once a year with a nontoxic, biodegradable cleaner that will not harm the quality of the water is highly recommended.

Size Matters

It is vitally important that you properly size your rain barrel or cistern, or you will quickly have water pouring out of it all over the garden. Choosing the right size barrel or cistern depends on a few factors. The three main factors to consider are how large your roof is, how much rainfall you get on average, and how much space you have. As a general rule, for every 1,000 square feet of roof space, you will collect 600 gallons of water for every inch of rainfall. That can quickly add up to a lot of water, so you have to plan ahead. One solution would be to have a rain barrel at each downspout, so the water is dispersed to several locations.

With high amounts of rainwater and not enough capacity, barrels will overflow, and you will need to determine where the water will go once it does overflow. At the very least, overflowing rain barrels should diffuse the water flow so it doesn't gush out all over the garden at once. You will have to carefully plan where the rainwater will go when it overflows. Maybe you will direct the excess water to your rain garden or dry stream. Another solution is to upgrade to a larger barrel or cistern to increase the storage capabilities of your collection devices. If you switch from barrel to cistern, be aware that cisterns can be quite a bit more complex than rain barrels. You should consult a professional engineer or local water authority to make sure you choose and use a cistern properly.

Catch Basins: Routing Water in the Right Direction

Installing a catch basin is another way to collect and direct water where you want it to go rather than letting gravity decide. Water always runs downhill using the path of least resistance, and if that path happens to include your patio, lawn, or flower beds, then you will have one soggy garden when it rains. Water coming off the roof and down a downspout has to go somewhere when it reaches the soil. If it's misdirected, this water can find its way into your basement or could damage the foundation of your house. Misdirected water can also create a very soggy situation near your foundation plantings, causing them to perform poorly. But installing a catch basin will allow you to reduce runoff and erosion and recharge the groundwater supply.

Catch basins come in several shapes and sizes, but for homeowner use, you can purchase a plastic catch basin and install it at the base of your downspout. It is usually a square box with a grate on top to catch the rain as it comes off the roof. This catch basin in then connected to a pipe, usually 4-inch-diameter PVC, that is attached to a dry well placed in the ground. The dry well should be in a well-drained area with gravel at the base, so the water percolates through the well and into the ground. Dry wells should be at least 10 feet from the house. The best way to determine where you need a dry well is to observe where rain puddles during a storm. Before you dig a dry well, you will need to check with your utility company to ensure that there are no underground utilities in the area where you want to dig.

Catch basin grates should be placed in low areas where water collects.

Dry wells can be made of cement or plastic and come in a wide variety of sizes. Determining the size of your dry well depends on the square footage of your roof and how much rain typically falls in a rainstorm. One easy way to install a dry well in the landscape is by using a system called a flow well. It is a plastic tank that holds about 50 gallons of water. It has drainage holes in it so when water flows to it, it will disperse the water gradually into the soil.

> "Strategically place rain barrels near the house at the end of your downspouts so you can catch rainwater for watering your garden when you need it."

RECYCLING WATER: REUSING AND SAVING

In certain areas of the country where water is scarce, recycling water is an important part of everyday life, but anyone in any climate can benefit from reusing water. Recycled water is not just for industrial uses, such as factories and making clean energy, anymore. More and more homeowners are utilizing recycled water for irrigation and household uses, such as toilets and washing

A small gray water recovery sink that drains automatically to a reservoir makes it easy to reuse gray water for watering plants or gardens.

clothes. In fact, today there are entire water supply systems that can be installed in homes that will capture, store, filter and distribute recycled water to supply water to an entire household. There are systems in place now where rainwater can be collected and used as needed. If treated properly, and filtered according to local health standards, recycled rainwater can even be used for drinking. While costly upfront, over time these systems can provide an economical and efficient way to use a free source of water. Local water companies in certain cities also have systems in place that provide recycled water to homeowners.

Grey Water: How Does It Work?

Grey water is wastewater generated from household uses such as sinks, showers, baths, dishwashers, and washing machines. Grey water does not include toilet water, which is considered black water and is plumbed directly to the septic system. Grey water is also quite different from rainwater and is primarily used for irrigation. Grey water can also be used to flush toilets to save water. Grey water can be collected by simply catching it with a bucket and watering plants and lawns with it. Elaborate collection and filtration systems can be installed to disperse and reuse grey water as well. These may be expensive initially but over time will pay off, since they save a lot in water and energy bills. As supplemental water for irrigating lawns,

ornamental plants, trees, and shrubs, grey water does have value. Here are a few significant benefits of grey water for irrigation:

- Grey water reduces domestic water use, energy use, and expense.
- Grey water reduces strain on your septic system or cesspool.
- Grey water recharges groundwater.
- Using grey water helps conserve drinking water.

Grey water should not be stored, as it will encourage the growth of bacteria. If you cannot afford an elaborate system to catch, filter, and disperse grey water, you simply pour it on the lawn. Grey water can be disposed of this way as long as there are not high amounts of chemicals, grease, or detergents in it. With a biologically active soil environment, soil bacteria and other organisms will quickly break down and filter grey water to be used by plants. However, there are various rules and regulations regarding grey water that may be unique to your area. Please consult with your local water district or health department on updated grey water regulations and recommendations before using grey water.

How Much Is Too Much?

While grey water can be beneficial, like everything else, too much of a good thing can be harmful. Grey water may contain food particles, detergents, grease, and other household waste. While these substances are biodegradable, using grey water in the same areas over and over again can harm plants and soil. As a general rule, it is a good idea to rotate where you use grey water in your garden or rotate watering with fresh water. Applying grey water to the same area every other week will also help reduce overuse. Or you can limit the amount of grey water used in a given area. As for amounts to use, well-drained loamy soils can absorb about ½ gallon of grey water per square foot a week. So if your lawn or flower garden is 600 square feet, you should not apply more than 300 gallons of grey water per week. Checking your soil pH regularly in these areas will reduce the buildup of sodium, which is evident in high pH soils. Applying gypsum (calcium sulfate) at the recommended rate on the side of the bag will also help prevent any sodium or other harmful impurities from accumulating in the soil.

Here are a few other recommendations when using grey water in the garden:

- Avoid using grey water on vegetable crops.
- Apply grey water directly to the soil and avoid contact with leaves of plants if possible.
- Evenly spread grey water over a large area instead of concentrating on the same area. Apply grey water to a flat surface, avoiding steep hills.
- Use grey water in flower beds with mulch, as it will be absorbed quicker by natural decomposition.
- Use grey water on established plants, not young plants, and avoid applying to acid-loving plants such as rhododendrons, azaleas, and hollies.

"You should investigate the feasibilty of recycling household grey water to reduce the strain on your water supply, septic system, and wallet. This information can be obtained from your local water authority or a licensed plumber."

WHAT'S ALL THE FUSS?

While the majority of Americans are just catching on to all the possibilities for conserving water to protect the environment, other countries are a bit ahead of us. In Australia, for example, water-wise gardens have been encouraged for years, allowing homeowners to apply many of the water conservation practices discussed in this chapter. In certain areas the government will even offer rebates for water-wise initiatives, such as rain harvesting, use of gray water, and household water recycling equipment, plumbing repairs and installations that save water. Water conservation issues are clearly a global concern that cannot be ignored anymore.

For centuries we have known that water is essential to our survival. But now more than ever, with climate change a serious reality, we're becoming aware that protecting and conserving water is vital to our quality of life. Water conservation is a major factor in the long-term sustainability of humans. It is also very important in the viability of our landscape, since so many living organisms rely on water. Through new and innovative technology and our own common sense, we can save oceans of water each year and put it to good use. Proper irrigation techniques, reducing runoff, and recycling our water supply can all have significant impacts on our water consumption. While there are serious water restrictions already in several areas of the country, the threat of global warming and increased severe weather patterns mean it is likely that extended droughts are going to affect many parts of the country. Even in areas of the country where water shortages are currently not an issue, it should be a common practice to handle water as if there were such restrictions. Sustainability requires all of us to treat water like the precious commodity that it is. If each of us starts today to implement even some of the recommendations highlighted in this chapter, think of the possibilities.

CHAPTER 6

Sustainable Lawn Care

Doing Less and Still Having a Beautiful Yard

It is no secret that lawns are one of the most popular features of the American garden. Lawn care has become embedded in American culture as much as family barbecues and summer vacation. Many homeowners will spend hours tending to their lawn each week, trying to outdo their neighbors. To some, lawn care is like an Olympic sport, with the gold medal going to the best-looking lawn on the block.

But this type of passion and dedication comes at a serious cost. The fact of the matter is that the traditional high-maintenance lawn is one of the least sustainable things on Earth. It offers little diversity, and as we know from natural biological systems, diversity is the key to long-term survival. Lawns require a substantial amount of regular care, including mowing, watering, fertilizer, pesticides, and most importantly, time. This exorbitant amount of resources spent on lawn care can be done by homeowners themselves or by hired landscape contractors. While I am all for supporting the landscape industry, there are many ways you can reduce the amount of resources that go into caring for a lawn and focus them in other areas of the garden. The resources that you save—time, money, energy, and so forth—can and should be directed towards other critical areas of the landscape, such as tree maintenance, wildlife habitat management, organic vegetable gardening, and other more critical (and fun) garden needs.

ANATOMY OF A LAWN

Traditional lawns have become artificial landscape features that are all about aesthetics and nothing about conservation. Americans spend billions of dollars each year to achieve horticultural bliss by having the perfect lawn. It is estimated that Americans spend about $40 billion dollars annually on lawn care and other garden-related improvements to weed, mow, water, and fertilize nearly 30 million acres across the United States. That is more than the United States spends each year in foreign economic aid.

What is the history of lawns, anyway? Lawns date back to sixteenth-century Europe. At that time, lawns were found mostly on large country estates owned by wealthy landowners. Because there were no motorized lawn mowers back then, human labor was used to maintain these lawns, and only the rich could afford the hired hands to do it. Then in the nineteenth and twentieth centuries, as Europeans started emigrating to America, they brought their idea of manicured lawns and the seed from their cool-season grass species with them. At first, expansive lawns were popular amongst rich Americans, such as industrialists. Lawns became popular in mainstream America when mechanical innovations allowed the average American to mow and maintain a lawn. The reel mower, invented by Edwin Beard Budding in 1830 with a series of blades that spun around a cylinder, became the first push mower. Rotary mowers, which have a single blade powered by an engine, became available in the early part of the 1900s.

But our obsession with the modern lawn really gained momentum after World War II. With the development of suburbs and the American dream of carving out a space in the community to call one's own, the residential lawn was born. A very popular builder in the late 1940s and early 1950s, Abe Levitt, developed an entire community called Levittown on Long Island. It was the first suburb with mass-produced housing, and it featured new, carpetlike lawns. Lawns became an extension of the living room or den, and families would eat, play, and congregate outside on their lawns during the summer months. Not much has changed on that front since then. We just have bigger houses and more expensive garden tools to play with now.

THE PROBLEM WITH LAWNS

The main problem with lawns is that by nature, they are nonnative ornamental species, which require a great amount of care to maintain at a high level of quality. Lawns are really a monoculture of the same or similar species of grass or blended species with similar characteristics. This contrived planting is foreign to the natural landscape and therefore requires a whole lot of care, including regular watering, fertilizer to keep it green, pesticides to keep it healthy, and mowing the keep it neat. Lawns also pose a problem to other plants in the landscape. Trees and shrubs do not encounter lawns in their native habitat in a woodland setting and are surrounded by compatible species and organic matter that feeds them and supports their biology. But lawns typically suck up much of the water and nutrients that are applied to them, and they also compete with the root systems of other plants in the area. While these other plants adapt, it is by no means an ideal or even suitable situation for plants in general.

Cool- and Warm-Season Grasses As a Monoculture

There are several popular species of grass found in lawns across the United States. Certain species of grasses are adapted to and thrive in

A reel mower requires more labor but is better for the environment.

cool climates, while others are more suited for warmer climates. Cool-season grass areas consist of the Northeast, Midwest, and Pacific Northwest, while the warm-season grass areas consist of the South, Southeast, and Southwest. Good examples of cool-season grasses are fescues, rye grass, and bluegrass. Popular cool-season species include perennial rye grass (*Lolium perenne*), Kentucky bluegrass (*Poa pratensis*), and tall fescue (*Festuca arundinacea*), all of which are native to Europe. In addition, there are various other species of fescues, called fine fescues (*Festuca* spp.), which are native to a range of places around the world. Bermudagrass, centipede grass, and Saint Augustine grass are examples of warm-season species. Bermudagrass (*Cynodon dactylon*) and centipede grass (*Eremochloa ophiuroides*) are both nonnatives, while Saint Augustine grass (*Stenotaphrum secundatum*) originated in the southern part of North America and tropical and subtropical regions of the world. Zoysiagrass (*Zoysia* spp.) will grow in both southern and northern climates.

Grass species that typically make up a lawn are either cool- *or* warm-season grasses. Warm-season grass species actively grow in the heat of the summer and go dormant in the cool winter months. Cool-season grasses are more adapted to grow actively in the cooler temperatures and plentiful rainfall of spring, early summer, and fall. Cool-season grass tends to stay green during the dormant winter months, while warm-season grasses often turn brown while dormant in winter. Cool-season grasses can be planted in fall or spring by planting seed or laying down pregrown sod. Cool-season grasses are usually quick to establish in the right conditions. Warm-season grasses are more often planted by laying sod or planting plugs as they germinate slowly from seed, and they take time to establish. However, warm-season grass is more heat- and drought-tolerant than cool-season grass.

Cool-season grass is made up of either a blend or mixture. A blend includes related species and cultivars of grasses, while a mixture includes different species and types of grass. Even though both contain some diversity—especially a mixture—I would still consider cool-season grass a monoculture because it contains essentially the same crop. Warm-season grass is not usually blended, as there is often too much variation within the species.

Whether a lawn is established by seed, sod, or plugs, it is the ultimate monoculture. Monoculture is the practice of growing a single crop or species of plant over a wide area for consecutive years. The main problem with monoculture is that you put all your eggs in one basket.

Some of the most stable and healthy ecosystems can be found in the local forest. The main reason they are so healthy is because they include a diverse selection of native plants that work together and provide benefits to one another along with wildlife. In a sustainable garden, even though it's not necessarily all native, our goal is also to diversify the ecosystem by incorporating a wide variety of plant types and species, because by nature, diversity leads to a healthier ecosystem. A lawn is totally contradictory to this theory and practice. If a disease or insect is specifically targeting a lawn, often the entire lawn is in jeopardy, because its plantings are not diverse enough to handle the pressure from the pests. In a more diverse planting, such as a mixed border or evergreen screen composed of five or six unrelated species, if a pest problem arises, it is unlikely to wipe out the entire planting.

The ultimate goal with lawns is to create a lush surface that can be maintained at a uniform height by mowing. This uniformity, along with the lack of diversity, is what makes lawns less desirable in a sustainable garden. Lawns are an artificial and often unhealthy landscape feature that ultimately requires intensive care to maintain. Manicured lawns are an example of human detachment from the natural world around them. Finely sheared lawns delineate the area that we have created to separate us from the rest of the neighborhood. Lawns can also represent a status symbol and a statement of wealth and creativity.

But it doesn't have to be that way. A successful sustainability program, if implemented correctly, with common sense, and with reasonable expectations, allows gardeners to have lawns with less maintenance. There will have to be some compromises, though, and accepting that a large, perfect lawn is not in the best interests of a truly sustainable landscape. Having a modest lawn—or maybe even something better, such as low-maintenance groundcovers to replace a lawn—is worth considering. With thoughtful planning, you can have your cake and eat it, too.

THE NOT-SO-BIG LAWN MOVEMENT

Lawns have been a popular part of American life for many years, but that is slowly changing. Several decades ago, a conversation began about the challenges lawns create for our environment and what management techniques could be put in place to mitigate the ill effects of the traditional lawn. But over the last five to ten years, this debate has intensified. Now the public is starting to put lawns in better perspective from a landscape point of view. It is impossible to criticize or lament the use—and sometimes abuse—of pesticides and fertilizers that make their way into groundwater supplies without discussing homeowners who can't live without a putting green-quality lawn. The blame cannot be placed solely on the shoulders of golf courses and farmers, who require such chemicals to maintain their unique crops and landscapes.

Do homeowners really need to go to such great lengths to maintain beautiful lawns? Hardly. The average American lawn is too big these days, dominating any other landscape or green space in the garden. Perhaps it is time to look at reasonable alternatives to the great American lawn. Gardeners would be better served by focusing their efforts on creating diverse, well-landscaped gardens that feature a wide variety of herbaceous and woody plants with four seasons of interest. At the very least, reducing the size of your lawn can create opportunities to develop and enhance new garden features with far more long-term benefits. Gone are the days where homeowners feel obliged to flex their horticultural muscles by maintaining an oversized lawn as a status symbol. Your neighbors and friends will not be green with envy if you keep your lawn, and they won't think any less of you if you don't. I'm sure many homeowners will say, "Where are my kids going to play if I reduce or eliminate my lawn?" Well, maybe there is a way to accomplish both. Read on.

"Reducing or replacing your lawn with low-maintenance alternatives can save time and backbreaking work, allowing you to spend more time enjoying your garden. Each season, try to eliminate a little more of your lawn—maybe 10 percent—and replace it with flower beds, groundcovers, or native grasses."

WEED LAWS

Lawns have been so embedded in our way of life for so long that we have created laws to protect against unkempt, weedy properties. These weed laws were created to enforce aesthetics and really had nothing to do with reducing the invasion of noxious weeds in the landscape. The premise of early weed laws was that landscapes allowed to grow wild would encourage damaging insects and rodents and potentially become fire hazards, causing human health risks. A 1945 ordinance in the city of Chicago was an early example of such weed laws. It outlawed weeds taller than 10 inches. The problem with this language is that first, what is a weed? And second, only plants that grow taller than 10 inches are considered weeds? In Madison, Wisconsin, a weed ordinance from the early 1980s was modified to require homeowners to submit an application to landscape their garden in a more natural way with a less manicured appearance. The request would have to be approved by the majority of the neighbors in order to be approved.

But these established ordinances have softened over time, and some even have compromised to include setbacks or buffer areas, which allow for the growing of natural vegetation on most areas of the landscape. For example, the setback or manicured area around the perimeter of a garden creates a tended, maintained appearance that preserves curbside appeal. Providing this buffer zone also minimizes the risk that natural areas will impact neighboring yards with loose vegetation spreading in all directions.

You will still find many local villages, towns, and counties that regulate the maintenance and upkeep of home properties, but this mainly addresses extreme cases involving litter and lack of yard maintenance. Ordinances typically have general language that states property owners will prevent unhealthy accumulations of grass, brush, and other debris and that the municipality has the right to require homeowners to mitigate these issues if deemed necessary. It is a way for municipalities to regulate these types of landscape issues if needed.

It is unlikely that most local government authorities will allow 4-foot grass in your front yard, at least in suburban environments. But with reasonable setbacks and creative planning, you can have a combination of natural areas that are more sustainable along with more intensely maintained areas that give your garden well-differentiated zones. By no means am I suggesting that you should let your entire garden go wild—especially the front yard—evoking the wrath of the entire neighborhood. Using common sense and appropriate creative license will serve you well in this process.

NATURAL LANDSCAPING

Natural landscaping, or gardening with native plants, basically involves using all types of herbaceous plants, trees, shrubs, and so forth, that are indigenous to the area you live in. Native plants, unlike lawns, offer biodiversity and help filter impurities from water while protecting soil. Natural landscaping also provides much better habitat and food sources for wildlife, which lawns do not. Natural landscaping is by definition the complete opposite of a manicured lawn. I believe that this form of gardening in an informal context can also include noninvasive exotic

A diverse, well-balanced landscape with a variety of native species will help to create a sustainable landscape.

species that provide food for birds, beneficial insects, and other wildlife. This type of natural landscaping, within any setbacks that may be required by law, will help to build healthy plant communities, wildlife habitat, and aesthetic plantings that offer multiple seasons of interest. A more naturalistic landscape design veers away from the traditional practice of a high-maintenance, time-consuming, and resource-dependent landscape toward a more self-sustaining, low-maintenance, and functional garden.

> "You should designate a portion of your yard and make that a more naturalistic landscape to support wildlife and create a lower-maintenance garden. This can be accomplished by leaving the less-visible areas of the garden more wild while maintaining the front yard so your landscape offers natural beauty but does not turn into a jungle."

FERTILIZING YOUR LAWN

In a sustainable landscape, an ideal situation is to use chemical fertilizers only if necessary. Let's face it: we are accustomed to fertilizing our lawns once in the spring and once in the fall in order to keep them looking green and lush. But using chemical fertilizers at such a high rate is not always necessary if we use creative measures and sound gardening practices. For example, if you have a mulching mower, which chops up the grass clippings into fine particles and leaves them on the lawn, that will alleviate the need for fertilizer. These grass clippings will break down and add nitrogen back to the soil. I urge you to use a mulching mower or compost your grass clippings whenever possible to reduce the amount of chemical fertilizer you add to your lawn. But there *are* situations where processed fertilizers are needed.

A broadcast spreader can be used to apply the right amount of fertilizer, lime and other materials needed to keep your lawn healthy.

Processed fertilizers consist of different percentages of nitrogen (N), phosphorus (P), and potassium (K). On each bag of fertilizer, three numbers represent these main nutrients that promote plant growth. The first number is percentage of nitrogen, the middle number is phosphorus, and the last number is potassium. So a 40-pound bag of 10-6-4 has 10 percent nitrogen (4 pounds), 6 percent phosphorus (2.4 pounds), and 4 percent potassium (1.6 pounds). (Fillers make up the remainder.) Fertilizers can be fast- or slow-release, depending on their formulation. Fast-release fertilizers are generally applied at a lower rate than slow-release ones, because damage may occur to your lawn if you fertilize too much at once. (Soil fertility and nutrients are covered in more depth in Chapter 7.)

The best way to handle fertilizing your lawn is to first take a soil sample to determine soil pH and the levels of nutrients that are in the soil. (You can use a home pH test, or send the sample to your local county agricultural Extension office, or to a commerical facility, to test it.) Nitrogen is the element that greens up the lawn and is the most soluble, leaching to the soil fairly quickly. Phosphorus moves very slowly in the soil and primarily encourages root growth. Potassium is not usually needed in large quantities and is responsible for physiological processes, including the more efficient use of nitrogen, increased vigor, and tolerance of physical and environmental stresses. More often than not, to keep lawns green and healthy, nitrogen should be fed at a reasonable level to ensure that your lawns stay green. Choosing a fertilizer may be a bit challenging given the fact that there are so many choices. The results of your soil test will help you narrow your options.

When to Fertilize

Typically, lawn soils are depleted of nutrients in the early spring after a long dormant season, especially in cold northern climates where cool-season grasses are prevalent. Lawns can be fertilized in the spring and the early summer, until the temperatures get hot. You can also apply fertilizers as the weather cools down in the fall. There is research to suggest that applying high-nitrogen fertilizers too early in the spring will encourage leaf growth and not enough root growth. One good solution might be to apply a lower dose of nitrogen early in the spring to green up your lawn and then apply fertilizers with higher rates of nitrogen as the season goes on. But remember: do not apply high-nitrogen fertilizers in the heat of the summer in cooler climates. It is better to wait for cool weather at the end of summer or in the fall. At this time, it is also wise to use lower-nitrogen fertilizers, such as 5-10-5 or 10-6-4. Some communities have restrictions on when you can apply fertilizer to your lawn. Check the regulations in your area to ensure you are complying with all local and state fertilizer application laws.

The warm-season grasses that grow in the southern areas of the country have different fertilizer requirements. Warm-season grasses benefit from fertilizing after greening up in the spring and once again in the late summer or fall as long as conditions are favorable. You should not fertilize too late in the season, as that may stimulate a flush of soft, fleshy growth, which is vulnerable to an early frost. For this reason, higher amounts of nitrogen can be applied in the spring and lower doses can be applied in the fall.

An example of a higher-nitrogen fertilizer would be 20-0-8 or 24-0-5, while lower doses of nitrogen are contained in 10-6-4 and 5-10-5. As a good rule of thumb, an acceptable ratio for spring applications of fertilizer for cool-season grasses is 3:1:2 or 21-7-14. In the fall, a lower dose of nitrogen such as 10-10-10 (1:1:1 ratio) can be applied. With warm-season grasses, fertilizing in the spring and summer is acceptable depending on your lawn's needs and the existing environmental conditions. However, before applying fertilizer it is wise to take a soil test to ensure your fertilizer rates and ratios are appropriate. Fast-release fertilizers tend to be cheap and short lived while slow-release fertilizers tend to be longer lasting and more expensive.

If you have the resources and the time, a slow-release fertilizer is the best option for the first fertilizing of the season. You can always go back later in the spring and follow up with a quick-release fertilizer if you need fast greening.

Setting Up a Schedule

It is helpful for gardeners to set up a fertilizer schedule in order to organize and keep track of seasonal fertilizer applications. The advantages to doing this are that you can track what you have done in the past and note successes or

Fertilizer Schedule–Example

Date of Application	Fertilizer Formulation	Rate	Total Amount of Fertilizer Used	Comments
APRIL 14, 2013	20-10-10	1 LB. OF N PER 1,000 SQ. FT.	15 LBS.	LAWN GREENED UP WITHIN 2 WEEKS.
MAY 28, 2013	10-10-10	2 LBS. OF N PER 1,000 SQ FT.	40 LBS.	LAWN IS LUSH AND GROWING QUICKLY.
OCTOBER 25, 2013	5-10-5	1 LB. OF N PER 1,000 SQ. FT.	40 LBS.	LAWN IS A BIT SPARSE; RESEEDED.

Keeping grass taller, especially in times of drought, is better for your lawn.

failures for future consideration. On page 143 is a chart that illustrates basic information and priorities you can include in a fertilizer schedule.

By following these simple guidelines, reading the instructions on your fertilizer bag, and applying fertilizer at the proper rates and time of year, you can maintain a healthy lawn without a lot of fuss.

Fertilizer Rates: How Much Is Too Much?

Just like pesticides, fertilizers must be used carefully and should not be applied without reading the instructions on the fertilizer bag first. Just eyeing how much fertilizer you think you need and applying that much is not a responsible or sustainable way to apply fertilizer. This informal way of applying fertilizer will result in either too much or too little being applied to your lawn, which can cause a variety of problems. Overfertilized lawns may grow at an excessive rate, become burned or damaged, or (in extreme cases) be stunted, and excess fertilizer will leach into the soil, possibly making its way into water supplies. An underfertilized lawn tends to be weak, underperforming, and prone to invasive pests. If your fertilizer instructions recommend 5 pounds of fertilizer per 1,000 square feet, 10 pounds is *not* necessarily twice as good. As an example, statistics show that during the 1970s to the mid-1990s, midwestern states were plagued with overfertilization. During that period, tons of excess nitrogen and phosphorus found their way to the Mississippi River and the Gulf of Mexico. This influx of nutrients caused significant algae growth in those water bodies. This algae growth reduced oxygen in the water, which had a major environmental impact on that region. Since the 1990s, improved farming techniques and better technology have increased yields and decreased water pollution.

The lesson to be learned here is that implementing responsible fertilizing practices at home is important. Besides the environmental impact of using too much fertilizer, overfertilized lawns tend to be more prone to pests, and in extreme cases, can be burned from too much chemical fertilizer. This burning is caused by a buildup of salts, which chemical fertilizers contain. One simple rule is to apply no more than 1 pound of nitrogen on average per 1,000 square feet of lawn for fast-release fertilizers and up to 2 pounds per 1,000 square feet for slow-release fertilizers. Although lawns can often absorb more nitrogen at certain times of the year, it is not in your or your lawn's best interest from a sustainability standpoint.

> "Using too much nitrogen can cause lawns to grow too fast, make them more vulnerable to pest problems, and harm your lawn. Make sure you read the fertilzer bag carefully before you apply fertilizers to your lawn and apply these products only at the recommended rate on the bag."

NEW MOWING METHODS FOR BETTER SUSTAINABILITY

If you cannot take the leap to remove all your lawn or transform it into a natural planting, then another alternative is to explore less traditional, more eco-friendly mowing methods. These mowing practices are designed to reduce stress on your lawn, increase vigor and plant health, reduce noxious weed invasions, and reduce maintenance.

The bottom line is that a sustainable lawn is a healthy lawn. By practicing sound mowing, your lawn will require less water, be more lush and full, and be less prone to insect and disease infestations. The absolute worst thing to do to a lawn is to mow it too short. The growing point at the base of the grass plant is called a crown. If you cut your lawn too short, the crown could be damaged, resulting in poor growth or death of your lawn. Lawns that are mowed too short are more stressed and more prone to pests, and they dry out a lot quicker. The more foliage you leave on your lawn, the longer the soil will take to dry out. Also, lawns that are mowed too short can easily be overrun by invasive weeds. The recommended mowing methods that follow will save time, labor, chemicals, water, and money!

Lawns are typically mowed between 1 and 2½ inches in height, depending on the species. Most lawn species will tolerate this, but by no means is this an ideal situation. A much more sustainable way to manage your lawn is to raise the mowing deck of your mower to a height of 3½ to 4 inches. Or just put your mower deck at the highest setting, and that will suffice. At first this will be a bit of a shock to the gardener who is used to a putting green-type lawn, and the lawn may look a bit shaggy just before it is cut, but this will ultimately reduce maintenance and save money. Lawns that are left higher like this in the summer months will grow thicker, have deeper root systems, and will compete with weeds more effectively. The key to success with raising your mower height is to mow often, at least once a week, so that you don't have too much of an accumulation of grass clippings. The one-third rule is a good guide for gardeners; it states you should never remove more than one-third of your lawngrass height at one time when mowing. It is also important to mention that you never should mow your grass during times of drought and heat. A drought-stressed lawn is extremely vulnerable, and by mowing it you are multiplying that stress tenfold. You should stop mowing until your lawn is adequately watered. Drought-stressed lawns could take weeks or more to recover from a serious drought.

For years many public gardens, universities, corporate headquarters, and other large commercial sites have been mowing this way in order to create a more sustainable landscape. Even right-of-ways and lawn areas along highways and local roads are mowed this way. Although your front yard needs to be handled a bit differently than a traffic median along a busy public road, the same types of mowing principles apply.

> "Raise your mower deck to the highest setting or at least to 3 ½ inches high, which will produce a thicker lawn with fewer weeds, requiring less water and fertilizer."

Types of Mulching Mowers

There are various types of mowers that can be purchased for the home garden. Either a walk-behind push mower or a ride-on tractor mower will do the job. Both are considered rotary mowers, as they have single or multiple blades that

Using a rotary mower without a bag but with a mulching blade is a great way to recycle grass clippings.

rotate along the lawn surface, shearing off the tops of grass blades. Rotary mowers can range from 20 inches wide all the way up to 72 inches or more, depending on the type and model. These mowers can be designed to catch grass clippings or leave the clippings on the lawn. One excellent feature that gardeners have available to them today are mowers that have a special mulching blade. A mulching blade will chop up the grass clippings very finely and spread them evenly on the lawn. This type of blade is not expensive, and it simply replaces the conventional blade on an existing mower. Mulching and dispersing grass clippings on your lawn is highly beneficial because it is a type of composting. As the clippings decompose, they add nitrogen and other nutrients back to the soil. This sustains your lawn quite well and reduces the need for chemical fertilizers. Studies show that lawns maintained this way need 30 percent less fertilizer over the course of a year. More mulching and composting of your grass clippings will save time and money and will also reduce the chance of chemical fertilizers leaching into the soil.

Today's rotary mowers can be gas-powered, battery powered, or electric. While gas-powered mowers are still the most efficient for large lawns, electric and battery-powered mowers can be quite suitable for a small parcel of lawn. Electric mowers are available with cords or cordless. Since the goal is to reduce the size of your lawn anyway, there is no reason why mowers powered by clean energy cannot be effective.

Regardless of the type of mower you decide to use, it is very important that you keep your mower blades sharp and in proper working order. Over time, blades can become dull and even bent if you occasionally hit rocks and other debris. Make sure your blades are sharp and in good condition at the start of the mowing season, and have them sharpened again at least once during the summer. In warmer climates where you mow the lawn most of the year, you should have your blades maintained every few months. This is especially true if you opt to mow your lawn at raised heights and/or at a higher frequency. Dull blades will shred and severely damage grass foliage, causing brown tips and increasing the potential for disease. Check with your local hardware store or landscape supplier for your mower and blade sharpening needs. This type of work should be done by a professional who has the proper equipment and training for the job.

OTHER THINGS YOU CAN DO TO MAINTAIN A SUSTAINABLE LAWN
Dethatching and Aerating

Another way to keep your lawn healthy is to dethatch it occasionally. Thatch is a layer of dead grass that can build up and affect the heath of your lawn. By using a dethatching machine or even a wire rake, you can remove or reduce the buildup of thatch. Aerating the lawn pokes holes in the lawn, allowing for better root growth and penetration of water and nutrients. A lawn with heavily compacted soil will eventually become sparse and even devoid of grass. After dethatching or aerating the soil, overseed your lawn by spreading grass seed and raking it in. Overseeding once or twice a year will help keep those sparse areas full, so weeds do not establish

themselves in the lawn. Aerators can be rented or purchased and will keep grass roots healthy and growing. Both of these methods probably need to be done only occasionally, as needed. Remember, a happy lawn is a healthy lawn and is less susceptible to drought and pests.

Sustainable Watering Techniques

Proper watering techniques are critical in the maintenance and care of a lawn. One must be mindful of soil type, plant needs, local water restrictions, and water conservation opportunities. New technology has afforded home gardeners the opportunity to operate irrigation systems with less water and less electricity than ever before, using improved watering methods that provide better results. Irrigation systems installed twenty or thirty years ago are far less efficient and more wasteful than new ones. If you have an older irrigation system, you should change the irrigation heads to more modern ones to save water and increase effectiveness. In most cases, the two best types of irrigation heads are rotor (rotary) or mist heads, also known as spray-type heads. Rotary heads are most commonly used directly in the lawn; when the system is turned on, the water pressure causes them to pop up and rotate as they spray a stream of water. They can be adjusted to apply water at different angles, widths, lengths, and flow rates. Gardeners should always be sure that their rotary sprinkler heads water in overlapping areas to cover the whole lawn and garden. Some of your walkways and driveway may get wet, but that's better than having pockets of your garden be underwatered.

Mist heads are generally used in narrow strips of grass, islands, or areas where a rotary sprinkler would be overkill. Mist heads supply a light, even application of water in a very concentrated area.

The same basic rules apply for watering your lawn that you would use for the rest of your garden. Watering for long periods of time infrequently is far better than watering for short periods of time frequently. Too many times I have seen lawn irrigation systems that are programmed to water thirty minutes a day, seven days a week. This not only wastes water, but it also encourages the development of a shallow, weak, and vulnerable root system. It is much more responsible to program your irrigation system or to simply turn it on manually a few times a week for several hours. This type of watering will encourage a deep-rooted lawn that is more able to handle drought and pests. It will also save water over the long -term, because the water gets down to the roots of the plants rather than evaporating at the soil surface. Here are a few helpful hints to follow when watering your lawn:

- If you want to keep your lawn from going dormant during a drought, water when grass looks blue-gray and you can see your footprints on it.
- Water your lawn in the early morning to discourage disease.
- Water your lawn to a depth of 4 to 6 inches to encourage deep root establishment.
- Avoid light, frequent watering and afternoon or evening watering.

> "Proper irrigation techniques will not only help develop deep-rooted, drought-tolerant, and healthy lawns but will also save water."

Testing Your Equipment

Modern irrigation sprinkler heads can be adjusted and manipulated to meet your specific needs. Special irrigation adjustment keys can be used to ensure that your sprinkler applies water at the correct angle and rate. These adjustments will also enable you to adjust the degree of rotation on your sprinkler heads. Your irrigation equipment does require regular maintenance. You should closely monitor these sprinklers every so often while they are in use. Sprinklers

A natural, water-wise garden will save time, money, and water.

may need to be adjusted every so often, and they can get clogged, causing them to work improperly. When you turn on your irrigation system at the beginning of the growing season, you should test each zone to make sure that everything is working properly. Ignoring malfunctioning irrigation heads will only lead to wasted water and improper watering of your lawn. It is also important in cold climates to winterize irrigation systems. Winterizing requires the system to be drained and blown out with an air compressor to remove any water from the system. This type of service is normally provided by local professional irrigation companies. Systems that are not properly winterized may be damaged severely, making them inoperable the following spring.

DROUGHT-TOLERANT GRASS TYPES

Over the past few decades there has been a tremendous improvement in the quality of grass species and varieties for lawns. These grasses have been improved in many ways, including pest and drought tolerance, durability, and adaptability to a wide variety of growing conditions. New grass selections are more adapted to shade, heat, and humidity and more tolerant of wear and tear, but this varies greatly among species. There are certain species of grasses that are by nature lower-maintenance than others. For example, Kentucky bluegrass, highly prized for its lush, green color, is not particularly tolerant of shade or drought. Fescues, such as tall and fine fescues, are typically much better for shade, drought, and traffic. Warm-season grasses, such as bermudagrass and Saint Augustine grass, are adapted to perform well in heat. The chart below outlines both cool- and warm-season grasses and their tolerance to drought, wear, and shade.

AN ECO-FRIENDLY LAWN

Believe it or not, lawns don't have to be the high-maintenance, water-guzzling, and wallet-siphoning entities that they have become. We created the lawn monster, and we can change it. There are many innovative and creative ways to transform your lawn into an environmentally friendly, easier-to-maintain landscape feature. But managing an eco-friendly lawn does come with a price. It requires gardeners to compromise and give up traditional methods for new ones. The recommendations below do not require the use of chemicals but do require more hands-on attention from the homeowner.

Steps to Planting an Eco-Friendly Lawn

- Check soil type and pH to make sure they are appropriate for growing a lawn. If your lawn is happy, it is more likely to compete successfully with weeds and pests and survive hot, dry weather.
- Identify any bare areas in your lawn in early spring and reseed or replant those areas before noxious weeds take over. Once weeds like crabgrass have infiltrated your lawn, the only recourse is to pull them by hand.
- Fertilize several times a year with an organic fertilizer. There are many to choose from, and most have low amounts of nitrogen in them, but corn gluten is high in nitrogen.

Cool- and Warm-Season Grasses

	Kentucky Bluegrass	Perennial Rye	Tall or Fine Fescue	Bermudagrass	Saint Augustine Grass
Drought Tolerance	GOOD	GOOD	GOOD	EXCELLENT	EXCELLENT
Wear Tolerance	GOOD	FAIR TO GOOD	GOOD	GOOD	POOR
Shade Tolerance	FAIR TO GOOD	FAIR TO GOOD	GOOD	FAIR TO POOR	GOOD

If you're using corn gluten, make sure it is applied after any seed has germinated, as corn gluten will inhibit germination.

- Mow high, mow often, and leave the grass clippings. Also, during times of drought, you may decide to stop watering and mowing and let your lawn go dormant. In severe cases, you can water every few weeks just to sustain your lawn; once the weather cools down in late summer or fall, your lawn should come back with full force.

- In patios and cracks of walkways, pour boiling water on weeds to kill them rather than weedkillers. Acetic acid (vinegar) and clove oil are sold in formulations that are organic, nonselective weed killers. In high-traffic areas where soil gets compacted and lawn is sparse, think about replacing the lawn with steppingstones, permeable pavers, or gravel.

Should You Plant a Native Front Lawn?

I am suggesting that home gardeners move away front traditional lawn maintenance practices, such as mowing short, watering a lot, and pumping pounds of chemical nitrogen into the landscape, but having a grass meadow in your front yard is not usually practical. Leaving your front lawn unmowed for the summer will likely horrify your neighbors and may violate some local ordinances. But there is always a healthy compromise in most landscape situations, and in this case there may be a way to achieve more than one objective. I have seen resourceful gardeners around the world that treat their lawn like the rest of their garden, rather than a separate entity. For example, in Australia a water-wise gardener let his front yard go natural, and it was both beautiful and functional. This area became a combination of grasses, wildflowers, and strategically placed shrubs and trees that all worked together nicely. Water-wise gardens are now popping up all over the United States, especially in the western states and along the West Coast.

You may want to consider planting native grasses, such as switchgrass (*Panicum* spp.) or fine fescue (*Festuca* spp.), in your front yard, occasionally cutting it at a high setting every few weeks or even less often. If you maintain this native grass at a height of less than 10 inches, you can prevent it from turning into a meadow while reducing maintenance. If this is not what you expected, you can always mow it more often, but still higher than 3 inches.

With warm-season grasses, newly developed seed mixtures of native grass species are available for use in lawns. These species are already adapted for warmer climates and are able to coexist in a diverse plant community. If properly used, these multispecies mixes can provide an appearance and function similar to their nonnative monoculture counterparts. The idea is that by using these native species, lawns will require much less pesticide, fertilizer, water, and mowing. These are species native to the Great Plains of the United States, such as buffalograss (*Buchloe dactyloides*), blue grama (*Bouteloua gracilis*), and curly mesquite (*Hilaria berlangeri*), just to name a few. While this is a newer trend, it is certainly something to explore further for gardeners who want to think outside the box.

> "Be bold; tear out your existing lawn or at least a portion of it and try some new native lawn species and new drought-tolerant species and varieties of grass."

Can I Have a Garden without a Lawn?

It may be hard to believe, but yes, you can have a garden with no lawn if you choose. The lawnless garden is slowly becoming popular in many home gardens as we trend away from landscapes dominated by lawns. Many homeowners, especially those with a small enough lawn to convert easily, are choosing to replace their lawn with something else. I have seen natural stone pavers, gravel, mulch, and groundcovers all used in place of lawns. All these options can be more sustainable than lawns and just as functional if you prepare the area correctly and monitor it for invasive weeds, erosion, and other issues.

Russian arborvitae is a dense, fast-growing groundcover.

Now, we all know there are creative ways to use hardscape or softscape materials such as wood chips, gravel, and bluestone pavers and other products to replace your lawn. If you use your lawn for recreation, these products may not be the best option, but perhaps using some of the lower-maintenance grass species would be. These products are probably best in more of a passive-use area than an active-use area.

Since this is a book about gardening, I prefer to offer some plant-related alternatives to a lawn.

In areas where you are looking for an aesthetic yet functional feature and do not need an open area to play catch with the kids, groundcovers are a good option. There are many good, durable, and hardy groundcovers that can add the lush foliage you are looking for without all the mowing and such that goes with it. Once groundcovers are established, watering, fertilizing, and other lawn care activities should slow to a bare minimum, depending on what you select. The use of groundcovers will still require occasional

Weed-Suppressing Lawn Replacements

Plant	Habit	Height	Ornamental Value	Culture
CREEPING JENNY (*LYSIMACIA NUMMU-LARIA* 'AUREA')	CREEPING GROUNDCOVER	3–4 IN.	LUSH, ROUNDED, GOLDEN YELLOW LEAVES AND A SPRAWLING GROWTH HABIT. VERY FAST-GROWING, NEEDS MONITORING TO MAKE SURE IT STAYS IN BOUNDS.	PREFERS MOIST SOIL AND PARTIAL SHADE BUT WILL GROW IN FULL SUN WITH ADEQUATE WATERING. ZONES 4–8.
BLUE WOOD SEDGE (*CAREX FLACCOSPERMA*)	CLUMPY GRASSLIKE PERENNIAL	6–12 IN.	BLUE-GREEN GRASSLIKE FOLIAGE AND INTERESTING SEEDHEADS THAT DEVELOP IN THE SPRING.	PREFERS SHADE AND WELL-DRAINED SOIL. LOOKS BETTER IF IT IS CUT BACK IN LATE WINTER. ZONES 5–8
RUSSIAN ARBOR-VITAE (*MICROBIOTA DECUSSATA*)	EVERGREEN GROUNDCOVER	8–12 IN.	BRIGHT GREEN FOLIAGE TURNING SHADES OF BROWN TO PURPLE IN WINTER	PREFERS MOIST, WELL-DRAINED SOIL AND SUN BUT TOLERATES DRY CONDITIONS. ZONES 3–7
COMMON PERIWINKLE (*VINCA MINOR*)	EVERGREEN GROUNDCOVER	4–6 IN.	DARK GREEN LEAVES AND PERIWINKLE BLUE STAR-SHAPED SPRING FLOWERS.	PREFERS MOIST, WELL-DRAINED SOIL AND PARTIAL SHADE. ZONES 4–8.
TWO-ROW STONE-CROP (*SEDUM X* 'JOHN CREECH')	SUCCULENT GROUNDCOVER	3–6 IN.	SMALL, SUCCULENT, EVERGREEN LEAVES; CREEPING HABIT; AND ATTRACTIVE PINK FLOWERS IN LATE SUMMER AND EARLY FALL	FULL SUN OR PARTIAL SHADE AND WELL-DRAINED, EVEN DRY SOILS. ZONES 3–8.

weeding and blowing to remove debris, but it will still be a far cry from the horticultural marathon of lawn maintenance.

> "If you are sick of a lawn, remove it and replace it with low, durable perennials and evergreen groundcovers. If you are afraid to take the big leap and remove the entire lawn, try replacing a smaller section first."

The weed-suppressing groundcovers highlighted in Chapter 4 will certainly do the job to replace your lawn, but below I offer you a few more options.

These are just a few examples of groundcovers that could be used to replace a traditional grass lawn. You can choose from many types of groundcovers that grow in your area. Just remember to choose a noninvasive groundcover that is medium- to fast-growing with a dense habit and the ability to choke out weeds, so you do not have to constantly remove weeds. Planting one or maybe two species that are compatible is acceptable, but don't plant a menagerie of plants that do not belong together. One of the best combinations of groundcovers I have seen in place of a traditional lawn is creeping Jenny (*Lysimachia nummularia* 'Aurea') and black mondo grass (*Ophiopogon planiscapus* 'Nigrescens').

The contrast between the fine, blackish purple grass and the lush, rounded, golden yellow foliage of the creeping Jenny was striking. Whatever you choose, once established, your ground-hugging

Creative use of groundcovers can eliminate the need for a lawn.

plants should reduce maintenance and look good without all of the fuss that a lawn requires.

In the past, lawns were a significant reason why landscapes were not sustainable. More than any other component of a garden, lawns demand too many resources to make them practical. But a high-maintenance lawn does *not* need to be perpetuated in a more modern, sustainable landscape. Today, gardeners have a wide variety of resources at their fingertips to make the most of their lawn. A sustainable lawn, unlike a traditional lawn, can be an asset and not a burden to our environment. Commonsense maintenance practices, increased mowing heights, mulching

mowers, proper irrigation and fertilizer techniques, and choosing the right grass species are all great steps to a more sustainable lawn. For home gardeners, the pressure to have a perfect putting green-quality lawn should be a distant memory. If you insist on still having a traditional lawn, please hire a landscape professional to care for it. Leaving that in the hands of a professional will allow you to concentrate your efforts on other areas of the garden. Another option if you still crave the flawless green carpet under your feet is to take up golf. In the long run, it will be far less expensive and much more enjoyable than taking care of a lawn at home!

CHAPTER 7

Maintaining a Healthy Garden from the Ground Up

What You Need to Know about Composting, Soil Management, Planting, and Pruning

Composting is one of the easiest and best ways to feed your plants. It is environmentally friendly and is safe and natural, unlike conventional chemical fertilizers, which can damage plants if applied too heavily. Compost is organic material, such as plant matter and animal manure, that has been aged (recycled) to create a finished product known as humus. Recycling is critical for long-range sustainability. By recycling, we can reduce toxic wastes and environmental pollution. Recycling also conserves natural resources, protects natural ecosystems, and encourages biological diversity, all of which enhance the long-term sustainability of the environment as a whole. Waste is simply energy that has been transformed, but not used, in the process of doing something useful. By recycling, we can transform waste into something useful.

It is important to point out that composting is only one part of having healthy, sustainable soil. It is equally important to perform regular soil tests, which will tell you the type and contents of your soil. Soil test kits are relatively inexpensive and easy to use, and store-bought tests will provide basic information about your soil. Or your local agricultural Extension agent can perform a more elaborate soil test.

Regular and proper mulching of your garden beds will help with the long-term health of the soil while also enhancing the aesthetics of the garden. Nothing is more satisfying than a new spring planting with a fresh blanket of clean, soft mulch to finish the job. As this mulch decomposes, it slowly adds vital nutrients to your soil.

Fertilizing your soil, whether with homemade compost, mulch, or processed fertilizer, can be done to boost plant growth and vigor. Seasonal fertilization of your garden will keep plants lush and beautiful. While there are many products on the market to choose from, my best advice is to use only what you need. A current soil test will guide you in that decision.

Other important things to consider in order to maintain a healthy garden are proper planting and pruning techniques. Sustainable gardening requires careful handling of your valuable plants. By following proper planting and pruning practices, gardeners can enjoy watching the development of their garden into a beautiful showplace right before their very eyes.

COMPOST: YOU SCRATCH MY BACK, I'LL SCRATCH YOURS

Compost is not just fertilizer. It can also be used as a soil amendment. Incorporating it into the soil during or after planting will enhance plant growth, because compost improves the soil's water-holding capacity.

Compost also encourages the presence of beneficial microorganisms in the soil. These microorganisms include bacteria, fungi, worms, and other microbes that help break down organic matter and help plants absorb nutrients and water. For example, mycorrhiza is a partnership formed between beneficial soil fungi and plant roots. This partnership allows the fungi to extract carbohydrates from the plants. The fungi colonize plant roots and become extensions of the root systems, helping plants absorb nutrients and water more effectively. This colonization can very often be found in mulch or compost piles, and it looks like small, white threads. Mycorrhizae are essential in the success of certain plant species and are most present in rich, organic soils. The addition of compost or some type of mulch to your garden beds will encourage this symbiosis (mutually beneficial relationship) between fungi and plants.

It is important to point out that, although finished compost looks like soil, it is not soil. Compost is organic matter that's been broken down. Soil is composed of rock particles and minerals that have certain chemical components useful for growing plants. Compost can enhance soil's chemical makeup, nutritional value, and drainage capabilities, but it does not replace soil. Planting in pure compost is not recommended for this reason (because it lacks all the rock particles and minerals of soil).

Elements of Compost

Composting and the use of organic products to enhance soil biology and improve plant growth is a very complex procedure. It is important for gardeners to know how to compost, including what raw materials to use and how to best use the finished product. Composting and the reuse of organic products to make a natural form of fertilizer do require specific materials and

Finished compost ready to use

environments to produce a tangible benefit. A healthy compost pile needs adequate oxygen and water to support the microorganisms necessary to break down the fresh organic material.

Air and Space

By providing ample room and regularly turning your compost pile, you can properly manage and aerate this material. The turning process supplies oxygen to the compost and helps the decomposition process. Turning your compost pile every few weeks, on average, is recommended.

Moisture

Moisture is an important component for a healthy composting system. Adding water to a compost pile as needed will encourage microorganism growth. Adding water is only required during dry, hot weather. The best way to determine whether water is needed is by digging into your compost pile and checking how mosit it is. If it is very dry or dusty, then add water. If it is soggy, then let it dry out a bit. You want to mainatian a compost pile that is niether too dry or too wet but somewhere in the middle.

Heat

Another important factor in facilitating the decomposition of compost is heat. As your compost pile grows in size and begins to decay, this process naturally generates heat. Heat helps to accelerate the decay process while killing off harmful pests and weed seeds. The combination of oxygen, moisture, and heat all encourage the presence and growth of beneficial fungi and bacteria. These fungi and bacteria are microorganisms that are vital to the decomposition process needed to produce compost. Fungi are important because they break down tough debris that is not easily consumed while bacteria decompose material that is easier to consume. This is discussed in more detail on previous page.

> "You should make the most of your yard and kitchen waste by building a compost bin in the backyard. You can use wire fence, snow fence, wooden pallets, or a more elaborate store-bought bin to recycle your organic material. By following a few easy steps, you can make free, nutrient-rich natural fertilizer for your whole garden"

Brown and Green Products

In addition to space, water, oxygen, and heat, you also need products to compost. This is an important decision for gardeners to make. There are several schools of thought on what to put in your compost pile. Some gardeners like to mix kitchen waste such as vegetables, coffee grinds, and leafy materials with grass clippings, leaves, and wood chips. This will produce compost that is appropriate for a wide variety of uses. Another method is to separate compostable materials into different compost piles, which allows gardeners to create certain types of finished compost for specific uses. For example, green products, such as herbaceous material, grass clippings, or kitchen waste, can be separated. Herbaceous material is soft, fleshy plant growth from annuals, perennials, and other plants. Bacteria will mostly decompose green products. "Brown" products, such as wood chips and leaves, can be composted separately and will be decomposed by fungi. These brown products are an important source of carbon. Once composted fully, these two different types of compost can be applied to specific plants to meet their specific needs. Green compost can be used on turf, vegetable gardens, and herbaceous borders. Brown compost can be used on shrubs and trees. The benefit of separating compost is that if you mostly have specific landscape plants such as herbaceous borders and lawns, then green compost will be most beneficial to them. If you are mostly adding compost to trees and shrubs, then brown compost will be most beneficial. If you have a little of both in your garden, which most of us do, I recommend you mix the green and brown materials and let nature take its course. This way your plants can have the best of both worlds! This can easily be done by alternating layers of your green and brown raw materials.

Composting Methods

Within the general framework of composting, there are more specific ways to compost organic products in your garden.

Vermicomposting

Vermicomposting is the use of earthworms to transform garden and kitchen waste into high-quality compost. This form of composting is handled quite differently than traditional composting methods, because worms require specific conditions. Environments that are too hot or excessively wet can be counterproductive to vermicomposting.

Organic kitchen waste is an excellent raw material to add to your compost pile.

Worm compost is referred to as castings. Castings are the waste left behind by worms. Worm castings are high in nutrients and typically low in contaminants, making them an excellent source of compost and soil conditioner. Vermicomposting is also very efficient. Adding small amounts of moist kitchen scraps to a large compost pile in the garden daily can disrupt the decomposition process so that the compost is never really finished. But using smaller, more manageable bins for worms to decompose organic matter is a great way to recycle kitchen waste without disrupting the composting process. Bins need to be shallow, because worms typically feed in the top layers of the organic matter. A bin that is too deep will not be as efficient and can produce bad odors. Bins do require holes, so that the compost drains and is properly aerated. Bins are usually made of wood or plastic and can be homemade or store-bought. Plastic is lighter and lasts longer than wood. Plastic containers work quite well for this purpose.

Worms are excellent at turning your raw materials into usable compost.

"You can create your own worm composting bin for very little money, and this is a great way to create free, high-nutrient compost in a relatively short period of time."

When you're choosing a vermicomposting container, estimate the amount of food scraps or yard waste you have to dispose of or that you wish to compost. Depending on how much raw material you produce and the conditons, it will take approximately three to four months for the worms to decompose all the kitchen waste. Also think about where the ultimate location of the bin should be. An ideal sized bin, especially for anyone new to vermicomposting, is 5 to 10 gallons. The bin is usually rectangular, and a good example is approximately 24 X 18 X 8 inches. At least a dozen holes ¼ to ½ inch in diameter should be drilled in the bottom of the container for proper drainage. The bin should have a cover that fits firmly to secure and protect the contents. Another method is to use the 1-2-3 method, which recommends making a bin that is 1 foot deep by 2 feet wide by 3 feet long.

If a worm bin is kept outdoors, place it in a sheltered position away from direct sunlight. The bin should also be protected from frost in winter. This is easy; just nestle the bin into the ground in a protected location near the foundation of a house or move it into an unheated garage or cold frame.

Besides a bin, vermicomposting requires bedding (shredded newspaper or cardboard) for the worms and regular, even moisture. The amount of bedding to use depends on the size of your bin. For example, a 2 x 3-foot bin will take 9 to 14 pounds of bedding. If this seems like too much material, you can always reduce the amount to fit your specific needs. Your bedding should be moistened before it goes into your vermicomposting bin, and the bin should be filled to two-thirds of its capacity. You should add your acceptable kitchen waste and other compostable items slowly. Then add your worms and let nature take its course.

Regular maintenance of bins includes replenishing bedding as it decomposes and separating worms from their castings. Gardeners can harvest the worm castings when it contains few or no scraps of uneaten food or bedding. There are three methods you can use to harvest worm casting from bins. You can dump the entire contents of the bin once the compost is ready and seperate worms from compost by picking them out by hand; you can divide the contents of your bin between fresh material and finished compost; or you can scoop castings from the top.

The first method simply requires dumping out your worms and castings onto a clean, dry surface and separating as many worms as possible from the compost by hand. The majority of the worms that are separated can be put in a new bin with fresh bedding and new raw materials.

The second method is to push the black, decomposed material to one side of the bin and fill the other side with new, moist bedding and kitchen scraps. For the next few weeks, place only compostable items and fresh bedding on the side with the fresh material. Then wait several days. The worms should migrate to the freshly filled side of the bin, and you can just scoop out the finished compost minus the majority of the worms. Make sure you pick out any wigglers or worm eggs (opaque cocoons) and return them to the bin.

The third method is to remove the top layer of worm castings by hand or with a sieve. Worms are sensitive to light, so each time you remove some material, the worms will be exposed to the light and will migrate toward the bottom of the bin.

Rather than harvesting worms from your yard, it is preferable to purchase worms to aid your vermicomposting process. It is believed that harvesting worms from your yard may adversely disrupt their population numbers. The worms most commonly offered are red worms or red wigglers (*Eisenia foetida* and *Lumbricus rubellus*). There is some debate over whether some exotic species of worms pose a threat to our native soils, and you should keep up on this topic by checking with your local agricultural Extension service or university website to ensure you are not using an invasive species to make compost. There are several mail-order catalogues and garden supply companies that carry worms and vermicomposting supplies as well as various worm farms that sell these beneficial critters. (See page 186 in Resources.)

Worm compost (castings) can be incorporated into soil as an amendment or mixed with water as part of a compost tea. Castings add nutrients to the soil and improve drainage and overall health of the soil. Brewing compost tea is covered on pages 160–161 in this chapter.

A few pitfalls to avoid when vermicomposting are:

- Do not put plastic, aluminum, or glass in your bin.
- Make sure your pets do not have access to your bins, as cats may use open-top bins as litter boxes.
- Do not use pesticides in the vicinity of your bin, as worms are sensitive to chemicals.
- Do not use garden soil in vermicomposting bins.
- Do not use manure in your vermicomposting bin.

"If you are serious about composting, the key to success is to use only good-quality raw materials such as clean leaves, grass clippings, and organic kitchen waste. Part of that success also depends on your ability to be a master chef, managing the cooking process with equal parts moisture, aeration, and natural heat."

Bin Composting

Bin composting is another type of composting method. It is the most accepted, popular method of turning organic material into useable fertilizer. It requires gardeners to either purchase or build a bin for holding organic materials, which are then aged. The naturally cooked and finished compost is eventually harvested for use. A circle of wire fencing is a simple, inexpensive way of composting your yard waste if you want to make your own bin. The circle can be any size you desire, based on how much space and material you have on hand. Other homemade systems include using snow fencing or wooden pallets nailed or tied together. While all these options are inexpensive and offer great flexibility, they are rather unsightly and should be placed in hidden areas of the garden.

How to Brew Your Own Compost Tea

Compost that has been properly aged, also known as finished compost, can be mixed with potting soil, incorporated into soil as an amendment, or used to brew compost tea. Compost tea is a biologically active liquid that is used to improve soil biology and enhance plant vigor.

Brewing compost tea is a complex process that involves using composted materials in a solution that can be applied to landscapes. Essentially it gives gardeners the ability to apply compost in liquid rather than solid form. The advantage is a quicker absorption of nutrients and presence of millions of beneficial bacteria and fungi for plants. This brewing process requires gardeners to have a general understanding of how to make good-quality compost. Compost tea brewers can be homemade or purchased preassembled. Typically the compost tea brewing system requires a bucket or holding tank, air pump and tubing to aerate the mixture, a stick to turn the mixture, unsulfured molasses, and a strainer or fine mesh to steep the compost. For prefabricated brewers, there are local suppliers as well as online sources that make these systems. If you regularly make large amounts of compost tea, purchasing a prefabricated brewer that is already set up may be a more efficient and cost-effective option.

A properly brewed compost tea can be sprayed or applied as a drench onto the soil, turf, or on plant leaves. (A drench is a liquid used to soak the soil or the entire plant.) Take note that compost teas are not pesticides and are not marketed as ways to control harmful diseases. They are, rather, a more efficient way to introduce beneficial organisms into your garden and help plant vigor. Because it is a liquid, compost tea makes nutrients and micro-organisms more readily available than solid compost does. This is similar to how liquid fertilizers work compared with granular fertilizers. Spraying a solution of 20-20-20 liquid plant fertilizer gives quicker results than applying a granular form of 15-16-17 to the garden. Compost tea brewing is a relatively new science that requires some time and research in order to get positive results, but believe me, you can do it!

Scientific research continues on how to properly implement and maximize the benefits of compost tea. There are conflicting opinons and a continuing debate amongst horticultural and arboricultural experts on how effective compost tea really is. Therefore, you should do some research yourself to see if compost tea brewing is right for your specific landscape situation.

A homemade compost tea brewer

You don't need fancy equipment to brew your own compost tea. This set up includes a plastic garbage can, a mesh net for compost, an air hose and a wooden board to secure a garden hose, which will gradually fill the barrel with water when you are ready to brew.

This well-made compost bin provides the necessary air and light needed to turn yard waste into compost.

Prefabricated compost bins come in all shapes and sizes.

Compost bins can also be purchased ready-made and come in a variety of styles and materials. A simple holding bin, usually made out of lightweight, durable plastic, is simply a barrel that you put your organic matter to be composted in. It does not require turning, but material in this type of bin can take six months to two years to break down completely, due to lack of aeration. Some units have a ventilation system to help the aeration process, but overall these types of compost bins make it more difficult to turn and harvest usable compost.

Rotating bins or barrels, usually made from plastic or metal, are fastened on a stand of some sort, making them easy to turn regularly. This turning motion will aerate your compost, causing faster breakdown of the material inside. It is important to have enough materials to fill the rotating barrel and to not add new material to an existing batch being processed. Otherwise your compost will have material in different stages of decompositon, and this will delay the finished product. These types of composting systems can be more costly and require assembly.

> "You can turn your compost bin once a week with a long-handled cultivating fork, pitchfork, or shovel. This aeration process will keep your compost pile active."

Binless Composting

There are also composting systems that do not require bins at all. A binless system is simply a loose pile of organic materials that can be turned regularly—or not at all. While some time will be spent keeping the heap from sprawling out far from where you want it to, it is simple and costs nothing to the resourceful gardener who is willing to put the extra work into it. Another binless method is just to bury yard waste and organic material in the ground. Dig a hole large enough to accommodate all your waste with at least 8 inches of soil covering it. Over time, the material will decompose, and the fertile soil in this area

A Recipe for Compost

- Compostable materials: wood chips, grass clippings, weeds and herbaceous trimmings, hedge trimmings, coffee grounds, eggshells, fruit and vegetable trimmings, animal manures (except dog and cat)
- Compost bin or pile
- Thermometer

Pile up yard and kitchen waste, the more the better, to generate heat. A pile 3 x 3 feet or more will retain enough heat to kill any plant pathogens and weed seeds. The optimum temperature range is 130 to 140 degrees Fahrenheit. Watch the temperature! Do *not* exceed 160 degrees for an extended period, because few beneficial organisms actively decompose organic material at temperatures higher than this. Regularly turn your compost pile to aerate it. Keep your compost pile "cooking"—you will need to add new raw materials regularly to feed the pile. If you have one main area where you pile debris, and you are constantly adding material, your compost pile is never really done. One solution is to locate two compost bins next to each other. When one compost pile is well aged and decayed, add new raw materials to a second bin. When thoroughly cooked, "serve" the compost to your garden.

A special thermometer can be used to measure how hot your compost gets.

can be planted at a later date. This process does require hand digging, and decomposition may take up to a year, since aeration is not an option. Gardeners should avoid planting in this area for at least that long so the composting process has time to finish.

> "Take some time to seperate your desireable kitchen waste, such as leafy material, vegetable matter, and coffee grounds, and stockpile it in a small can or container for easy transport to the compost pile."

A wide variety of raw materials can be used in your compost pile.

Compostable Materials

Whether you decide to separate green products from brown products or mix them together, there are rules governing what to add to your compost pile and what to avoid. Check out this table of common materials to compost and ones to throw in the trash.

During the composting process, the cooking of raw materials is essential. The optimum temperature range is 130 to 140 degrees Fahrenheit. By piling up and layering yard and kitchen waste, the composting *process* will naturally generate heat. Compost has relatively good insulation properties, and a large enough pile (3x3 feet or bigger) will retain heat. High temperatures are

essential to destroy pathogens and weed seeds. Also, decomposition is more rapid at higher temperatures. Since few beneficial organisms actively decompose organic material above 160 degrees Fahrenheit, I don't recommend that you exceed this temperature for an extended period of time. Regularly turning or aerating your compost pile will reduce any extended periods of high temperatures while aiding the decomposition process. In order to keep your compost pile cooking, you will need to regularly add new raw materials. This will continuously fuel the pile. One disadvantage of this is that if you have one main area where you pile debris, and you are

Compostable Items Versus Trash

Good	Not Good
WOOD CHIPS	BONES
LEAVES	CAT LITTER
GRASS CLIPPINGS	CHARCOAL AND BRIQUETTES
HERBACEOUS MATERIAL	COOKED FOOD
HEDGE TRIMMINGS	DAIRY PRODUCTS
COFFEE GROUNDS	OILY OR GREASY FOODS
EGGSHELLS	MEAT
MOST FRUITS AND VEGETABLES	GLOSSY PAPER
ANIMAL MANURE	FISH SCRAPS

constantly adding material, your compost pile is never really done. Here's a solution: put two compost bins next to each other. As your existing compost pile in the first bin nears the point at which most of the raw materials are well aged and decayed, you can add new raw materials to the adjacent second bin. This is a good way to keep older matreial seperate from new material that hasn't been composted yet. This way you'll have a new compost pile started for future use while the finished compost from the first bin is still being used in the garden.

FERTILIZERS, MULCH, AND COMPOST: WORKING TOGETHER
Fertilizers

There are many formulations of fertilizer on the market, designed specifically for turf, trees and shrubs, or herbaceous plants such as annuals and perennials. Fertilizers are generally divided into two groups, inorganic and organic, with inorganic formulations being composed of chemicals. Inorganic fertilizers can certainly serve a valuable role in gardening, but choosing organic fertilizers first is a more sustainable approach to gardening. An organic fertilizer is derived from plant or animal sources, such as composted or processed plant parts or manure. Fertilizers can be either slow-release or fast-release depending on their makeup. Organic fertilizers tend to be slower-release, because microorganisms in the soil typically have to break down the organic fertilizer into a more useable form. Inorganic or chemical fertilizers can either be slow- or fast-release depending on their formulation.

> "Organic fertilizers are a safe, reliable, and long-term method of feeding your garden."

While composting allows you to make your own fertilizer, there are many organic fertilizers on the market that can be purchased. While compost is cheap to make and offers long-term benefits, it is a slow-release form of plant food that takes time to work. Commercial, processed organic fertilizers that you buy from the store are also typically slow-release but tend to work faster. These processed fertilizers may also come in specific formulations for specific crops or plant needs. These commercial fertilizers come in many forms, such as bloodmeal, bonemeal, amino acids, seaweed extracts, fishmeal, microbial inoculants (mycorrhizae), and feather meal. Corn gluten meal is a feed byproduct that provides an organic form of nitrogen as it breaks down (and it can also be used as a natural herbicide). While there is obviously a cost involved with using these fertilizers on a regular basis, the advantage is that they are relatively safe and effective products and can be used for specific purposes. For example, if your soil test reveals that the soil in your garden is deficient in phosphorous, you can purchase bonemeal to effectively add a natural form of this nutrient to the soil. It is imperative to follow the application instructions on the label, and it may take more than one application to see tangible results, but there are a wide variety of products available to address specific plant needs.

Much About Mulch

Another way to naturally feed your plants *and* improve soil biology over an extended period is to mulch your garden. Mulch is a general term that can apply to many types of products. Most mulch is applied to the surface of the ground in planting beds and around trees, shrubs, flowers, and vegetables. Often the mulches used in the garden are influenced by the area where you live and the raw materials that are available in your part of the country. Typically the types of mulch used in a garden are wood chips, pine straw, cocoa shells, shredded leaves, or sifted compost. Mulch has many benefits, including reducing weed growth, moderating soil moisture and temperature, and enhancing the aesthetics of the garden. But the most important function of mulch is to slowly add nutrients and support the growth of beneficial microbes in the soil. Mulch functions the same way as compost and is also quite effective as a soil amendment. The main difference is that mulch is used as a topdress rather than being incorporated into the

A 1 to 2" layer of mulch will offer a neat, mani-cured appearance to shrubs, trees and other ornamentals.

soil, and mulch has usually not gone through the composting process yet, so it is in a more raw form. I recommend mulching at least once a year depending on how fast the material you are using decomposes. Different mulch products vary in the time it takes them to decompose, so mulching application frequency will vary.

Too Much of a Good Thing

It is important not to overdue mulch. In this case, too much of a good thing can be quite harmful. Mulch should be applied at a depth of 1

to 2 inches either in the spring or the fall. Mulch-ing at depths of 3 inches or more, or mounding mulch around the base of your plants, especially trees and shrubs, can have catastrophic results. Why? Plants need oxygen, just as we do. Too much mulch causes an anaerobic condition, or a low-oxygen environment, around the plant's roots. This causes plant roots to grow toward the surface of the soil in search of oxygen. As these surface roots grow and become established, they can eventually grow around the base of a tree or shrub until the root cuts off the water flow and nutrient uptake of the plant. This "strangling" effect can even cause plants to weaken and fall over in windstorms. In addition, overmulched plants can develop a secondary root system close to the surface of the soil, which stresses plants even more, making them more sensi-tive to drought and other weather extremes. Plants in the rhododendron family (*Ericaceae*) are examples of plants that are quite sensitive to overmulching and burying roots too deep.

Timing of Mulching

Mulching your landscape should be done at appropriate times during the growing season. Mulching your garden in very dry, hot weather or very wet conditions is not recommended. When mulching, soil should be evenly moist. Plants can be damaged if mulch is applied when they are stressed from heat and drought. In addition, if soil is too wet, mulching over that soil can encourage harmful diseases. Certain plant groups, such as oak and beech, benefit greatly from the presence of mulch, as it pro-motes beneficial soil organisms such as worms and mycorrhizae.

The sources from which you get your mulch is crucial to the success of your gar-den. Adding poor-quality mulch is a waste of time and resources. There are several ways to ensure you're getting a clean, reliable source of mulch that can be used in garden beds, around vegetables, and in shrub borders.

Clean, shredded mulch is ideal for many garden applications.

Developing a clean edge and using a high quality mulch will keep weeds at bay and protect the vulnerable roots of your valuable garden shrubs.

> "Mulching is a form of composting, because it provides organic matter and nutrients to plants while also suppressing weeds, regulating soil moisture and temperature, and enhancing the aesthetics of the landscape. Mulch your garden with a 1- to 2-inch layer once or twice a year, and your plants will be very happy."

Gardeners can purchase a small shredder that can accommodate small branches and leaves. These fairly inexpensive machines can be either electric or gas-powered. The advantage of at-home shredding is that you can recycle yard waste and reuse it very efficiently.

Another option is to contact your local town or village landfill. Most municipal landfills recycle yard waste—and often even shred it—and then offer it back to local residents. As long as this material is properly managed and stored by the municipality, it can be another reliable source of mulch.

Beware of processed mulch, which can be purchased from local hardware stores or retail outlets. Gardeners should avoid processed mulch that has been dyed a specific color, such as red, blue, black, and so forth, as those products contain chemicals and are *not* consistent with a truly sustainable garden strategy.

IT ALL BEGINS WITH THE SOIL

Soil health and biology is, without question, the most important factor in growing plants successfully. Plant life begins in the soil, and without a good growing medium, plants will die. Poor soil conditions can suppress plant growth, reduce flowering and fruit production, and cause plants to be more susceptible to drought, pest problems, and other environmental challenges. When creating a garden, it is essential to look at the landscape from the ground up, with soils being the first and most important aspect. It doesn't particularly matter whether your garden is in sun or shade, is windy or protected, or has a great view of the coast. If the soil is of poor quality, compacted, or infertile, in most cases plants will not grow successfully. Too often we tend to overlook or underestimate the value of

Rich, organic soil is ideal for growing a wide variety of plant life.

soil biology. But great gardeners spend a lot of time cultivating and enriching the soil, knowing that this time investment will pay long-term dividends. This type of long-range planning is very complementary and consistent with sustainable landscaping.

Life Within the Soil

Soil biology, or life within the soil, is quite complex and is vital to growing plants successfully. While it is not necessary to have a chemistry degree to know your soil makeup, there is some basic information that gardeners need to know. Gardeners who ignore or underestimate the importance of healthy, viable soil are doomed to fail. There are several key factors that one should be aware of regarding soil. These factors include soil type, drainage, soil pH, soil horizons or layers, organic matter content, and levels of primary and secondary minerals in the soil. This sounds like a lot to consider, but it really is fairly easy to ascertain this information—and it is critical before moving forward.

Soils are fascinating materials that vary greatly in their structure, texture, chemical makeup, biological components, and other characteristics. The three main components of soil are sand, silt, and clay. Sand is the coarsest, with the largest particle size, and clay tends to be the finest, with the smallest particle size. Soil *structure* consists of pore spaces and a mixture of solids (minerals), water, and air (gas). Because of their particle size, soils with clay or silt components are typically more prone to compaction than sandy soils. Compacted soil can suppress plant growth, limit root expansion, and predispose plants to disease.

Plant Like with Like

It is very important to group plants with like needs in the same areas of the garden. In general, most of the plants outlined in this book (unless otherwise noted) will perform best in moist but well-drained soil. It is also important to know the soil makeup because different soils react in different ways. That is, soils all have various levels of reactivity, or cation exchange capacity (CEC). CEC refers to soil fertility and capability of the soil to retain nutrients. Soils higher in clay or organic matter (humus) have higher CEC and in general tend to do a better job of retaining nutrients; thus, they're considered more fertile. There are a wide variety of plants that require a specific soil type in order to thrive. Soil can vary greatly in many regions of the United States—even within the same state. See the maps at www.nationalatlas.gov/geology.html to find your soil type..

"Be sure to take a soil test at least once every few years or as needed to ensure that your soil is balanced and healthy. You can buy a soil test kit or take a sample to your local nursery or agricultural Extension office."

Because soil and plants are so diverse, ensuring that your garden will thrive in the soil you have must be a priority. It is essential that you test your soil pH and nutrient content and determine soil texture before planting or cultivating the soil. The most efficient way to do this is to send a soil sample to your local agricultural extension office. A full soil analysis will reveal pH, soil fertility, and the amount of organic matter in the soil. Typically these tests recommend what to add to the soil to address any deficiencies.

The three main nutrients in the soil that are vital to plant growth are nitrogen (N), phosphorus (P), and potassium (K). There are also several important secondary and micronutrients that are essential to plant life, such as calcium (Ca), magnesium (Mg), and iron (Fe). It's necessary to know the levels of these nutrients in the soil at any time and how to properly add them if needed. Soil nutrient levels depend on many factors, including type of soils, drainage, climate, and rainfall. Nutrient availability is affected by soil pH, soil type, rainfall, and other factors. Depending on the

situation, these nutrients can either be deficient or abundant in the soil. For example, in some parts of the northeastern United States, phosphorus is not usually deficient in the soil. Phosphorus also moves very slowly in the soil. So adding phosphate products to the soil around newly planted trees is often unnecessary. However, nitrogen is usually quickly absorbed by plants and is leached through soils rather quickly. So nitrogen can be deficient at certain times of the year and may need to be added through fertilizers. Plants will often show physical signs of nutrient deficiencies such as poor growth, yellowing or chlorotic leaves, and so forth. Gardeners must keep a close eye on their plants and observe them before any problems become irreversible. Regular soil tests (once every year or two) will ensure that these types of problems do not become more challenging than they need to be. The following table offers a list of general soil nutrients tat are used by plants.

"You can check your soil's capacity to drain by digging a hole that is about I foot deep. Fill the hole with water and observe how long it takes for the water to drain. If your soil drains I inch or less in an hour, it is poorly drained; ideally it should drain I to 6 inches in an hour."

You Don't Need a PhD to Understand Soil pH

Soil pH (its relative acidity or alkalinity) is an important factor that will determine the plants you can grow. The pH of the soil is typically discussed in relative terms and based on different levels or ranges of alkalinity or acidity. Soil pH is measured on a scale from 1 to 14, in which 7.0 is neutral. Soil pH below 7.0 is considered acidic; soil pH above 7.0 is alkaline. For example, a soil pH of 6.8 would be considered slightly acidic, whereas a pH of 4.5 would be considered very acidic. It is relatively easy to determine your soil pH by purchasing a soil pH meter or test kit from a local retail garden center or nursery.

Once you have determined the pH of the soil, you can evaluate the needs of your landscape. Certain plant groups, such as dogwood, holly, and rhododendron, *prefer* acidic soil, whereas other ornamentals, such as lilac, prefer neutral or alkaline soil.

In the case of new plantings, you can measure the soil pH and select your plants based on that information. In the case of an established landscape, soil pH poses a much greater dilemma. Often gardeners must deal with existing plantings in poor health, trying to determine what the cause is. The first place to look is in the soil. If the soil pH is not adequate to grow the types of plants already in your landscape, you may have to take steps to alter the pH of the soil. Soil pH can be raised or lowered by adding products to the soil, but this is a slow and tedious process that takes time and patience. There is no quick fix for altering soil pH levels. Garden lime (calcium carbonate) can be added to raise the pH, whereas aluminum sulfate will acidify or lower the pH of the soil. Generally speaking, nitrogen compounds in fertilizers, such as ammonium nitrate, applied in in small intervals, will acidify soil over time. Natural products, such as animal manures and compost, also help acidify the soil. However, soil pH should be changed gradually, over an extended period of time. Trying to change soil pH too quickly can damage plants. In this scenario, too much of a good thing can be harmful. This is why it is so important to read and follow the directions on the label of horticultural products such as fertilizers, limestone products, and other soil amendments. For example, if the label on a bag of limestone (calcium carbonate) recommends applying the product at a rate of 50 pounds per 1,000 square feet, applying it at double the rate (100 pounds per 1,000 square feet) will not necessarily raise soil pH twice as fast. In fact, with many products, such as fertilizers, plants can become damaged, stunted, or even killed by applying these products incorrectly at toxic levels. With lime, even if plant damage does not occur, applying at the incorrect rate can waste time, product,

A soil pH test kit is essential for determining how acidic or alkaline your soil is.

and money. Remember that the main principle of sustainability is reducing waste. Throwing time and money away by overapplying garden products is counterproductive to that principle.

Soil Amendments

There are a wide variety of soil amendments that can be used to improve soil water-holding capacity, drainage, and CEC; add vital nutrients and minerals to the soil; or alter soil pH. Check out the following table listing some of the commonly used soil amendments.

"Instead of turning to chemical fertilizers all the time, try using organic soil amendments to improve the quality of your soil. Plant compost, manure, and worm castings are all excellent examples of these."

Organic soil amendments, such as compost and worm castings, provide nutrition to the soil and are typically rich in essential nutrients such as nitrogen. Animal manures can provide N, P, and K to the soil as well as micronutrients. Soil

Common Nutrients

Primary Nutrients	Secondary Nutrients	Micronutrients
NITROGEN (N)	CALCIUM (CA)	IRON (FE)
PHOSPHORUS (P)	MAGNESIUM (MG)	MANGANESE (MN)
POTASSIUM (K)	SULFUR (S)	BORON (B)
		ZINC (ZN)
		COPPER (CU)
		CHLORINE (CL)
		MOLYBDENUM (MO)

inoculants, also known as biostimulants, are beneficial bacteria and fungi such as mycorrhizae that can be injected or worked into the soil.

Inorganic soil amendments such as gravel, sand, vermiculite, and perlite are added to soils to improve drainage and create air space in the soil. Limestone and gypsum are inorganic products that add vital nutrients such as calcium to the soil. Gypsum can also be used as a soil conditioner and will improve soil structure and reduce compaction without altering soil pH. Limestone, which comes in several formulations, such as pulverized, granular, and pelletized, will raise soil pH over a period of time.

PLANTING CORRECTLY IS VITAL

In addition to knowing your soil conditions, you must plant your new landscape plants properly. It is not as simple as just digging a hole and placing soil around their root systems. There are several important steps that should be followed when you plant shrubs, trees, and herbaceous plants. Although woody plants are typically handled differently than herbaceous plants, the proper planting techniques and principles are similar. Give careful attention to the preparation of the planting site. Following the details of the guidelines below will ensure that your landscape plants thrive in their new setting.

First, **evaluate your site**, paying close attention to soil type, light exposure, wind conditions, and other environmental factors that will impact plant growth. Without this information, gardeners are left to make too many assumptions about what will work in their garden. Having hard facts will enable you to select the right plant for the appropriate location in the landscape. Too often we choose the plants we like first and try to make them work within the existing landscape conditions. This doesn't always work out the way we would like it to.

Timing is important when planting. In most areas of the country, the best time to plant is in spring or fall, while the air temperature is cool and the soil is moist. In hardiness zones 8, 9, and 10, where the climate is warm most of the year, the planting season is much broader. Exact timing of the planting season in your area depends on the

Common Soil Amendments

Organic	Inorganic
COMPOST (HUMUS), SOLID AND TEA	GRAVEL
WORM CASTINGS	VERMICULITE OR PERLITE
PEAT MOSS	SAND
ANIMAL MANURE	LIMESTONE
SOIL INOCULANTS (MICROBIAL)	GYPSUM

specific climate where you live and the species and type of plants you are planting. No planting should be done during the extremes of summer or winter.

Prepare the planting hole once you have determined the types of plants that will work in the locations you have chosen for them. The size of the planting hole depends on the size of the rootball or container of the plant. When shrubs are purchased from a garden center or nursery, they are typically growing as balled-and-burlapped plants or in containers. Sometime you will be able to buy plants bare-root, in trays, or as plugs. Containers can range in size and type but are often made of plastic or biodegradable peat pots. Burlap is a coarsely woven cloth that is used to cover and support the roots and soil of a nursery plant grown for transplanting into another location. Burlap can be biodegradable or treated, and gardeners should find out which type they have before planting. This is important, because treated burlap is designed to resist decay and can remain in the planting hole for an extended period of time. If not removed from the planting hole, treated burlap can impede root growth and establishment of the plant. Treated burlap is typically green in color, while natural burlap is a brown color. If you are not sure, ask your local nursery professional what type of burlap is on your plant before you make a purchase. Whether your plants are in containers, cell packs, or in burlap, the planting hole should be significantly larger than the root system of the plant. In the case of woody plants, dig the planting hole at least three times wider than the diameter of the rootball. This will allow the roots to establish in loose, fluffy soil. With your annuals and perennials, digging a large planting hole and backfilling with fluffy soil will help plants get established quickly.

Place plants at the proper depth in the soil, regardless of the types of plants you select for the landscape. *This is very important.* Plants that are planted too deeply can develop root problems, become more susceptible to disease, or grow poorly. While this can be less of an issue with herbaceous plants, it is critical to the success of growing trees and shrubs. In most cases, the top of the root system should be even with, or slightly above, the soil level. In addition, all rope, plastic, wire, treated burlap, and so forth must be removed from the plant once it is placed at the correct height in the planting hole. Although as much burlap should be removed as possible, leaving some of the burlap in the bottom of the planting hole is not a concern. Just fold it down underneath the rootball and cover it with soil.

Container-grown shrubs are handled a bit differently than those that are balled and burlapped. Plants growing in containers are very often pot-bound, meaning that a large number of roots fill the container. As roots reach the edges of the inside of the pot, they form a thick mesh. This fibrous web of roots should be carefully teased out or sliced with a knife to encourage roots to grow *out* into the soil rather than in a circular pattern. This technique is especially important on plants with fine root systems, such as rhododendrons.

Apart from whether your new plants are balled and burlapped or in containers, the planting procedure is basically the same. Often when plants arrive from the nursery, especially if they're balled and burlapped, the soil is pushed up against the main stems or trunk of the plant. Before placing the plant in the hole, be sure to expose the top of the rootball and clean off any excess soil that may have accumulated at the base of the plant during transport from the nursery. Once the planting hole has been prepared and the plant is at the appropriate depth, soil can be backfilled into the planting hole and lightly tamped. It is very important not to break or damage the rootball in any way. Leaning or standing on the rootball is a serious error because it can seriously damage the root system of the plant. If the rootball breaks, even partially, it could slow establishment of the plant or even cause the plant to die. Any excess soil that does not fit in the planting hole, rocks, or other debris can be discarded. The plant should be watered thoroughly and slowly so that the entire planting hole is evenly moist. After a generous drink of water, a thin layer of mulch added around the rootball will reduce soil water loss, fluctuating soil temperatures, and weed growth. Newly planted shrubs should be watered for at least two growing seasons after planting to ensure they have established a healthy root system and can survive on their own.

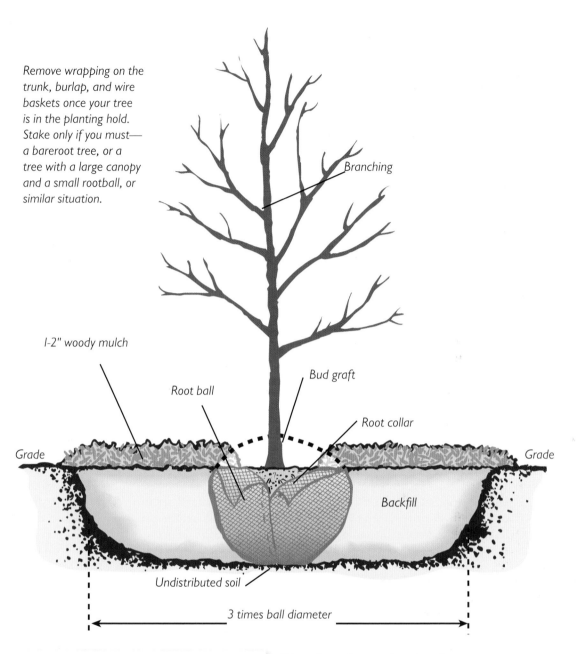

Remove wrapping on the trunk, burlap, and wire baskets once your tree is in the planting hold. Stake only if you must— a bareroot tree, or a tree with a large canopy and a small rootball, or similar situation.

Branching

1-2" woody mulch

Root ball

Bud graft

Root collar

Grade

Grade

Backfill

Undistributed soil

3 times ball diameter

"When planting a new tree or shrub, make sure you find the root flare or top of the rootball and position your new plant an inch or two above the grade of the soil."

Planting above the Grade

As a general rule it recommend that plants be placed slightly above the grade of the soil. With trees and shrubs, I recommend planting 1 to 2 inches above the soil surface. This will aid in proper drainage, reduce the chances for girdling roots, and helps reduce the chance of plants that are planted too deep due to the settling of the soil.

With trees, one good rule of thumb that will help guide you as to the proper height to plant is finding the root flare of the tree. With few

The wide root flare at the base of a tree is easy to find on mature specimens. On smaller plants, you must look more closely.

exceptions, most trees have a naturally occurring swollen area where the tree trunk meets the soil, known as the root flare. It is usually most evident in trees with trunks 2 inches or thicker. If the root flare of your newly purchased tree is not visible, it could be an indication that the soil in the rootball is covering it. Gently remove soil from the rootball closest to the base of the trunk to expose its root flare.

This root flare planting tip can also help you with an established tree that is planted too deeply or that has had soil accumulate against its trunk over time. Again, gently remove any soil from the trunk to expose the root flare. This method does not apply to herbaceous plants or even shrubs, but it can be the difference between life and death when planting trees.

Planting Procedures Are the Same

Whether your new trees or shrubs arrive balled and burlapped or in a container, the planting procedure is similar. Once the planting hole has been prepared, and your tree or shrub is set at the appropriate depth, the soil can be backfilled

into the planting hole and lightly tamped. Any plastic twine, wire, treated burlap, excess soil, rocks, broken roots, or other debris should be discarded. Water the tree thoroughly and slowly, so that the entire planting hole is evenly moist. Gently tamp the soil and slowly water to remove air pockets in the newly disturbed soil. Depending on your soil type, the planting hole may or may not require soil amendments such as compost, manure, and so forth. If the soil you are planting in is well-drained topsoil or garden loam, no soil amendments may be needed. If the soil is sandy or clay, and the specific tree or shrub being planted would benefit from amendments, then compost may be incorporated into the existing soil. Peat moss is not as effective as compost, because it does not add significant nutritional value to the soil. When amending the soil, don't drastically change the soil backfilled into the planting hole. With a few exceptions, herbaceous plants such as perennials, annuals, and bulbs tend to be easier to handle and plant than woody plants. They are usually transported from a small container or are sold as bare-root plants. Like trees and shrubs, however, it is important to prepare the soil properly when planting your new herbaceous plants but the process tends to be less complicated than handling a balled-and-burlapped plant. Just make sure the bases of your new herbaceous plants are level with the ground and the roots are not exposed. Also, don't fertilize at the time of planting. It is better to allow the plant time to establish itself and fertilize later. For example, if you're planting in the spring, wait until the fall to fertilize plants, and vice versa. This applies more to woody plants than herbaceous plants. Lightly fertilizing when planting your new annuals and perennials will help them grow. A thin layer of mulch covering the soil surface will reduce soil moisture loss, temperature fluctuations, and weed growth. New plantings should be watered regularly for at least two growing seasons to ensure they establish.

PRUNING HELPS SUSTAIN YOUR GARDEN

Proper pruning techniques are an important aspect of garden maintenance and the long-term sustainability of the landscape as a whole. Plants that are poorly maintained are more likely to become prone to pest problems and will perform poorly. A regular pruning schedule will result in vigorous plants that will maximize growth, flowering, and fruit display.

> "You should prune your garden regularly, removing any dead wood or broken or damaged branches, or to prevent overgrown or overcrowded plants."

Consider these factors before pruning your trees and shrubs.
- What species of tree or shrub do you have?
- What is the current health your plants?
- What is the desired outcome (mass planting, foundation planting, specimen)?

Knowing the species of plant you are pruning is important, because many plants have specific growth and flowering traits and specific needs. For example, flowering shrubs that flower on new growth would be pruned differently than ones that flower on previous season's growth. Panicle hydrangea (*Hydrangea paniculata*) flowers on the current season's growth. Therefore, you should prune these plants in spring to encourage new growth, which will then encourage more flowers.

Bigleaf hydrangea (*Hydrangea macrophylla*) typically blooms on the previous season's growth; therefore it should be pruned soon after flowering to avoid disrupting the flowering process. If the shrubs are overgrown or are not producing ample flowers due to poor vigor, selective pruning in the late winter or early spring while plants are still dormant will invigorate them. These flowering shrubs can be selectively pruned by removing weak or unproductive stems and leaving vigorous young stems. This technique may reduce flowering for one year, but shrubs will be stimulated to produce more flowers next year. This type of pruning will also keep shrubs to scale and encourage a more compact growth habit.

To adequately address the second question you must evaluate the health of the plant you are planning to prune. Plant vigor will influence the type and severity of any pruning that you do. Plants in good health have a better chance of recovering from severe pruning than ones in poor health. However, proper pruning can also reenergize plants that lack vigor or that have developed poor growth habits.

The third question is probably the most important, because gardeners must have a good understanding of their goals when pruning. In addition, knowing the function of these plants is critical and will dictate the types of pruning that will be needed to maintain them. For example, plants used as a hedge may have different pruning requirements than those that are used in a perennial border as individual specimens.

Good Tools Have No Substitute

It is important to know what types of pruning tools are necessary to maintain garden plants. Proper pruning tools are essential in maintaining handsome shrubs, trees, evergreens, tropicals, and herbaceous plants that will produce loads of showy flowers and lush foliage. While there are many valuable tools that gardeners may use at any given time, none are more important than hand-pruning shears, lopping shears, and a handheld pruning saw.

> "Use high-quality hand shears and lopping shears that are lightweight and sturdy and have the bypass-type cutting blade. High-quality tools cost more upfront but will last a long time and help you maintain your garden properly."

Lopping shears

Lopping shears are long-handled pruners that allow more leverage in order to cut larger branches. The handles can be made of metal, wood, or fiberglass, and the blades should also be bypass-type for a clean cut.

Folding handheld saw

Bypass pruner

A good hand pruner is one of the most important tools a gardener will have in his or her toolshed. There are several types of handheld pruners, including anvil- or bypass-type pruners. Bypass pruners are most preferred because they work like scissors, cleanly cutting branches without crushing them as anvil-type pruners often do.

Handheld pruning saws are used to prune large branches that are typically too large for lopping shears. A sharp, thin saw, also known as a pistol saw, will enable gardeners to effectively reach tight areas within branches on shrubs and trees. Saws can be nonfolding and folding type. The folding type is quite portable and can be carried or stored easily.

All these tools should be kept clean, sharp, and well lubricated. Tools that are regularly maintained will work properly and last a long time. Failure to properly maintain your tools may result in unnecessary damage to your plants and expensive repairs or replacements.

Types of Pruning

There are several types of pruning that can be performed to keep plants healthy and productive while achieving your desired outcome. These include selective pruning, rejuvenation pruning, and shearing. Each of these techniques requires knowledge and skill. Gardeners learn these techniques by the hands-on experience gained through maintaining the landscape. No one knows your landscape better than you, and you should use that knowledge to your advantage. There is no greater way to learn about how to prune than in-the-field experience.

Selective pruning is a method in which certain parts of a plant are removed. For example, selective pruning may be necessary on a forsythia that is not flowering heavily. Older, dead, or unproductive branches can be selectively removed, leaving the younger, more vigorous branches. Regular selective pruning on woody plants every few years will keep plants productive and in scale with their surroundings. For the best results, selective pruning should be performed in late winter or early spring while trees and shrubs are dormant.

Rejuvenation pruning is the most severe form of pruning, because it involves cutting shrubs or herbaceous plants close to the ground. This drastic method of pruning will rejuvenate plants and is usually done when plants are dormant. In the case of herbaceous plants, this type of pruning is often done in late fall or early spring.

Selective pruning requires removal of select stems that are not needed.

Drastic rejuvenation pruning in early spring will revitalize shrubs.

Shrubs will typically recover quickly from rejuvenation pruning.

Rejuvenation pruning means *nonselective* pruning of plants, usually within 6 to 12 inches from the ground. This type of pruning will encourage growth from the base or crown of the plant as it comes out of dormancy in spring. On shrubs, this nonselective pruning is commonly done each year on plants that bloom on current season's growth, such as butterfly bush (*Buddleia davidii*), Hidcote Saint John's wort (*Hypericum* x 'Hidcote'), and bluebeard (*Caryopteris* x *clandonensis*). Rejuvenation pruning can stimulate shrubs that flower on previous year's growth, such as viburnum and forsythia, but it will take at least one year for plants to recover and flower reliably. This is usually done when selective pruning is not a viable option.

Shearing is another form of pruning that is performed during the growing season to maintain more formal, manicured plants. Hand shears or trimmers are used to prune off new growth and keep the plant dense and evenly shaped. Trimmers can be handheld type, electric, or gas-powered. I don't recommend shearing as part of maintaining a sustainable landscape, because it does not encourage optimum plant health, and it can compromise flower and fruit production. Over time, shearing can cause plants to become weak with thin or no interior growth. Unless you are creating a specific formal look, plants should not be sheared regularly.

Trees Are Pruned Differently

Trees are typically handled a bit differently than shrubs, because they grow and function differently in the landscape. While shrubs are often trained as hedges and used in mass plantings, foundation plantings, or in mixed borders with herbaceous plants, trees are used as single specimens, in small groupings, or along a pathway in an allée. Because the growth habit of trees is unique, pruning practices are different as well.

For example, flowering trees that bloom on the previous season's growth, such as dogwood, ornamental cherry, or crabapple, are usually pruned after flowering. With shade trees, the goal is to remove deadwood or weak branches and to encourage a strong, stable growth habit. Pruning shade trees is often done in late winter or early spring. Evergreens such as conifers and broad-leaved shrubs present their own unique set of challenges, because they grow quite differently than deciduous trees. Evergreens are best pruned while they are dormant, and only shearing with hedge trimmers or a hand shearer should be done while the plants are actively growing.

As a general rule, pruning trees to stimulate new growth in late winter or early spring can be more rigorous, while pruning after flowering or the spring growth spurt should be more modest. Pruning after the flowering cycle should not be severe, because the tree may be damaged.

The Three-Cut Pruning Method

Start by undercutting from beneath the limb with your bow saw or chainsaw.

Finish the cut from above. This keeps the bark from tearing when the limb breaks loose.

Trim the stub from the limb so it's flush with the branch collar.

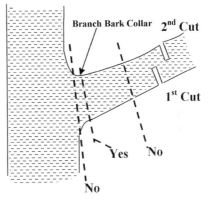

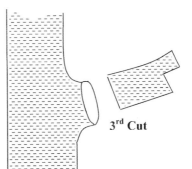

Pruning also will be dictated by plant species or a specific landscape situation. For example, crabapples have a reputation of developing a large amount of vegetative growth known as suckers and water sprouts. By removing a percentage of them in summer, their regrowth will be suppressed. Removing one-third of sucker and water sprout growth each year over a three-year period is more effective than removing everything at once.

As a general rule, younger, more vigorous trees should be pruned more often to train them to develop a strong structural habit. With any tree, pruning dead, diseased, or broken branches can be done at any time of the year with little negative impact. However, doing this type of pruning in winter is better because the plant is dormant, and any problems or issues on deciduous trees are easier to detect. Pruning late in the season (late summer and fall) is not recommended because it can stimulate plants to grow, and this new growth can be damaged by frost.

Unlike shrubs, trees have larger limbs that require specific pruning techniques. On limbs that require a pruning saw, the three-cut method of pruning is used. This method is used to remove branches that exceed 1 inch in diameter. This proper pruning technique will ensure that the wounds created heal properly.

The first cut is made by making the initial pruning cut on the *underside* of the branch, only partly through, 1 to 2 feet from the larger limb or main trunk that it is attached to. This cut will reduce the chance of the next cut causing the branch to pinch your saw or tearing the bark off the branch or main trunk. The second cut is made on the top of the branch farther out on the limb past the first cut. As the second cut is made, the weight of the branch will cause it to break as it reaches the first cut.

With the majority of the weight lifted from the limb, the third and final cut can be made close to the main trunk or branch. It is important to locate the branch bark collar before making this cut. The branch bark collar is the swollen area where the branch meets the larger limb or trunk. Preserving the branch bark collar will ensure that the wound heals properly. If the branch is cut too close to the main stem or trunk, the collar will be removed, and proper healing will not occur. Leaving too much of the limb, such as a short stub of the branch and the collar, will also result in improper healing. The part of the limb that is left will likely decay.

For smaller limbs that are a 1 inch in diameter or smaller, hand-pruning shears or lopping shears can be used for pruning or removal. Branches of this size do not usually cause problems, because they do not weigh as much.

A Well-Pruned Garden

While the best time to prune trees and shrubs is during the plant's dormancy, modest pruning during the growing season can be done to control a plant's size or alter a plant's growth habit. Use hand-pruning shears or loppers to shape or maintain the growth habit of a tree or shrub during the late spring or summer. Specific timing for this type of pruning depends on the specific species and the region of the country where you garden. It is important to note that only a small amount of growth should be removed while plants are growing. As a general rule, less than one-third of plant growth should be removed during the growing season. If more than one-third of the plant growth must be removed at once, it should be done while the plant is dormant in winter. Another good practice is to prune plants gradually over a three-year period by one-third each year. This gradual method of pruning will allow gardeners to be selective about what is pruned and will also reduce plant shock. No significant pruning should be done during extended periods of extreme heat, drought, ice storms, or other situations when plants are typically under stress.

Obviously, herbaceous plants grow quite differently than woody plants and are pruned differently as well. Annuals and perennials are generally deadheaded, which is a technique used to remove dead flowers from plants. In addition, the soft, fleshy branches and foliage of these flowering plants can be pruned at the end or beginning of a growing season to remove dead plant tissue. For example, ornamental grasses can be left to overwinter, leaving cover for birds and other wildlife, and can eventually be pruned in early spring, before the onset of warm weather. Failing to prune herbaceous plants may affect plant growth and the overall aesthetics of the plants. The best types of pruning tools to use when you are pruning herbaceous plants are hand shears, garden scissors, or hedge trimmers.

RECYCLING FOR A SUSTAINABLE LIFESTYLE

Living a sustainable lifestyle reaches far beyond just the garden setting and can influence all aspects of your life. Sustainability affects what we eat, what we wear, how we spend our free time, what we drive, and even where we live. In addition to cultivating and maintaining a healthy garden, many consumer products today are geared toward living a more sustainable lifestyle. A significant component of sustainability is using green products. These green products include everything from recycled wood products to recycled plastic that can be used as building supplies to more energy-efficient lights. For example, new technologies today make it possible to manufacture bamboo as boards, flooring, and decking material. Bamboo is hard, resists decay, and most important, is a renewable resource that will grow back within a few years. Regular harvesting and transformation of the bamboo into a useable form is an excellent way to manage potentially invasive species and still put the harvested product to good use.

Another recycled building product that offers a green alternative to conventional wood products

Recycled wood, plastic and even bamboo is now being used to manufacture decking for home use.

Low voltage or solar-powered garden lights come in all shapes and sizes.

is composite wood, which can be used for a number of outdoor applications such as decking material, landscaping lumber, outdoor furniture, and planters. Composite building product is often made from recycled plastic, wood fibers, fiberglass, and other recycled products. Composite lumber is durable and does not require stain, paint, or any other treatment. However, it is more expensive than wood and over time it will fade and scratch, and it does not have a wood appearance as it ages.

> "Incorporate green products, such as recycled building supplies and innovative lighting systems, into your garden plan. In the end, this will save time and money and will help the environment."

Even the playgrounds that our children play in may have recycled products in them. Several companies now manufacture playgrounds that use recycled plastic not only for the structures, but also for the material on the ground. Matting or flooring that is made from recycled tires can be used as a soft surface in playgrounds and other public areas. These materials can be installed as individual tiles that are pieced together or as single pieces like carpet. These products come in a wide variety of colors and patterns and are both low-maintenance and durable. In addition, rubber mulch can be used in these playground areas. It looks similar to real mulch, will blend into the landscape well, and is soft and durable. Rubber mulch is made from 100 percent recycled rubber products and is about five times heavier than wood mulch, so it doesn't move around a lot in the landscape.

SUSTAINABLE LIGHTING ADVANCES

Significant advances in the technology of energy-efficient lighting has now made it quite easy for homeowners to save money while contributing to the sustainability movement.

Light bulbs such as compact fluorescent lamps (CFLs) and light-emitting diodes (LEDs) may cost more, but they also have a much longer lifespan than standard incandescent lights. CFLs use one-fifth to one-third less electricity and last eight to fifteen times longer than incandescent bulbs. LEDs can last twenty-five thousand to fifty thousand hours or more, but that is often dictated by temperature and current. Higher temperatures and current can actually degrade the quality and longevity of the LED lamp. In addition, solar-powered garden lighting is becoming popular for residential landscapes. These fixtures are relatively inexpensive and easy to install, and they come in a wide variety of colors and styles. It is important to note that both CFLs and LEDs should not just be thrown in the garbage when you are done using them. CFLs contain small amounts of toxic mercury, and LEDs are recyclable. These specialized bulbs can be brought to a local waste collection center or a local retailer; some manufacturers offer a mail-back service.

All these examples highlight the importance of technological advancements with green products. Although these products cost more upfront, this investment will pay long-term dividends. Like many sustainable practices, using recycled products requires an initial investment of time and money, but with a little patience, gardeners can reap the benefits in the near future. With recycled products in and around the home and a sound gardening plan, gardeners can enjoy the rewards provided by all these innovations.

Sustainability offers so many opportunities for gardeners to live a greener life. Going green provides us with the products and the tools necessary to better maintain and sustain a healthy garden. Sound garden maintenance practices—proper pruning and planting, recycling, reducing waste, and paying close attention to our soils—can provide lasting benefits. With new scientific disoveries and innovative trends that reduce our needs and the consumption of our natural resources, we can all reap the benefits of an effective sustainablity plan.

BIBLIOGRAPHY

American Horticultural Society. "AHS Plant Heat Zone Map." *American Horticultural Society.* 2013. http://www.ahs.org/gardening-resources/gardening-maps/heat-zone-map.

American Nursery and Landscape Association. "American Standard for Nursery Stock: ANSI Z60.1-2004." *American Nursery and Landscape Association.* May 12, 2004. www.anla.org/docs/About%20ANLA/Industry%20Resources/ANLAStandard2004.pdf.

American Rainwater Catchment Systems Association. *American Rainwater Catchment Systems Association.* 2013. www.arcsa.org.

Aquascape. "Sustainable Water Management Solutions." *RainXchange.* 2010. www.rainxchange.com/downloads/rainxchange-rainwater-capture-system-solutions-guide.pdf.

Armitage, M. Allan. *Herbaceous Perennial Plants: A Treatise on Their Identification, Culture, and Garden Attributes.* Athens, GA: Varsity Press, 1989.

Association of California Water Agencies. *Save Our Water.* 2013. www.saveourh2o.org.

Beddow, Victoria. "A Brief History of Water and Health from Ancient Civilizations to Modern Times." *IWA Water Wiki.* February 8, 2010. www.iwawaterwiki.org/xwiki/bin/view/Articles/%2DABRIEFHISTORYOFWATERANDHEALTHFROMANCIENTCIVILIZATIONSTOMODERNTIMES.

Boyd, Robert, and Peter J. Richerson. "Complex Societies: The Evolutionary Dynamics of a Crude Superorganism." *University of Zurich.* June 1997. www.geser.net/richerson.html.

Brown, Carol Sevilla. *Ecosystem Gardening.* 2013. www.ecosystemgardening.com.

Bruneau, A. H., and D. L. Osmond. "Caring for Your Lawn and the Environment." *North Carolina State University.* 1999. www.soil.ncsu.edu/publications/waters.pdf.

Calhoun, R. N, et al. "Mowing Lawn Turf." *Michigan State University Turfgrass Science.* 2010. www.turf.msu.edu/mowing-lawn-turf.

California Department of Water Resources. "Irrigation Controllers for the Homeowner: Recommended Water Saving Features." *California Department of Water Resources.* 2003. www.water.ca.gov/wateruseefficiency/docs/irrigation_controllers_0903.pdf.

Chinery, David. *Organic Lawn Care Plan: Fact Sheet 7.51.* Ithaca, NY: Cornell University Cooperative Extension of Rensselaer County, 2001.

Cochran, Soni. "Vermicomposting: Composting with Worms." *University of Nebraska-Lincoln.* 2013. http://lancaster.unl.edu/pest/resources/vermicompost107.shtml.

Colorado State University. *Colorado State University Extension.* 2013. www.ext.colostate.edu/.

Cornell University. *Home Gardening.* 2013. www.gardening.cornell.edu/homegardening/.

Cornell University. *Cornell Lab of Ornithology: All About Birds.* 2011. http://www.allaboutbirds.org.

Cornell University. "Cornell Organic Lawn Care Course." *Cornell University: New York State Integrated Pest Management Program.* 2013. www.nysipm.cornell.edu/landscapes/org_lawn_course.asp.

Cotter, D. J., et al. "Landscaping with Native Grasses." *New Mexico State University Gardening Advisor.* 2013.

Cranshaw, W. S. "Lady Beetles: Fact Sheet No. 5.594." *Colorado State University Extension.* November 2006. www.ext.colostate.edu/pubs/insect/05594.pdf.

Cottingham, Donna. "Creating a Butterfly Garden." *Virginia Department of Game and Inland Fisheries.* 2013. www.dgif.virginia.gov/habitat/butterfly-garden.asp.

Culp, David, and Adam Levin. *The Layered Garden: Design Lessons for Year Round Beauty from Brandywine Cottage.* Portland, OR: Timber Press, 2012.

Cummins, A., and J. E. Klett. "Sustainable Landscaping: Fact Sheet No. 7.243." *Colorado State University Extension.* October 2011. www.ext.colostate.edu/pubs/garden/07243.pdf.

Dirig, Robert, et al. "Gardening to Attract Butterflies." *Cornell University Cooperative Extension: Rockland County.* 2007. rocklandcce.org/PDFs/Horticulture_Fact_Sheet_043.pdf.

Dirr, Michael A. *Manual of Woody Landscape Plants, Fifth Edition.* Champaign, NY: Stipes Publishing, 2009.

Elliot, Lang, et al. *Frogs and Toads of North America: A Comprehensive Guide to Their Identification, Behavior, and Calls.* Boston: Houghton-Mifflin Harcourt, 2009.

Ferraro, Dennis. "Bats Are a Gardener's Best Friend." *Fine Gardening.* 2013. www.finegardening.com/how-to/articles/Bats-are-gardeners-best-friend.aspx.

Fong, Jen, and Paula Hewitt. "Worm Composting Basics." *Cornell Composting: Composting in Schools.* 1996. http://compost.css.cornell.edu/worms

Garden Academy. "Site Analysis." *The Garden Academy.* 2009. www.thegardenacademy.com/site-analysis.

Gardening for Bats. Bat Conservation website. 2013. www.batconservation.org/

Gashler, Krisy. "Native Bees Are Better Pollinators, More Plentiful than Honeybees, Find Entomologists." *Cornell University Chronicle Online.* October 24, 2011. www.news.cornell.edu/stories/oct11/nativebees.html.

Harmon, Heather. "Farming for Native Bees." *Delaware Department of Agriculture.* July 28, 2006. http://dda.delaware.gov/plantind/forms/publications/Farming%20for%20Native%20Bees.pdf.

Harvest H20. "Regulations and Statutes." *Harvest H20.com.* 2013. www.harvesth2o.com/statues_regulations.shtml.

Horn, Bevin, and Brett Rappaport. "Weeding Out Bad Vegetation Control Ordinances." *Wild Ones.* 1998. www.wildones.org/weedlaws/weeding.html.

Ingham, Elaine. "Brewing Compost Tea." *Fine Gardening.* 2013. www.finegardening.com/how-to/articles/brewing-compost-tea.aspx.

Interlocking Concrete Pavement Institute. "Permeable Interlocking Concrete Pavement (PICP): Design Professionals Fact Sheet." *North Carolina State University.* 2008. www.ncsu.edu/picp/FactSheets/DesignProfessionals-PICP.pdf.

Johnson, Holly, and Ted May. "Worm Composting or Vermicomposting." *University of Wisconsin Milwaukee.* 2013. www3.uwm.edu/Dept/shwec/publications/cabinet/pdf/wormcomp.pdf.

Johnston, Cory. "Lawn Wars Review." *Lawn Wars: The Struggle for a New Lawn Ethic.* 2009. www.lawnwars.com/cory-johnston-lawn-wars-review.html.

Koski, Tony. "CMG Garden Notes #564: Fine Fescues for Lawns." *Colorado State University Extension.* December 2010. http://cmg.colostate.edu/gardennotes/564.pdf.

Kress, Stephen W. "Twelve Ways to Design a Bird-Friendly Garden." *Brooklyn Botanic Garden.* September 1, 1998. www.bbg.org/gardening/article/a_bird-friendly_garden.

Lady Bird Johnson Wildflower Center. "Native Lawns." *Lady Bird Johnson Wildflower Center.* 2013. www.wildflower.org/nativelawns/.

Lawn Reform Coalition. "Why Lawn Reform?" *Lawn Reform Coalition.* 2013. www.lawnreform.org/why-lawn-reform.html.

Lee, Sharon A., and Donald Rakow. *Public Garden Management.* Hoboken, NJ: John Wiley and Sons. 2011.

Low Impact Development Center. "Rain Barrels and Cisterns." *Urban Design Tools: Low Impact Development.* www.lid-stormwater.net/raincist_sizing.htm.

Marinelli, Janet. "Box Turtles in the Garden—Close Encounters of the Reptilian Kind." *Brooklyn Botanic Garden.* June 1, 2006. www.bbg.org/gardening/article/box_turtles.

Masarik, Kevin. "Lawn Irrigation Systems." *Cornell Cooperative Extension of Nassau County.* January 2003. www.ccenassau.org/hort/fact_sheets/c134_lawn_irrigation_systems_jan03.pdf.

Mauldin, David. "Nonpoisonous Snakes." *Trailquest.* 2013. www.trailquest.net/SNnonpoi.html.

Menunkatuck Audubon Society. *Menunkatuck Audubon Society.* 2013. www.menunkatuck.org.

Missouri Botanical Garden. "Plant Finder." *Missouri Botanical Garden*. 2013. www.missouribotanicalgarden.org/gardens-gardening/your-garden/plant-finder.aspx.

National Conference of State Legislatures. "State Rainwater Harvesting Statutes, Programs, and Legislation." *NCSL*. 2013. www.ncsl.org/issues-research/env-res/rainwater-harvesting.aspx.

Nature Conservancy. "What's My Carbon Footprint?" *The Nature Conservancy*. 2013. www.nature.org/greenliving/carboncalculator/index.htm.

New York State Department of Environmental Conservation. "Create a Rain Garden: Plant a Lush Oasis and Stop Polluted Runoff." *New York State Department of Environmental Conservation*. 2013. www.dec.ny.gov/public/44330.html.

North Carolina Cooperative Extension Service. "Carolina Lawns: A Guide to Maintaining Quality Turf in the Landscape." *North Carolina State University TurfFiles Centere*. August 2008. www.turffiles.ncsu.edu/PDFFiles/004175/Carolina_Lawns.pdf.

North Carolina State University. *North Carolina State University Cooperative Extension*., 2013. www.ces.ncsu.edu.

Obropta, Christopher, et al. "Rain Gardens." *New Jersey Agricultural Experiment Station: Rutgers Cooperative Research and Extension*. 2006. water.rutgers.edu/Fact_Sheets/fs513.pdf.

Olkowski, W., et al. *Common Sense Pest Control, First Edition*. Newtown, CT. Tauton Press, 1991.

People Powered Machines. "Cleaner Air: Gas Mower Pollution Facts." *People Powered Machines*. 2008. www.peoplepoweredmachines.com/faq-environment.htm#environment.

Pollan, Michael. "Why Mow? The Case Against Lawns." *New York Times Magazine*, May, 28, 1989.

Polomski, Robert. "Information Leaflet 55: Rainwater Runoff: Protecting Your Landscape." *Clemson University*.December1997. www.clemson.edu/psapublishing/pages/hort/IL55.pdf.

Rain Gardens. Suffolk County Soil and Water Conservation District, 2013.

Rain Gardens in Connecticut. UCONN Cooperative Extension System. http://nemo.uconn.edu/

Rain Gardens Fact Sheet. Rutgers Cooperative Research & Extension. http://water.rutgers.edu/Fact_Sheets/fs513.pdf.

Rain Gardens: A How-to Manual for Homeowners. Wisconsin Department of Natural Resources. http://dnr.wi.gov/runoff/pdf/rg/rgmanual.pdf.

Rainwater Management Solutions. *RMS*. 2013. www.rainwatermanagement.com/index.html.

Rakow, D., and R. Weir, R. *Pruning: An Illustrated Guide to Pruning Ornamental Trees and Shrubs, Third Edition*. Ithaca, NY: Cornell University Press, 1996.

Rappaport, Brett. "Green Landscaping: Greenacres: The John Marshall Law Review." *EPA*. 1993. www.epa.gov/greenacres/weedlaws/index.html .

Rossi, Frank. "Lawn Care without Pesticides." *Cornell University Cooperative Extension*. July 2005. http://ecommons.library.cornell.edu/handle/1813/3574.

Sarver, Matthew J. "Farm Management for Native Bees: A Guide for Delaware." *Delaware Department of Agriculture*. 2007. http://dda.delaware.gov/plantind/forms/publications/FarmManagementforNativeBees-AGuideforDelaware.pdf.

Schatz, Robin D. "How Obsession Fueled a Forty Billion Dollar Industry." *Bloomberg*. April 2006. www.bloomberg.com/apps/news?pid=newsarchive&sid=atWbvxYV3vVk.

Seattle Public Utilities. "Soaker Hoses: Good for Your Garden, Your Wallet, and Our Environment."*Saving Water Partnership*. 2005. www.savingwater.org/docs/successwithsoakerhoses.pdf.

State of Georgia. "Georgia Grey Water Recycling System Guidelines." *Environmental Protection Division: Georgia Department of Natural Resources*. April 2, 2009. www.gaepd.org/Files_PDF/GA_GrayWaterGuidance_%20FinalDraft_040209.pdf.

Sturgul, Scott J. "Soil Micronutrients: From B to Z." *University of Wisconsin-Madison*. 2009. www.soils.wisc.edu/extension/wcmc/2010/ppt/Sturgul.pdf.

Tallamy, Douglas. *Bringing Nature Home*. 2013. http://bringingnaturehome.net/.

Taunton Press. "Fine Gardening Magazine Plant Guide." *Fine Gardening*. 2013. www.finegardening.com/plantguide/.

Texas Water Development Board. "The Texas Manual on Rainwater Harvesting, Third Edition." *Texas Water Development Board*. 2005. www.twdb.state.tx.us/publications/reports/rainwaterharvesting manual_3rdedition.pdf.

"The History of Lawns in America." *American-Lawns.com*. 2013. www.americanlawns.com/history/history_lawn.html.

Tsontakis-Bradley, Irene, et al. "Weed-Suppressive Groundcovers." *Cornell University: New York State Integrated Pest Management Program*. 2007. www.nysipm.cornell.edu/factsheets/n_gh/groundcovers.pdf.

Trautmann, Nancy. "Compost Physics." *Cornell Composting: Science and Engineering*. 1996. http://compost.css.cornell.edu/physics.html.

United States Department of Agriculture. "Sustainability in Agriculture." *United States Department of Agriculture National Agricultural Library*. April 11, 2013. http://afsic.nal.usda.gov/sustainability-agriculture-0.

United States Department of Agriculture. "Plant Hardiness Zone Map." *United States National ArboretumI*.website. January 24, 2012. www.usna.usda.gov/Hardzone/ushzmap.html.

United States Department of the Interior. "Water Use in the United States." *Nationalatlas.gov*. January 14, 2013. http://nationalatlas.gov/articles/water/a_wateruse.html.

United States Environmental Protection Agency. *EPA*. 2013. www.epa.gov.

United States Environmental Protection Agency. "Heat Island Effect: Green Roofs." *EPA*. 2013. www.epa.gov/heatisland/mitigation/greenroofs.htm.

United States Environmental Protection Agency. "Lawn and Garden (Small Gasoline) Equipment." *EPA*. 2012. www.epa.gov/otaq/smallsi.htm.

United States Environmental Protection Agency. "Water Recycling and Reuse: The Environmental Benefits." *EPA*. 2013. www.epa.gov/region9/water/recycling/.

United States Geological Survey. "The USGS Water Science School." *United States Geological Survey*. 2013. http://ga.water.usgs.gov/edu/.

University of Connecticut Plant Database website. 2013. www.hort.uconn.edu/plants/

University of Florida. "Saving and Using Rain Water." *UF/IFAS Extension: Solutions for Your Life*. 201w. http://solutionsforyourlife.ufl.edu/hot_topics/lawn_and_garden/harvest_rain_water.html.

University of Illinois Board of Trustees. "Building Your Compost Pile." *University of Illinois Extension: Composting for the Homeowner*. 2013. http://web.extension.illinois.edu/homecompost/building.html.

University of Minnesota Extension. "Best Management Practices for Nitrogen Use in Minnesota." *University of Minnesota Extension*. 2008. www.extension.umn.edu/distribution/cropsystems/DC8560.pdf.

Vestel, Broydo, Leora. "The Legislation of Rainwater Harvesting." *New York Times*, June 29, 2009.

Washington State University. "Compost Fundamentals: Why Compost." *Washington State University: Whatcom County Extension*. 2013. http://whatcom.wsu.edu/ag/compost/fundamentals/needs_aeration.htm.

Water-wise Action in Central Australia. Power and Water Corporation. 2009. www.power-water.com.au/search?queries_all_query=water+wise+garden

Whit Gibbons. People Have Questions About Frogs. Savannah River Ecology website. October, 2008. http://srel.uga.edu/ecoviews/ecoview081012.htm

Whole Farm Planning. Department of Primary Industries website. 2013. www.dpi.vic.gov.au/agriculture/farming-management/business-management/whole-farm-planning

GARDEN RESOURCES AND PLANT SOURCES

This list highlights a few of my favorite garden websites and plant sources that will expand your knowledge and appreciation for plants. These resources will also provide helpful information on garden supplies while also offering valuable information on environmentally friendly practices that will help you along the way to becoming a more sustainable gardener.

A Way To Garden www.awaytogarden.com

American Horticultural Society www.ahs.org

American Public Garden Association
www.publicgardens.org

Arrowhead Alpines www.arrowhead-alpines.com

Brent & Becky's Bulbs www.brentandbeckysbulbs.com

Broken Arrow Nursery www.brokenarrownursery.com

Camellia Forest Nursery www.camforest.com

Collector's Nursery www.collectorsnursery.com

Cooks Garden www.cooksgarden.com

Cornell Cooperative Extension www.cce.cornell.edu

Fairweather Gardens www.fairweathergardens.com

Fancy Fronds www.fancyfronds.com

Flower Factory www.theflowerfactorynursery.com

Forest Farm www.forestfarm.com

Garden's Alive www.Gardensalive.com

Gardener's Supply Company www.gardeners.com

Greer Gardens www.greergardens.com

Heritage Perennials www.perennials.com

Heronswood Nursery www.heronswood.com

Joycreek Nursery www.joycreek.com

Klehm's Song Sparrow www.songsparrow.com

Mail Order Gardening www.mailordergardening.com

Niche Gardens www.nichegardens.com

North Carolina State University Fact Sheets
www.ces.ncsu.edu/depts/hort/consumer/factsheets

Old House Gardens www.oldhousegardens.com

Online Plant Guide www.onlineplantguide.com

Pine Knot Farms www.pineknotfarms.com

Plant Finder www.plantfinder.com

Plant Ideas www.plantideas.com

Plant Delights Nursery www.plantdel.com

Plant Introductions Inc.
www.plantintroductions.com/aboutus.html

Prairie Nursery, Inc. www.prairienursery.com/store

RareFind Nursery www.rarefindnursery.com

Sandy Mush Nursery brwm.org/sandymushherbs

The Down to Earth Gardener www.suzybalesgarden.com

The Nature Conservancy www.nature.org

Uncle Jim's Worm Farm www.unclejimswormfarm.com

UCONN Plant Database www.hort.uconn.edu/plants

United States Department of Agriculture
www.usda.gov/wps/portal/usda/usdahome

United States Environmental Protection Agency
www.epa.gov

University of Georgia Trial Gardens
http://ugatrial.hort.uga.edu

We-Du Nursery www.we-du.com

Woodlanders Nursery www.woodlanders.net

Yucca Do Nursery www.yuccado.com

INDEX

MEET VINCENT A. SIMEONE

Vincent Simeone is an experienced lecturer, instructor, and horticultural consultant, and has worked in the horticultural field for nearly three decades. He has spoken to hundreds of groups nationwide and has appeared on several garden shows including *Martha Stewart Living* and shows on HGTV. Vincent annually presents an average of fifty horticultural lectures, workshops, and tours to garden clubs; plant societies; professional landscape, nursery, and arboricultural trade associations; and academic institutions. Lecutre topics range from plant identification, woody plant selection and use, historic landscape preservation, and general plant maintenance and care. As if that's not enough, Vincent teaches horticulture classes at the New York Botanical Garden. Over the last fourteen years, Vincent has assisted the renowned Dr. Allan Armitage, leading garden tours throughout the world. He is very active in local and national organizations including The American Public Garden Association, New York Hortus Club, New York State Arborist, Long Island Arboricultural Association, Long Island Holly Society, American Rhododendron Society, Nassau Suffolk Landscape Gardeners Association, and the Long Island Nursery and Landscape Association.

Simeone received an AAS degree in ornamental horticulture from SUNY Farmingdale, Farmingdale, New York, and a BS in ornamental horticulture from the University of Georgia, Athens, Georgia. While at UGA, Vincent studied under well-known professors Dr. Michael Dirr and Dr. Allan Armitage. Vincent also obtained a Masters Degree in Public Administration from C.W. Post-Long Island University.

For the past two decades, Vincent has served in public horticulture at Planting Fields Arboretum State Historic Park in New York, where he is the Director. At Planting Fields, Simeone helped coordinate several large horticultural and educational symposia and special events including several national flower shows and conventions, landscape preservation conferences, tree conferences, and conferences to promote new garden trends in the field of horticulture. He has written and contributed to various gardening articles for magazines and newspapers including the Long Island based newspaper, *Newsday*. In addition to this book for Cool Springs Press, Simeone is the author of four other books on plants. In 2010 Vincent contributed to a first-ever textbook on public garden management. For all his accomplishments thus far, the Long Island Nursery and Landscape Association honored Vincent as Man of the Year in 2010.

You may contact Vincent Simeone at: vasimeone@aol.com

vincentsimeone.com/Vinnie_S/Welcome_to_the_Website_of_Vincent_Simeone_-_Home.html